"THIS HAS GOT TO BE THE DEFINITIVE BOOK ON HOLLYWOOD."

Bob Hope

"This book is filled with vicious innuendoes spawned by a few disgruntled reporters, like Jim Bacon, whom I happened to run down with my car. Only kidding. Jim has written **the great book on Hollywood.** I don't care what he says about me. He's still my friend and one hell of a newspaperman. **He says it all."**

Frank Sinatra

"**It's a great book because it was** written by the man who was there when it all **happened."**

Lucille Ball

"**The best book ever done on Hollywood's boudoir shenanigans.** I predict it will sell a million."

Harold Robbins

James Bacon
HOLLYWOOD
is a Four Letter Town

AVON
PUBLISHERS OF BARD, CAMELOT AND DISCUS BOOKS

To my wife, Doris,
without whose relentless nagging
this book would have been
completed years sooner

AVON BOOKS
A division of
The Hearst Corporation
959 Eighth Avenue
New York, New York 10019

Copyright © 1976 by James Bacon
Published by arrangement with Contemporary Books, Inc.
Library of Congress Catalog Card Number: 75-32960
ISBN: 0-380-01671-0

First Avon Printing, October, 1977

AVON TRADEMARK REG. U.S. PAT. OFF. AND IN
OTHER COUNTRIES, MARCA REGISTRADA,
HECHO EN U.S.A.

Printed in the U.S.A.

Contents

Foreword

I ALMOST CALLED THIS BOOK *Breakfast in Tamaqua*. The title would have had nothing to do with its contents, but no less a literary giant than John O'Hara once suggested that I use that title for my book—if I ever wrote one.

John, an old friend from the Bogart days, and I both came from central Pennsylvania. We were also Irish drinkers until John, in his last years, reformed.

One morning I had breakfast in Tel Aviv, Israel, and then got on a jet. With the time change, I had supper in New York that evening. In those days my mother was still alive, living in Lock Haven, Pennsylvania, and I decided to visit her. Well, Lock Haven is not New York or Paris. Allegheny Airlines, which flew to that part of Pennsylvania, had no plane after 4 P.M., and the one train had already left. Finally, I checked with Lakes-to-Sea bus stages and took a bus leaving at midnight.

Tired from my long trip, I immediately fell asleep. I was awakened by the bus driver shaking me.

"Breakfast in Tamaqua," he yelled at everybody, and then he made sure they all got fed. It must have been 5 A.M.

Now Tamaqua is maybe fifteen miles from Pottsville, which to any O'Hara buff is Gibbsville, the locale of most of the O'Hara novels. I got to Lock Haven two or three hours later and called up John, who was then living in Princeton, New Jersey.

"I had breakfast in Tamaqua this morning," I told him.

"Breakfast in Tamaqua," he repeated. "What a great title for a book. If you don't use it, I will."

I told him to go ahead, but he never did. I'll use it one of these days if I ever write a novel.

It took me almost as long to go 300 miles on that bus trip as to cross half the world by jet. When I had left my little hotel in Galilee to drive to the airport in Tel Aviv, I passed the original Mount Carmel. And now, within less than one day's elapsed time, my bus took me through Mount Carmel, Pennsylvania. That must give me some kind of status. How many times have you ever heard place dropping like that?

The book you are about to read covers my own peccadilloes in twenty-eight years of covering Hollywood. It's an unusual book because, with one exception, I personally knew all the people I wrote about. I was there. You would be amazed at how many of the Hollywood books are written by people who never got closer than a newspaper clipping to the stars they write about.

My chapter on W.C. Fields is the exception. Fields died before I arrived on the scene, but George Marshall, the director from whom I got the story, was a dear friend of his.

It has been a fun life with the stars. It was a thrill for me, a small-town boy, to come to Hollywood and suddenly be thrust—thanks to the worldwide circulation of Associated Press—among many of my idols: the Gables, the Coopers, the Waynes, the Crosbys and the Hopes and all the great feminine stars of the Golden Era.

The big ones, like Cary Grant, never disillusioned me. Some had artistic temperaments—you need that to be a star—but there wasn't a prick among them. I loved them all.

Writing this book seems a far cry from the time my Aunt Clare took me on an excursion to New York City, my first visit to the big city. While she went shopping, she dropped me off at the Roxy Theater, then the great cathedral of moviedom. Being a little kid, I went to the men's room first and came out into a huge room with chairs and settees. I sat there for a half hour and then turned to a man and asked him what time the movie started, explaining how long I had been waiting. The man laughed and told me I was in the lounge, took me upstairs, and showed me the main theater.

Believe it or not, the Roxy's lounge was bigger than the movie house in my hometown of Jersey Shore, Pennsylvania.

P.S. Pardon the overabundant use of the first person pronoun in this book, but no other writer is ever going to write about me. Not that I haven't had my share of glory. I've acted in more movies than Robert Redford. Counting both movie and TV films, it's around 320. Duke Wayne maybe has been in more, and with better results, but I'm faster. Duke seldom works less than three months in his movies; the longest I've ever worked in one is about five days. Forgettable as my scenes may have been, I've worked with hundreds of biggies—stars and directors and producers. And I've done something few stars ever have. Arthur P. Jacobs cast me in his ultrasuccessful *Planet of the Apes* and its spin-offs. I think I made good. After I had played an ape in four of them, in the next one he let me play the U.S. Air Force Chief of Staff.

I have played reporters in *Al Capone* and *Black Tuesday*, my first movie role, but I hate playing reporters—it's real lousy typecasting. I played a corporation giant in *High Velocity* and a lecher in *Half a House*. Either one is more me. I played a bookie in *The Outfit* and, in *Black Samson*, a drunk at the bar looking up at a beautiful, nude go-go dancer. Many times I have played myself; in *How to Seduce a Woman* I was the only one who did not get seduced or do any seducing. How typical!

But acting is an asset for a columnist. You get in on some big stories that happen on sets, and you get on the talk shows—Merv Griffin, Mike Douglas, and the like.

The show that gave me the most public recognition was "77 Sunset Strip," in which I played myself. A few months later I was in Brigitte Bardot's villa in Cuernavaca, Mexico, where she was making *Viva Maria*. Suddenly we both stared at the TV set. There I was, speaking perfectly dubbed Spanish.

Brigitte commented: "You are as good ze actore as you are ze lovair."

I still don't know whether that was meant as a compliment or not.

PART I

The Funny Men

And that includes Jack L. Warner,
who has $75 million and is
envious of Henny Youngman.

I

You Can't Cheat
an Honest Man

VAST, SPRAWLING UNIVERSAL STUDIOS today is the busiest of all the Hollywood majors. The word depression is unknown to its 6,000 employees. No studio grinds out more television products and few, if any, make more movies.

But it was not always so. In fact, one day in 1938 W.C. Fields, in a drunken stupor, saved the studio from bankruptcy with just eight words.

It is sometimes hard for outsiders to comprehend the ups and downs of moviemaking. The movie industry is probably the only one founded on waste and run like a floating crap game. A string of bombs at the box office can put the studio in hock faster than a Las Vegas high roller.

So it was with Universal in the days of the Roosevelt Recession. Nate Blumberg, who was running the place, suddenly found himself with the prospect of payroll checks bouncing.

He went to the bank for a loan. The bank looked over the collateral and said that Universal could keep operating only if it started a picture with Fields—its only bankable asset.

The studio had lured Fields from his native habitat at Paramount with a four-picture deal—the last such deal he would ever make—at $125,000 a picture, plus an extra $25,000 for writing them under one or more of his assorted noms de plume. One of his favorite pen names was Mahatma Kane Jeeves. Another was Charles Bogle.

For Fields, it was a deal that could be compared with Robert Redford's current price of $1 million plus 10 percent of the gross. In Fields's day, the dollar went a long way. And the fact that such a fabulous deal was made by a studio unable to meet its payroll went virtually unnoticed in Hollywood. That's how the town operates.

Fields, the most difficult of comics to work with because of his two-fifths a day consumption of alcohol and a general distrust of the whole human race, was considered a good risk by Universal. Blumberg knew Fields's doctor and had been told that the great comedian had been ordered on the wagon—and off the martinis he downed by the Mason jar.

"What Nate didn't know," recalled Director George Marshall, "was that Fields's idea of going on the wagon was to drink a special brand of sherry instead of gin. I once took a sip of that sherry and it almost took my head off. I hadn't tasted anything that potent since the days of bootleg hooch."

Blumberg, fresh from his meetings with the bankers, called George into his office and told him that a Fields picture had to be started immediately, if not sooner.

"Fine," said George. "Where's the script?"

"Well," answered Blumberg, somewhat hesitantly, "Fields is writing it. Go see how he's coming along."

George recalled that his heart sank at these words. Not five minutes before, passing by Fields's bungalow, he had observed that the comedian was drunk on the front porch. Sherry can get you as wildly drunk as martinis. It may take a half hour longer, but the effect is the same.

"I mentioned this fact of life to Nate, who didn't seem too surprised," the director said.

"But then he confided about the bank loan and how urgent it was that the movie with Fields get started. So I called on Fields."

Bill was far gone. When George asked him about the script, he muttered something about "this fellow who inherits a circus from his . . ."

"Then," as George recalled, "he would become openly belligerent, start mumbling incoherently, and pass out."

No director in the history of the movies had ever started a movie with so little, so George kept coming back to Fields.

"Every day for a week, it was the same scene. He would utter 'Well, there's this fellow who inherits a circus,' another swallow or two from that Mason jar of sherry, and the fadeout mumbling."

In panic, Blumberg called George into the front office again. The picture had to start, script or no, and Marshall had never seen Blumberg so frantic or so depressed.

"I knew he meant every word he told me. What the hell else could I do? I started the picture with eight words of story as told by a drunken comedian."

Marshall knew that if Fields was too drunk to write the script, he also would be too drunk to do much acting. The director cast Edgar Bergen and Charlie McCarthy, then very hot on radio, as co-stars. Those of you who have seen *You Can't Cheat an Honest Man* on the late, late show may have wondered why Bergen and McCarthy had more screen footage than the star. Well, the ventriloquist drank little and the dummy not at all.

The cameras turned, and somehow Marshall talked Fields the writer—he was "Charles Bogle" this time—into hiring an assistant. A young writer by the name of Everett Freeman was brought into the act. Everett, now a producer, once made a picture with Jackie Gleason that is a career saga in itself.

As Freeman recalls:

"Here I was, a young, dewy-eyed kid fresh from New York, being thrown to a lion like Fields, who hated all writers except Charles Dickens. But I was so eager that I stayed up all night writing dialogue for the next day's scenes. Then I would come in trembling and show it to the Great Man. Invariably, he would crumple it, throw it back to me, and growl demandingly: 'When do I play the death scene with my wife?'

"I tried to explain that he didn't even have a wife in the movie, let alone a death scene with her. It was no use. He wanted to play a death scene with a wife he didn't have."

George told Freeman to forget about it, to just keep writing. Somehow the young writer kept about fifteen minutes ahead of the camera.

Meanwhile, Fields kept getting drunker and nastier. George concentrated on the other actors and brought in

Eddie Cline, the old-time Mack Sennett director, to work with Fields. The comedian's abuse just bounced off Eddie, and there are those who say that the off-camera exchange between Fields and Cline would have made a classic movie in itself.

Fields wasn't drunk all the time and on these days, George would shoot film twice as fast as on Fields's less sober days, getting it while he could. But another problem arose.

"Bill would listen to the radio at night and come in the next day with one-line jokes. They were the type of things that a Jack Benny or a Fred Allen would do.

"Bill," I would plead, "why the hell do you want to imitate these guys? Do you realize they would fire all their writers tomorrow if they could do the kind of comedy you do? You're the world's greatest master of comic frustration. No one is as funny as you."

As Marshall remembers it, "Some days, it would take up most of the shooting schedule trying to talk Fields out of turning into a George Burns. It's amazing how this greatest of all comedy talents could be so insecure. And always there was the drinking. On the days that he tapered off, we shot as many scenes as we could with him because he might not be around the next day. Surprisingly, we kept fairly close to schedule. If we had had Fields's buddy, John Barrymore, working on the picture, it never would have gotten finished."

Constance Moore, then a teenager fresh out of Texas, made her debut in the movie as Fields's daughter. She says today:

"After that experience, my whole career in show business was anticlimactic. I still can't believe what happened."

The movie rolled on and got down to its final weeks. Then came the worst crisis of all, as George Marshall recalls:

"Bill came on the set early in the morning really soused and fighting mad. He told me he either played a death scene with his wife or he quit the picture. What could I do? He had no wife in the movie, so I shut down production for the day before making my next move. Fields staggered over to his limousine, which was equipped with chauffeur in front and bar in back. He didn't come back.

"We still needed a few thousand feet of film—else we had the world's longest short subject. I hired a double for Fields and shot him only in long shots."

Everett Freeman, eager to make good on his first job, kept on turning out pages like a mimeograph machine.

"Suddenly, with Fields gone for good," Freeman recalls, "the story—if that is the word—went out the window and the whole thing was a fouled-up mess."

But Blumberg and every other producer with a new picture on the lot were all delirious with joy. The bank, true to its word, had come through with a healthy loan—close to a million—and the lot was humming again.

Fields, meanwhile, was back on his Los Feliz Estate on De Mille Drive—a street he loathed because he thought Cecil B. De Mille was a hypocrite. He was always courteous, even tipped his hat, when he met neighbor De Mille on the street during the day, but he hated his guts.

Fields continued his version of being on the wagon by drinking two fifths or more of sherry day and night. It had a strange effect on him; he started seeing and hearing imaginary prowlers—nothing else to do but shoot at them with a shotgun. Bill, as a marksman *sober*, was no Daniel Boone. Drunk, he was a real hazard to his neighbors. When Bill would shoot, the neighbors would retaliate by throwing empty whiskey bottles at his house. Some mornings, the Fields's driveway looked like the city dump.

Bill immediately suspected De Mille as the chief bottle thrower. One night, in a drunken rage, he took all the empty bottles he could carry and hurled them through a huge bay window in the De Mille mansion. As he tossed them, one by one, he would curse: "Take that and that and that, you sanctimonious knave."

Later, Bill told writer Gene Fowler that he never had another empty bottle in his driveway after that night of bottled fury.

Occasionally he would call Marshall on the phone and demand to know about the scene with his dying wife. Marshall would appease him as best he could, never telling him that the picture had been finished without him.

George and his cutters, meanwhile, did what must be one of the great editing jobs in movie history. Long shots of Fields were intercut with close-ups. The audience never realized that a double was in half the scenes.

The movie finally was ready for critical preview. Freeman, new and wide-eyed in Hollywood, can recall the notices almost verbatim.

"All the critics," says Freeman, "referred to the movie's daring innovations, its departure from formula, and its inventive use of the camera—especially on the long shots intercutting to the close-ups."

One critic praised the story line, saying: "What Hollywood needs are more Charles Bogles."

Today Freeman says: "I often wonder about the connection between this early louse-up and the avant-garde picture techniques that critics rave about today."

The punch line, of course, is that *You Can't Cheat an Honest Man* is considered a Fields classic, admired by film buffs the world over.

The movie was also a box office success. I saw it not long ago on television. Of all the Fields movies, it was the only one shown twice in the week-long festival. This is because Fields drunk is funnier than other comedians sober.

I once asked Charlie Chaplin an obvious question: What is the basic secret of great comedy? His answer was direct: "You must kick pomposity in the ass."

Fields did this superbly in *You Can't Cheat an Honest Man* by the title alone—a Fields invention. Then there was the classic scene when Fields's daughter, who is about to marry into high society to save her father's circus from the sheriff, introduces him to her fiancé's snooty parents.

As Larson E. Whipsnade, Fields rides up to the Bel-Goodie Mansion in a circus chariot driven by a roustabout, himself in formal afternoon wear, complete with sleeveless sweater and opera cape. The white silk underside of the cape has emblazoned on it: "Larson E. Whipsnade's Circus Giganticus."

A pompously correct butler opens the door and presents a small tray for the calling card; Fields puts a dime in it. Then, as the butler takes his cape, Fields sees to it that it is spread out over a chair so that the advertisement is in full view.

In the midst of high society, Fields starts telling one of his preposterous stories. This one is about rattlesnakes. Everytime he mentions the word snake, the hostess faints. But he keeps on, with the aside: "The old bat's had too much to drink."

The story he tells has to do with how a rattlesnake once saved his life when he was attacked by culprits. Fields tells how he befriended the snake, which never forgot his kindness:

"As these ruffians attacked me, the little beggar stuck his tail out the window and rattled for a constable," Fields drones on as the rest of the guests fan Mrs. Bel-Goodie. The upshot of the scene is that Fields so alienates the high-society in-laws-to-be that his daughter, Constance Moore, flees back to her true love—Edgar Bergen.

It was probably the only time in his movie career that Bergen ever got the girl, but even that accents how desperate the script situation was with a writer like Charles Bogle.

After *You Can't Cheat an Honest Man,* Fields made *My Little Chickadee,* with Mae West. It's not generally known that Humphrey Bogart, feuding with Jack L. Warner, had originally been cast in the role of the sheriff, played by Joseph Calleia.

Bogey had come to a preproduction meeting at Universal and was handed a script. As he once described what happened: "I had one line, and then there would be thirty blank pages with the notation: 'Material to be supplied by W.C. Fields.' Another line or two for me and thirty more blank pages, 'Material to be supplied by Mae West.' I sat there reading that script by myself in an outer office and then I grabbed my hat and stole silently away. I think I went out a window. I don't remember."

Fields's genius for comedy was never diminished by drink. As Joe E. Lewis was to say years later on nightclub floors: "Some people drink to forget. I drink to remember." So did Fields.

But Miss West was taking no chances. A zealous non-drinker herself, she had it stipulated in her contract that should Fields ever get drunk during the filming of *My Little Chickadee* he was to be forcibly removed, else the Queen of Sex would walk off the set.

"I must say that Bill was quite good about it. He went almost all through the picture more sober than I had ever remembered seeing him. If he took a drink (which he did often), I couldn't notice it," recalls Mae.

"Then one day he showed up roaring drunk and kept getting fresh with me, calling me his 'little brood mare,' which I didn't particularly relish being called. Who wants to be compared with a horse?

"I called the director over and reminded him of my contract. He called a couple grips, who grabbed Bill under the arms and gently lifted him out the door.

"I must say he was kinda cute about it. He was all smiles as they carried him out and when he passed me, he made a deep bow and tipped his hat. He was a gentleman around the ladies."

Not long ago, Mae told me an amazing story concerning Fields. It had to do with the showing of *My Little Chickadee* on television some years after Fields's death—he died on Christmas Day, 1946.

"I got a letter from a lawyer in Illinois," Mae recounted, "who said he had a client who wanted to talk with me about the movie. She was going to be in California anyhow and, since the letter sounded kinda legal and urgent, I gave the OK for a meeting.

"Well, up to my apartment one day comes this woman with five good-sized kids. All you had to do was look at them and it was like seeing five W.C. Fieldses—even the girl.

"The woman told about her husband, a traveling evangelist, who had deserted her and the children about fifteen years previous. She had seen *My Little Chickadee* and was certain that Fields was her husband. He had given her some other name—something like the Rev. Lamar J. Lompoc or some such crazy name that only Bill could have thought up.

"There was nothing I could do, since Bill was long since dead."

After the woman left, Mae recalled hearing a story about

Fields's old vaudeville days—of how he used to change his name and work on the hick circuits like the Gus Sun Time.

"Vaudevillians only worked forty weeks a year in the big time. Rather than take that twelve-week layoff, Fields would work under another name. He liked a buck.

"I remembered years ago," Mae continued, "how he told me he once did a traveling evangelist act where he lectured on the evils of drink out in the sticks."

Whether the story is true or not doesn't really matter, but it sure sounds like the type of ironic joke W.C. Fields would pull on society—with his rum nose, preaching against the evils of drink.

2

And Away We Go!

JACKIE GLEASON, the sour-mash version of Diamond Jim Brady, cornered me one day in 1962 on the Paramount lot.

"Pal," he said, "how would you like to take a train ride across the country with me? It's the only way to fly."

Gleason then had a pathological aversion to airplanes. And the way he travels on trains, he was right. It *was* the only way to fly.

The Great One had been off television for a few years and had just finished making a movie called *Papa's Delicate Condition* in Hollywood. His next move was a return to Saturday night TV, and CBS-TV, in a great burst of generosity motivated by publicity, offered to pick up the train tab for Gleason and his friends, provided Jackie would make a few stops along the way and plug his show. At the time, the network had no idea that the final tab would be $100,000. Then, of course, no one from the network had ever traveled with Gleason aboard a train. Jackie, even when he's broke, lives luxury first cabin at all times.

Even the send-off party at Los Angeles's Union Station was hard to top. There were beautiful dancing girls, two swinging Dixieland bands, midgets, clowns, and movie stars, plus booze that flowed as only Gleason could make it flow.

As guests boarded the chartered train for the farewell shindig, they were greeted by Midget Billy Curtis, dressed like the son of Reggie Van Gleason. Col. Tom Parker, the colorful manager of Elvis Presley, was one of the guests— but not for long. Parker, who had already made millions off Elvis, saw a chance to make a few extra bucks off Gleason. The onetime circus and carnival barker grabbed some autographed pictures of Gleason and was soon hawking them on the station platform.

"Twenty-five cents. Pay no more!" he spieled. Later he sold some of Elvis's pictures for fifty cents.

In the two club cars reserved for the party stood Gleason, tipping the scales at his drinking weight of 280 pounds. He was resplendent in a red vest, with a red hankie and a red carnation in his lapel. In honor of the occasion, he took his first drink in some time—a triple screwdriver.

"I went without drink for three days," he pontificated. "It had to be. Even Muhammad Ali couldn't make this trip without going into training."

Some forty-five people—a usual Gleason entourage—and I were scheduled for the ten-day trip to New York. It was a journey that would follow as erratic a course as Gleason's homeward steps from Toots Shor's pub. Stops were scheduled at Phoenix, Denver, St. Louis, Chicago, Pittsburgh, Baltimore, and Philadelphia.

CBS-TV thought of such stopovers as promotion. Gleason called them fresh-ice stops. Jackie has a theory that all hangovers are caused by stale ice and, occasionally, potato chips—never booze.

The train was about three hours late pulling out of Union Station because of the party and several minor crises. One of the latter was caused by Col. Parker's greed. When he had sold out all his pictures, he miraculously produced hundreds of balloons, with Elvis's face imprinted on them, and inflated with some sort of gas that Parker just happened to have in a nearby container. The balloons were going for twenty-five cents, pay no more, with Billy the midget helping him.

But the colonel overloaded Billy with balloons, and suddenly those of us inside the train saw the weird sight of Billy rising from the ground. Gleason dashed out to the platform and grabbed him by the legs.

"The little bastard would have beaten us into San Bernardino by a half hour," said Jackie.

Then, just before the train pulled out, Jack Haley, an old Broadway pal of Jackie's, came by to make a periodic appeal for Gleason to give up his life of sin and return to the church of his Irish Catholic forbears.

"I know a priest who will forgive anything in confession —and no lectures or sermons," said Haley, who is devout and a favorite of Jackie's.

"One of these days, pal," said Gleason.

Haley, sensing that this was the wrong time for reconversion, then asked Jackie if he would buy a ticket to a $100-a-plate dinner to help Father Patrick Peyton and his Family Rosary Crusade. Instead Gleason wrote out a check for $10,000 and handed it to the amazed Haley.

"Give the tickets to some priests and nuns who haven't got a hundred bucks, pal," he said.

On that religious note, the conductor yelled, "All aboard."

Gleason, of course, with his famous burlesque move, yelled: "And away we go!"

Col. Parker, Billy the midget, and all the party guests waved as we pulled out. Only one band stayed on the train —Max Kaminsky's Dixieland Combo—and it never missed a beat. Max always plays for Jackie on trains. Also on board were June Taylor and some of her dancers—those gorgeous showgirl types always used in the billboard opening of Gleason's TV show—plus the writers, producers, and me.

All the ingredients were there for a first-class orgy: booze, women, and song, complete with first-class sleeping accommodations. But, other than the drinking, it was a circumspect trip all the way. Gleason always was a stern father to the girls. Whenever the party started getting a little rough, Jackie would nod to his choreographer and Miss Taylor would herd the girls off to their compartments. Their sleeping area was off limits and everyone knew it. Gleason had warned that hanky-panky meant instant dismissal from the TV show.

The girls gone, the club car turned into an Irish pub with New Orleans jazz. It was a time for serious drinkers, the hard core.

Somewhere in the middle of the Mojave Desert, Jackie waved to Max and told him to take five: believe it or not, the band had been playing continuously for eight hours.

As if by cue, writer Walter Stone moved to the piano. Walter, who won't work for anyone but Gleason, is house pianist and resident Irish tenor.

Walter knew that his boss was in a sentimental mood, a common one among Irish drinkers. That's when the piano player must play and sing the traditional Irish melodies. Walter knew them all and had just enough whiskey in him to sound good. With Gleason's glass atop the upright and his eyes fixed in deep study on the keyboard, the Irish hour began.

Irish tune followed Irish tune. Gleason never moved except to lift the glass to his lips and occasionally to ask a repeat of "Donegal Bay," his favorite.

Then, as suddenly as it had started, the Irish hour was over. Gleason now became Reggie Van Gleason, and Max picked up his horn and was soon swinging with a little "Strutters' Ball."

"You're ... ahh ... a good group," said Reggie between blasts. And it was New Year's Eve again at McSorley's Saloon as the Great Gleason Express rambled over a Mojave that no longer could be called dry.

By this time, it was well past midnight and no one had thought much about food. Now Gleason, with that gargantuan appetite, thought about it. A dining-car steward was summoned.

"Let's have a couple dozen barbecued ribs, pal," he said, disdaining the menu. The embarrassed steward named off a dozen midnight snacks; there were no ribs on the train.

Gleason assumed the hurt expression of the Poor Soul. This threw his staff into a panic. I have never heard Jackie utter as much as one cross word to any of them, but they all get very uptight when the boss wants something and it's not available.

Jackie yelled for his longtime secretary, Syd Spear, who, despite the name, is all girl. To digress, Syd was one of 100 applicants Gleason interviewed for the job. He asked each one the same question: "Do you take shorthand?"

Syd answered, "Yes, but it takes me longer."

So now you see why he called to her in this barbecued ribs emergency.

"Sydell," said Jackie, using her formal name, "how can we get some barbecued ribs in this joint?"

She glanced out the window at the vast desert reaches and the lonely moon and said: "It could take a little time, maybe a half hour or so."

"OK, pal," said Jackie, pouring himself another drink, "we'll be waiting at the bar."

Syd, to my amazement, was not the least bit ruffled by her boss's seemingly impossible request. As if it were the most normal situation in the world, she conferred in a low voice with the conductor.

In about 15 minutes, the train stopped at a siding, one of those water tank section stops in the middle of nowhere. Syd and the conductor got off the train, and soon a light went on in the little telegrapher's shack. You could hear the clicking of the Morse key in the still desert air.

Before long the train pulled back onto the main line, and Max and his band swung into a somewhat stirring rendition of "Tiger Rag." The Sour Mash Express chugged on.

About forty minutes later, we pulled into the station at Needles, California, on the California-Arizona border. There, standing alongside the tracks, was a little Chinaman, holding a half-dozen greasy boxes.

Jackie had his barbecued ribs, and as he shared them with some of us, he asked, "Now, was that so damn hard?"

Around 5 A.M., the party—which had begun about four the previous afternoon—petered out. Somehow we all got to our sleeping quarters just four hours before we were due in Phoenix for the big civic welcome by the governor, mayor, and God knew who else.

I was in the dining car at 8 A.M., and Gleason came in a half hour later, looking like a bad embalming job. He had a monumental hangover; no one spoke for fear of knocking off his head.

Jackie looked at the menu. One of the breakfast entrées was fried calves brains, typical ranch fare in the Southwest. "First guy who orders that—off the train!" said Jackie, with that grandiose, sweeping arm gesture. He put his head in his hands and ordered a screwdriver. Then another. He barely had a chance to get some bacon and eggs in him before the train pulled into Phoenix. Holding his head in his hands, he bravely made it to the train door. Well, you can't imagine the civic welcome Phoenix had on tap. It was more like the Gunfight at the O.K. Corral.

First off, the date was August 10—and by 9 A.M. in Phoenix, the August sun had shot the temperature past 100. Great hangover weather.

The welcome was one of those Wild West affairs with cowboys and Indians shooting at each other. Gleason was dying from all the noise, but, true to show business tradition, he was affable and funny. He did all of his drinking and hangover jokes, and every time he told a particularly funny one, the Indians would yell and the cowboys would shoot their guns in the air. It was pandemonium. And Gleason had the biggest head in town.

Then came the speeches—typically dull, welcoming speeches, complete with scrolls from the city council filled with whereases.

The sun was killing us.

Finally, when it was over, a fleet of air-conditioned limousines pulled up to take us to the hotel. Gleason started to get into one but was unceremoniously pulled away.

"We got a special conveyance for you, Jackie," said the local chargé d'affaires. And out of the alley came a stagecoach, pulled by two teams of spirited horses and filled with screaming cowboys and Indians.

"Here, Jackie," said one, "you ride shotgun up here." A couple of Indians pulled him up onto the coach. A crack of the whip, and Gleason bounced five miles to his hotel. Only a camel ride in the Sahara Desert could have been worse. The cowboys and Indians had visited a few bars, too, along the way, and they were in a playful mood. Jackie wasn't.

Finally, in the hotel at last, Jackie had barely got into his bathrobe before the Indians burst into his room to stage a tribal dance. Fortunately, there was no gunplay. Someone mercifully had failed to reload the pistols.

By the time the wild men left, it was too late for Gleason to take a nap. It was time, however, for the first of a series of breakfasts, luncheons, cocktail parties, and dinners. To Jackie's credit, he never refused a drink. "People expect it of me," he would say as he ordered a double. And at the luncheon testimonial given by the city of Phoenix, Jackie was in rare form.

"The governor just told me his salary is $18,000 a year," said Jackie. "That wouldn't buy the olives for my martinis."

Then he gave his views on drinking:

"There is nothing wrong with drinking if you know why you are drinking," rationalized Jackie. "I know why I drink. I drink to get bagged.

"I am no alcoholic. I'm a drunkard. There's a difference. I don't have to go to meetings. Ha! Ha!

"Drinking removes warts and other skin blemishes. Not from you, but from the people you are drinking with."

Then a hometown combo entertained. They were good —so good, in fact, that when they finished Jackie got up and announced: "You guys are on the first show." At this his producer winced. Guest stars were already set for the first five shows.

But Gleason's word is law. That unknown group was not only on the first show but also on five others that first season. Gleason's gesture eventually made the leader of the group a millionaire. His name—Wayne Newton.

Before the day was over, Gleason had met everybody and drunk with everybody in Phoenix. Since I was working for the Associated Press at the time, I had already filed several stories about the trip.

At one cocktail reception, a CBS public relations executive said he had just heard from his New York headquarters. Would I, he asked, please avoid mentioning Gleason's drinking? The usual reasons were cited—Bible Belt, sponsors, etc.

"What else is there to write about? The lore and romance of railroading?" I asked.

Later I mentioned the incident to Gleason.

"Write what you want, pal. I don't care if people know I drink."

Finally, around 10 P.M., we had worn out Phoenix and were all back in the club car of the train, which wasn't due to leave for Denver for several hours.

Gleason was in great form; it was party time again.

Max's band, which had played for most of thirty hours, was blasting away. There was dancing, singing, drinking.

Then a funny thing happened. The band collapsed—literally—they just couldn't blow anymore.

But this didn't stop Gleason. Once more he called on Syd.

She brought out albums and a record player. Most of the albums were Jackie's: mood music, mostly—music to drink slowly by. But someplace in the stack, someone had slipped in Dave Rose's great recording of "The Stripper." This piece is so low down, so dirty burlesque in its beat, that we all turned to Jackie to see what his reaction would be.

Jackie once again became Reggie Van Gleason. It doesn't take long to discover that the drinking Jackie goes in and out of these famous characters automatically. They are but moods of the real Jackie.

As Reggie, he unloosened the collar of his shirt and unknotted his tie. Then, in brilliant pantomime, he took the loose tie and worked it in perfect rhythm to the burlesque beat. Somehow he created the illusion of an Ann Corio or Tempest Storm doing her bumps and grinds on a Minsky runway. Chaplin on his best day could not have equaled that bit of mime.

When the music stopped, Jackie knew he couldn't top himself. How do you follow genius—even your own? Immediately he switched from Reggie to the Poor Soul. He got up and walked shyly toward his own compartment, looking about soulfully all the while. As he reached the end of the club car, he gave a backward glance and said: "You're nice people." A shy kick and he was gone.

Just about that time, the Golden State Limited, headed for Los Angeles, stopped alongside our train. I grabbed my bag and headed home. From Los Angeles the next morning, I wired Jackie aboard the Great Gleason Express: "Sorry, Jackie. I left with the first wounded."

3

The Comedians

THE COMEDIANS ARE, by far and going away, the most colorful and interesting animals in the Hollywood jungle.

Some, like Bob Hope, are more than mere comedians. Hope is an institution—like the Bank of America.

Others, like Red Skelton, are downright nutty.

"If I weren't making $2 million a year, I'd be in Camarillo (a local funny farm)," Red admits. He figures that the only thing keeping him out of Camarillo are the guys who pay him. "That would make them nuttier than me."

As a close friend of Red's, I have to go along with him.

Red hires a piano player who puts into music Red's humming. That way, Red composes a song every day, most of them heard only by him—and the piano player.

He also writes a love letter every day to his wife. That's not as romantic as it sounds because Red is already on his third wife. Too much is too much.

Once Red invited me to drop by his house in Palm Springs for a drink. I drove past and saw eight Rollses in the driveway; I thought he was having a party, so I didn't go in. But I found out—they all belonged to him.

"The ashtrays get full so I have to keep changing them," he explained. Somehow it seems sane when he says it.

Once, Red's wife Georgia tried to become a social pillar of Bel-Air society. She became very chummy with the late socialite Cobina Wright, who was a friend of the Queen Mother Nazli of Egypt—when King Farouk was still on the throne.

The Skeltons tossed a lavish dinner party for the Queen Mother at their Bel-Air hilltop mansion. It was such a fancy party that my one year at Harvard counted more for impressions than my 8,000 client newspapers.

Georgia screened the guest list. There weren't too many of Red's comedian friends. Instead the list read like a Who's Who of Beverly Hills and Bel-Air society—multimillionaire oilman Ed Pauley and the like.

The Queen Mother held court; whenever Georgia introduced a guest to her, Georgia would curtsy.

Finally, it came time to introduce Red, whom Georgia introduced thus:

"Your Majesty, may I present my husband, Richard Skelton?"

It was the first time I had ever heard anyone call Red by his given name.

"Queenie," said Red, "do you know your son is Farouking Egypt?"

That ended Georgia's social ambitions. She confided to me afterwards: "You can never reform a comic. I learned that tonight."

Red always delighted in saying and doing the most outrageous things at the most dignified events.

Once John Wayne threw a fancy party at the Beverly Hills hotel, and all the big names of the movie industry were there—from tycoons to stars. In the midst of all this was a beautiful foreign star who, at that time, was having an affair with Tyrone Power. Now, in those days, no one was more beautiful or sexy looking than this girl. She had a Nordic beauty that was unsurpassed. Wayne and a few others chorused: "Who is that?"

Humphrey Bogart made the comment: "Ty Power says she's the best cocksucker in town."

Red, standing with his wife, chided Bogey with mock-seriousness. "Ah, there. You've hurt Georgia's feelings."

Georgia was used to it. She had gone with Groucho Marx before she met Red. "Oh, Red, you're disgraceful," was all she said.

Skelton went on television in 1951 and did a weekly comedy show for almost a quarter-century—a record that is not likely ever to be broken. His show was probably the cleanest on the air—but you should have seen the dress rehearsals.

Over at CBS Television City, you couldn't find a secretary at her desk when Red did his dress rehearsal.

It was the filthiest hour you can imagine. Female guest stars put their lives up for grabs when they rehearsed with Red. But it served as a catharsis for the comedian. Like his character of the Mean Little Kid, he got it all out of his system.

No one was safe from Red. The first time he introduced me to his mother, he said: "Mom, tell Jim about the time you were a hooker in Chicago." His mother waved him off just like Georgia. He was absolutely incorrigible.

Red once got very much interested in photography. He soon owned every kind of camera and piece of equipment on the market—about $100,000 worth. One night he called me up to the house, which was high atop a hill in Bel-Air, and we went up to his bedroom. Red showed me a projection machine with a powerful telephoto lens and said, "Look down there on Sunset Boulevard. See that house on the curve with the white garage door? You see it?"

It could be seen, all right, but I was not prepared for what use Skelton would make of it. He took out a stag reel. I still remember the title—*The Little Sister*. It was one of those filthy reels where the wife's gorgeous little sister comes to visit. The wife leaves the sister with the husband to get better acquainted.

Well, in a matter of seconds, they are well acquainted indeed—both nude in bed and doing all the oral sex acts people do in stag reels.

Red had focused this reel on the white garage door on Sunset Boulevard. You could hear the brakes screeching all the way up the hill. Can you imagine driving down a busy street and seeing a girl going down on a guy on a garage door?

Showing this reel became a popular pastime of Red's—until the cops traced the light beams. Red got off with a warning, but the curve forever after has been called Dead Man's Curve.

One morning, about 2 A.M., I got an urgent call from Red to come up to the house immediately. The call sounded almost suicidal, so I dashed over from the Valley. He had also called Gene Fowler and a priest friend, and we all arrived there about the same time. We found Red up in a tree, trying to look in a bedroom window of his house.

When he finally came down, he took us over to the pool-house and showed us a remarkable sight. There was what looked like $10,000 worth of groceries: cases of beans and carrots, sides of beef, wine, whiskey—you name it, Red had it all.

"I bought out Jurgensen's," he explained. It was obvious that he had. Naturally, we asked why. "Georgia locked me out of the bedroom, and I'm going to make a siege of it."

That's America's most beloved clown—and I love him. There's only one Red.

Red's first wife, Edna, took him up from marathon dances of the thirties and guided his career until he became one of radio's and MGM's best comedians. He divorced her for Georgia, but he still held on to Edna as a writer. This used to infuriate Georgia, as it would any new wife. Edna finally let go, and now Red and Georgia have divorced, with Red now on his third wife. But Georgia is still president of his production company. Red goes over to their old home in Palm Springs every day and uses it as an office, even though Georgia still lives there.

My favorite Skelton story involves one of the screen's great beauties—still around—who at the time of this incident was a young contract actress at MGM.

For a major star like Red, having sex with a young actress on the lot is like belonging to the Book-of-the-Month-Club. It's that commonplace.

Red at this time was making a Civil War comedy called *A Southern Yankee*. The company was on a battlefield location, waiting for the special effects men to set off the charges for a battle scene. Red had a little time to kill between camera setups, so he had the beautiful young actress visit him in his portable dressing room.

As was her wont, she soon was on her knees, doing what came naturally. Just at the moment of climax, one of the special effects men accidentally set off a dynamite charge.

The portable dressing room rocked. Pictures fell from the walls. Clothes racks tumbled. It was like 9.9 on the

Richter scale. Red, satisfied, patted the head of the beautiful young actress and said: "Good girl."

A famous father figure star in his prime was one of the great cocksmen on the MGM lot. One day I was visiting Red on a set, where he was wearing a knight's full armor. The star came up to us and said: "Red, is that your Rolls Royce parked out there behind the sound stage?" It seems the star wanted to borrow it for a quickie with a starlet. As soon as the star left, Red said: "Let's go out and watch."

Trying to sneak up on somebody isn't easy when you're wearing armor. The Rolls was a scene of action, bouncing up and down on its wheels. Then it quieted down. Red sneaked up and tried to take a look inside, lifting his armored mask to do so.

With perfect timing, a used condom came sailing out of the car window, right through the opening in Skelton's armor. Such curses!

The star, much married, was very apologetic, but we all had to laugh—even Red. As I recall, the starlet didn't think it was so funny.

Hollywood used to be such a fun place in the old days.

If being a genius entails as much hard work as Charlie Chaplin used to put into it, who wants to be a genius?

Not long before Chaplin undertook his self-imposed exile abroad, I spent a week with him while he was making *Limelight*.

It was one of the more memorable experiences of my Hollywood career. In those days Sir Charles was only sixty-two, but he worked like a man in his thirties. In fact, he did the work of seven men. He was the star, the director, the producer, the writer, choreographer, conductor of the orchestra, and the composer of a score that included that hauntingly beautiful title song, a standard today.

I was doubly lucky that week because Chaplin was shooting a scene with Buster Keaton. Imagine watching these two great masters of silent comedy working together? It's one of those monuments of show business you never can forget. It was an old music hall routine in which Chaplin plays a comic violin solo while shrinking in his baggy pants to midget size before your eyes. The deadpan Keaton was at the piano, doing the trademark bits that made him one of the greatest.

Few members of the press ever got on a Chaplin set in those days. As I recall, the late James Agee, the famed author and critic, and I were the only ones there during *Limelight*. Agee was working for *Life* magazine.

I remember a profound observation from Keaton one day on the set. I asked him why he did such dangerous stunts in his silent comedies, notably the time he hung from the rear axle of a Model T Ford as it teetered precariously over the Pacific Palisades, 500 feet above the Coast Highway.

"I never used a stunt man," said Buster, "because stunt men don't get laughs."

That remark made such a lasting impression on me that I applied it to my own work. I have never used a legman, as do all the other Hollywood columnists. Some have two or three.

But back to Chaplin and his seven hats. As he stands in front of the camera in the baggy trousers as Chaplin the star, he suddenly becomes Chaplin the producer.

"Rest those lights. This is rehearsal only," he yells to the electricians.

Then Chaplin the director steps off the stage and sights through the camera lens. He decides that the camera shall remain stationary while he pantomimes the solo. The solo is hilarious—Chaplin at his best. He is a southpaw violinist, but he only pantomimes the playing; an offstage violinist plays the difficult piece, but Chaplin's finger and bow movements are perfectly synchronized with the music.

He is a violinist, but he says later he hasn't played for so long that he thought it better to hire a professional musician for the actual playing. Charlie also is an accomplished pianist and organist.

When Chaplin performs, everybody on the set, including the janitor, stops to watch.

After the rehearsal, Chaplin suggests to the violinist that the piece should be changed slightly. Right off the top of his head, he hums the change wanted. When the violinist agrees, Chaplin the composer sits down at the piano and makes the changes.

Soon it is a take.

He dances, he clowns, he grimaces and fakes the violin solo in hilarious tempo. Then Chaplin the director yells, "Cut."

The crew applauds spontaneously—first time I have ever seen that happen on a set. It doesn't happen that often in the routine of moviemaking where everybody is a critic.

He barks orders politely in that beautiful English voice of his. Sometimes he curses, "All right, you bastards, will everybody settle down? We're putting on a show here."

He rehearses the other actors in their parts and then orders a take. He believes in thoroughgoing rehearsals. That was his problem with Marlon Brando and Sophia Loren when he directed them, years later, in *Countess from Hong Kong*. Brando's talent is not comedy, and he needed all the personal rehearsal he could get. People who worked on that picture said that if they could have released a film that showed Chaplin showing the actors how to do the comedy bits, it would have been a hit.

You could never get Chaplin to discuss any of the other comics, dead or alive: "If I praise them, I'm called condescending. If I say they're horrid, I'm called jealous. So what can I say?"

This was back in the days when Joe McCarthy was finding Communists under every bed. Chaplin was under constant attack. He was anything but a Communist; for one thing, he was too damn rich. And his life-style was so grand that he could never give it up for such a Spartan life. I had dinner up at his home several times, and he truly lived like the king of Hollywood he really was.

Charlie's liberal views in those days—called leftist by some—were just a reflection of his comedy style. He loved destroying pomposity.

"During the First World War, I was on a bond tour, and a judge down South once told me: 'I admire you, Charlie, because your humor is so basic. When you go behind a dignified society woman and kick her in the ass —damn it, that's funny!"

So it was with some of Chaplin's politics. He loved kicking pompous politicians—are there any others?—in the ass.

Charlie told me of a great practical joke he once played on his friend Douglas Fairbanks, Sr., whom Charlie described as sometimes taking himself far too seriously. I know I will get a letter datelined Palm Beach, Florida, from Douglas Fairbanks, Jr., taking me to task on this, but here is the story Charlie told me:

"Doug and Mary Pickford, of course, were the king and queen of Hollywood, ruling from Pickfair. Now, there was nothing Doug liked more than entertaining royalty. Once, on a visit to Norway, he met the King of Norway and extended him an invitation to come to Pickfair, should he ever visit the United States. The meeting was a brief one, but the king thanked Doug and said he might just do that someday since he was very interested in Hollywood films. I got so goddamn sick of Doug telling this story and I also got sick of seeing Doug—who had the finest wine cellar in town—bring out the good stuff only for visiting crowned heads. He treated us like peasants when we dined up there.

"Finally, about a year after Doug's visit to Norway, I got a brilliant idea. It involved a few actors out of Central Casting and a few bucks, but it was worth it.

"I started first with a phony career diplomat from the U.S. State Department calling on Doug with a phony representative of the Norwegian monarch. The King of Norway, it seemed, was going to make an incognito visit to the United States and was going to accept Doug's kind invitation to stop by Pickfair. But there was to be no publicity of any kind while he was in the country—and especially while he was at Pickfair. Doug was not too happy about this but he didn't say anything.

"I next got an actor who was a perfect double for the King of Norway, especially after we outfitted him in wardrobe. This guy was born to be a king, but he was a ten-dollar-a-day extra. I surrounded him with an entourage befitting a king—all the flunkies. Then I went to Santa Fe and hired a private railroad car, which we attached to the regular train in San Bernardino. The train and the private car pulled into Pasadena as scheduled. No one important ever got off a train in downtown Los Angeles, not even movie stars. Always Pasadena.

"Doug was there with Mary and a fleet of limousines. I was there, too, because the State Department phony had said that the king was most anxious to meet me, since I was his favorite. This didn't set too well with Doug, but he liked royalty so much he overlooked it.

"The limousines drove the phony king and his party to Pickfair, where they stayed ten days. Actors used to be really hungry in those days, and all the king and his entourage did at Pickfair was eat and drink. Doug, of course, brought out only his best stuff. They drank it all, and when it was gone they took off. The king thanked Doug for his wonderful hospitality and, most of all, for keeping the visit so top secret.

"It took Doug a month or so to realize he had been taken and I, of course, got the blame—deservedly so."

That practical joke is the secret of the Chaplin comedy. As he defines it: "You kick dignity in the ass, add a little rhythm and tempo, and you have it. Isn't it wonderful that we can do that? Else, man would be so insufferably proud."

Chaplin, as great as he was, once had another comedian steal scene after scene from him. That was in *The Great Dictator,* in which Chaplin played a Hitler-like character and Jack Oakie the Mussolini prototype.

In the scene in which Mussolini arrives at the railroad station, Oakie walked away with it. And in the barber-chair routine, the same thing happened. I once asked Oakie how he did it.

"Chaplin only made that movie so he could deliver that long speech at the end. He got careless. He was of the silent comedy style, whereas I was a product of talkies. It was very easy to steal, and Chaplin didn't seem to mind. After all, he had final cut, and he left in everything I did."

I have become a student of those two scenes. Oakie, who is a close friend and a neighbor, likes to invite you over for a showing of *The Great Dictator*. But guests are always amazed at how short the picture is, but that's because Oakie shows only the scenes he is in.

"I can't stand the rest of the movie," says Jack. And that's an honest answer for an actor to make.

Oakie, of course, is one of the great scene stealers in movie history. Today in drama school that famous double

take expression is often called an Oakie. He was the master
of all little bits. For instance, he could walk out a door
and steal a whole scene. Watch some of those old Oakie
movies on the late, late show and you will see what I mean.

Oakie even stole a scene from the famous deadpan comic
Ned Sparks. Sparks's wry delivery usually stole every picture he was in.

"I studied for weeks how I would compete with this
guy," recalls Oakie. "Finally I hit on the idea of hitting him
on the shoulder every time he spoke. As long as I kept him
off balance, he was helpless with me."

But Oakie met his own Waterloo in *Murder at the Vani-
ties* with the great Victor McLaglen.

"I got careless because I dominated this one scene when
the big cop, played by McLaglen, comes into the girls'
dressing room to investigate the murder. "McLaglen didn't
do anything. They shot three times, and I was breezing.
McLaglen was even standing behind me in the scene. It
was like taking candy from a baby.

"But then they shot a fourth take. This is where I got
careless and didn't watch McLaglen. That big lug picked
up a powder puff and looked in the makeup mirror and
powdered his nose."

Oakie is one of the town's richest actors.

"I bought A.T.&T. when it was called American Smoke
Signals," says Jack, and he's not kidding. Oakie's mother
invested all his screen earnings in the stock market during
the Depression years. He lives on a ten-acre estate in
Northridge, which he bought from Barbara Stanwyck right
after she divorced comedian Frank Fay—Oakie asked Barbara if he should call his place Santa Barbara or Santa
Fay.

Robert Taylor, who later married Barbara, told me that
Oakie paid only $30,000 for the estate. Recently a sub-
divider offered him $1 million for just nine of the choice
acres; that would leave Oakie the big English Tudor mansion and an acre of ground. Oakie thought about it for a
while and then turned down the million. I asked him why,
because I know he likes money. "Well, if I sold off those
nine acres, it would mean that I'd have to put trunks on
when I go in the swimming pool."

The richest comedian, of course, is Bob Hope, who *Time* magazine says is worth $500 million. *Fortune* magazine places him among the 50 wealthiest men in the United States, at $250-300 million. I told Bob he should read *Time;* he's richer there.

"Ever since Dolores read that *Time* piece, she's been cutting up all the mattresses in the house, looking for the money," says Bob.

Bob once confided to me: "If I sold everything I have, I might come up with $300 million."

Bob doesn't like to talk about his wealth because he knows Nelson Rockefeller doesn't get laughs. But Bob has an uncanny knack for looking at a piece of worthless land, buying it cheap, and then holding onto it for years until the state builds a freeway through it.

He came out here in 1938 with $100,000 cash from his Broadway and vaudeville earnings. He had a friend, a partner in Lehman Bros., the famous Wall Street banking house, who advised putting the money into real estate. Hope bought half the San Fernando Valley at $30 an acre. Now it houses a million and a half population and Hope often can be seen strolling down Ventura Boulevard singing, "This Land is My Land." But Hope is mostly land rich. Each year he has to come up with $1.5 million, just for property taxes in Los Angeles County alone.

Bob is one of my close friends. I have been everywhere with him from Vietnam to Wilkes-Barre, Pennsylvania. It's hard to believe he's seventy-three. But it just goes to show you that age is really just a matter of attitude. Bob, on that basis, is the youngest man I know.

He's also the most genuine of all the superstars. People who work for him have a job for life. He never forgets a friend, and some of the people still working for him date back to his vaudeville days.

He's a friend of presidents and kings, but the most important thing in life for him is that monologue. That's his baby.

Bing Crosby once played a great practical joke on Bob, and it was the only time I ever saw Bob angry with anyone. Bing called Bob and asked him if he would be interested in a shipload of sailors for his studio audience.

Well, the whole world knows about Bob's love affair with the troops. He jumped at the suggestion.

Came showtime, and the first five rows were filled with sailors, all invited by Crosby. Hope started his monologue. No laughs from the sailors. Joke after joke died. Crosby was in the wings laughing his head off. They were sailors all right, but from the Dutch navy. None of them understood a word of English. Hope did not think it was funny.

I have heard critics of Hope say that he is strictly a product of writers. Wrong. Bob in person is funnier than any of his writers could make him. He's always cheerful, always funny. He could write his own material—he supervises the writing now—but he makes so many appearances that he has to have a $500,000-a-year staff of writers. I have seen Hope do a TV show and then use the hour or two break between dress rehearsal and show time to do a couple of benefits around town.

Hope has been criticized by the Jane Fondas of this world for using the taxpayers' money to finance his television shows during the Vietnam War. It's not generally known that those Christmas tours annually cost Hope himself anywhere from $250,000 to $500,000. The Defense Department furnished a plane for the Hope troupe, but that's about all. On rare occasions we spent the night on a military base and got free accommodations and food. I can remember that happening only one night in ten—at the Air Force Academy.

Hope put up eighty people at the Erawan Hotel in Bangkok, one of the finest hotels in the Orient. Each day we would fly to the various bases in Thailand, Singapore, and Vietnam, and then we'd fly back to Bangkok after the shows.

On Christmas Day, 1972, we flew six and a half hours by jet from Bangkok to Diego Garcia, a flyspeck in the Indian Ocean, halfway between Perth, Australia, and Mozambique, Africa. There we did a show. That same night we flew the six and a half hours back to Bangkok. It knocked out everybody but Hope.

I'm in my room, exhausted, and the phone rings.

"Let's go out and get some Chinese food," says Bob. The nineteen-year-old girls in the troupe all are dragging, and here is this comedian in his seventies wanting to go out after putting in a twenty-hour day. He's amazing.

Another dear friend of mine was the great Stan Laurel, whom I visited often in his later years, in his modest one-bedroom apartment in Santa Monica. Once I brought the famed French pantomimist Marcel Marceau out to meet Stan.

"I am in ze home of ze master," said Marceau, bowing in the direction of Stan. "I learned my art from watching Laurel and Hardy movies."

Then he did a perfect mime of the Laurel walk and the crying face. Stanley roared with laughter. Although Stanley gave the world a million laughs, he was always sad-faced in his comedy. In person, he was a belly laugher.

In his late years, about the only visitors Stan ever had, outside his family, were Jerry Lewis and me. Jerry wanted to make Stan a comedy consultant on Lewis Films. Once I got wind of a script that was so perfect for Stan that I swear he would have gotten an Academy Award nomination if he had played it.

"No use," he said. "I'm all washed up. If I was well enough to make a movie I'd be out chasing girls. You know my hobby. I married them all." Then he laughed uproariously. Stanley married four women a total of eight times and had a fifth sue to be declared his wife.

As Errol Flynn once observed to me: "I've always liked Stan because he lost all his money on women. His partner, Oliver, I could never figure. He lost all his on horses and golf."

Stanley had come to this country from England as part of a music hall troupe that included Charlie Chaplin. Stanley, in fact, was Chaplin's understudy.

"My first night in America, I put my black shoes outside the door, expecting them to be shined, as was the European custom. Some son-of-a-bitch stole them and I didn't have another pair. That night I went onstage in a full dress suit, wearing carpet slippers. It got such a big laugh that I continued doing it."

He eventually made it to Hollywood, where he acted and directed two-reelers. Oliver Hardy, at the same time, was mostly playing comedy heavies. One day a comic actor failed to show at the Hal Roach Studio, so Stanley stepped in to do some scenes with Hardy. Joe Reddy, who was Harold Lloyd's press agent, recalls that first day:

"It was electric when these two got together. Everybody on the set knew that comedy history was being made."

Stanley always directed anything he and Hardy did on the screen. "Babe was the easiest going guy in the world," he said. "All he ever said to me was 'OK, Stan.'" Their partnership lasted thirty years, until Hardy's death in 1957.

"In those thirty years we never had one cross word between us," said Stanley. And that's a record for comedy teams, most of whom usually hate each other's guts. "I guess it was because of our different hobbies," Stan laughed.

Virginia Ruth Rogers, Stan's second, third, and seventh bride, once observed, in a classic of understatement: "Stan's a good boy, really, but he has a marrying complex." He was just an earlier version of Mickey Rooney.

It may surprise a lot of people to know that Laurel and Hardy never made any really big money. "We were getting $300 a week most of the time," he told me. "And Hal Roach had all the Laurel and Hardy TV and merchandise rights." Fortunately, he lived long enough to see a whole new generation fall in love with his crazy antics. "They didn't have residual rights in our day," he said. "Now I'm all over TV, and Hal Roach is getting all the gravy."

But Stanley was never bitter. He enjoyed life, and he loved his fans: "Laurel and Hardy were always bigger in Europe and Asia than they were in the United States. We had a fan club once in Europe that numbered two million members." Even Marceau was a member of it.

Once, after an engagement in London after the war, their plane stopped at Shannon Airport in Ireland. "One counter was filled with Laurel and Hardy dolls," said Stan. "The manager told us it was the biggest-selling item in the Shannon duty-free shop. And we didn't get a cent from it. In fact, we each bought a set and had to pay four dollars apiece." At this, Stan laughed and laughed and anyone who can laugh at his own misfortunes in an $80-a-month apartment, while many of the lesser comedians are miserable in $500,000 Bel-Air mansions, is a wonderful man.

As Ollie would say, "What a fine mess you got us into this time, Stanley."

One of the funniest and wittiest men of all time never made it big outside of saloons. That's because he spent most of his time inside them. That would be the one and only Joe E. Lewis, one of my favorite drinking buddies—everybody else's, too.

Joe E. started out in show business as a singer, but some jealous mobsters in Chicago, fighting over his services, slashed his throat and left him to die. That ruined Joe's singing career, but doctors put him together enough so that some of the nation's most ribald jokes could pour out —and a staggering amount of scotch could pour in.

Then, midway in his career as a saloon comic, he had his stomach taken out because of a bleeding ulcer. His doctors told him to forget scotch. His answer to that: "I see more old drunks in nightclubs than I do old doctors."

It was not until a few years before his death that he tapered off. "Already I can see the handwriting on the floor," he said.

Joe used to attack all the institutions women hold dear —marriage, family, fidelity: "Double your pleasure, double your fun. Sleep with two chorus girls instead of one." But I never knew a woman who didn't adore Joe E., once they got to know him. In appearance he was like everybody's Uncle George. You know, the one who drinks. He was dapper of dress, medium of height, and florid of face. He was a barroom philosopher.

Plato once said: "Under the influence of either poverty or wealth, workmen and their work are equally liable to degenerate." Several thousand years later, Joe E. Lewis said: "Show me a man without money and I will show you a bum." Or: "Rich or poor, it's better to have money." Some of Joe E.'s material was written for him, but most of it was pure Lewis ad-lib.

Somehow, he never made it on television: "They once took a Nielsen rating when I was doing a TV show, and they found out that half the studio audience wasn't watching me."

Joe E. was a character right out of Damon Runyon—
and his traveling companions likewise: Swifty Morgan, the
peddler of hot cuff links, and Austin Mack, his pianist,
who always cued Joe E. through his act, no matter how
drunk he got.

"I never knew Austin drank," said Joe E., "until he
showed up sober one night."

Sinatra also was a Lewis buddy. He, too, is out of Damon Runyon. Once Swifty was locked in his Beverly Wilshire hotel room for nonpayment of rent. He wired Sinatra
for help—Frank sent him a parachute.

Joe E. always included me in his act, but one night he
kept referring to me as Jim Bishop. This is something that
has happened to Bishop and me for years. Same number
of syllables, plus we're both white-haired newspapermen.
When I first met Jim, he reached out his hand and said:

"Boy, am I glad to meet you. I've been getting this Jim
Bacon bit for years." The payoff came when the hostess
of the party at which Bishop was guest of honor introduced me to some arriving guests as Jim Bishop.

But when Joe E. did it, this confusion of names was
fairly new. He sensed that he had hurt my feelings. When
I didn't go back to his dressing room as usual, there at the
front door of the El Rancho Vegas was Joe E. down on
his knees, yelling: "I don't even know Jim Bishop. Why in
the hell can't you have a name like Westbrook Pegler?"
All was forgiven.

On Saturday nights, Joe E. used to do three shows at the
El Rancho. One night between the second and third shows,
he and I and a couple of the showgirls from La Nouvelle
Eve were drinking. Came time for the 2 A.M. show and
Joe E. couldn't make it. He was passed out in his dressing
room. Beldon Katleman, the owner of the hotel, was furious. He didn't blame Joe E., he blamed me. "You are an
evil companion for Joe E. That's why he can't go on."

Can you imagine having the image of an evil companion
for Joe E. Lewis? That's like calling Satan devilish.

I knew all the Marx Brothers well—Groucho and Chico
the best.

You never hear much about Chico, the eldest. He would

be around ninety now if he were still living. He was a compulsive gambler but a great guy. In his later years, he carried on a marathon bridge game at the Friars Club. In his lifetime he had made two fortunes and gone through a half-dozen.

I dropped in the Friars to see him for lunch one day. Swifty Morgan came in selling cuff links. He showed us one beautiful pair, gold with pearls.

"The reward's $300," said Swifty, "I'll let you have them for $100."

Chico peeled off a C note, took the cuff links and handed them to me. "In case I'm not around for Christmas this year (which he wasn't)," he explained. Then he joined his buddies in a bridge game. About two hours later, he borrowed fifty bucks from me to stay in the game. That was Chico. And he was always that way.

Groucho once told me that the Marx family couldn't keep anything in their house when the brothers were kids: "Chico was always hocking it to play pool." Once their father, who was a tailor, gave Chico a pair of pants to deliver to a customer. Chico hocked the pants.

Harpo, the darling of intellectuals, was the only one in the family who almost never made it through kindergarten. Yet he was an intellectual himself, self-taught. He was a kind man, very gentle. He went through life mostly unrecognized because his getup on stage or screen was the most outlandish of the trio.

Once, like all other actors in Hollywood, he applied for unemployment payments. This was after the Marx Brothers had broken up as a team. The young clerk at the unemployment commission didn't recognize him, especially when he used his right name, Arthur Marx.

"Have you worked at any time in the last month?" she asked.

"Yes," said Harp, "one day."

"How much were you paid?"

"Fifteen thousand dollars," Harpo replied.

And he wasn't kidding; he told me he had done a TV commercial that he finished in one day. The supervisor at the Hollywood office finally cleared him because he was used to such things: Adolphe Menjou would pick up his unemployment check while arriving in a chauffeur-driven Rolls Royce. After all, it's not charity. The actors have all paid into the fund. Why not take out ninety dollars a week?

Onstage, Harpo was the wackiest of the brothers. Offstage, he was the quiet one living the good life in Palm Springs. He had only one eccentricity—I first noticed it when I went to a movie with him in the newsreel days: He applauded all political orators, regardless of party. He would cheer and whistle for a Nixon speech and then, a minute later, do the same thing for a JFK speech. It used to drive the other people in the theater crazy.

"My brothers never let me talk in the act," he said. "It would prove to the world that I am the only sane one in the family."

Chico, who might be considered the family ne'er do well, was the only one to graduate from public school.

Sadly, I never really got to know the brothers until their last movie, *Love Happy,* in which they gave the young Marilyn Monroe a break. But I remained friends with them through the years. Chico and Harpo retired, for the most part, but Groucho went on TV with "You Bet Your Life." It was such a success that twenty years later it is in revival across the country and is still a hit. When the show first came on the air, I went over to Groucho's house in Beverly Hills to do an interview with him. NBC had scheduled it very early in the morning, and Groucho was in a bad mood —with some justification.

He was miserable. He was insulting—mostly to the NBC press agent—but not with the usual Groucho wit.

I was on a deadline and had to write the column that afternoon. I thought that if I wrote the interview the way it happened, Groucho would come out looking like a jerk. Many columnists would have done just that. Instead I took everything he said and put a little twist on it, a punch line, so that it came out as a very funny interview, which it was not. After all, if you write a column about Groucho Marx, it should be funny. This one got very good play.

I saw Groucho a few days after that in Romanoff's. "You know something," he said, "considering how early in the morning that interview was, I was goddamn funny, wasn't I?" I agreed that he was. That will tell you something about comedians.

Groucho is the only eighty-five-year-old with groupies. Wherever Groucho goes, teenage girls follow. He rewards them all with a kiss.

Groucho has groupies because young people today regard him as the first of the antiestablishment comics. He was that way back in the days when people didn't know what the hell the establishment was.

W.C. Fields, if he were alive today, would have groupies, too. He had the same iconoclastic type of comedy.

Once the Brown Derby had an artist sketch a caricature of Groucho, to be hung on its wall with those of all the other stars. He autographed it thus: "To Al Levy's Tavern (a competitor)—the best restaurant on Vine Street. Groucho." It was never hung.

One day Groucho and I had lunch at Romanoff's. After the lunch, a crestfallen waiter said to him: "Are you mad at me, Mr. Marx?" Groucho said he wasn't and asked why the question. "Because this is the first time I have ever served you and you didn't insult me."

The waiter handed him the check. Groucho looked at it and then delivered a famous line from one of the Marx Brothers movies: "This is outrageous. If I were you, I wouldn't pay it."

He handed the unsigned check back to the waiter and walked out. The waiter was smiling.

Groucho was once the victim of one of the great practical jokes in Hollywood history. Back in the early thirties, Boris Karloff took his first wardrobe test for the Frankenstein monster—the first time ever he wore the monster's complete getup, makeup and all. Then he dashed out of Universal Studios in the valley, got into a studio car, and told the driver to take him across the mountain to Groucho's house in Beverly Hills. Can you imagine other drivers at signal lights looking at this creature in the backseat?

Groucho told me the story: "I was up in a back bedroom of my house, playing the mandolin, when I heard the doorbell ring. My housekeeper answered it with a scream and then I heard a kerplop. She dropped in a heap on the floor in a dead faint.

"Next I heard these heavy steps coming up my stairs. I didn't know what the hell was going to happen. I really thought someone was out to murder me. Then the door opened and there stood this monster who calmly said: 'Hello Groucho, I just happened to be in the neighborhood and dropped in to say hello.' Then he left and drove back to Universal, scaring hell out of everybody on the way."

Recently I kept hearing that Groucho, plagued by a series of minor strokes, was a little bit out of it. It worried me some, until I saw him at a party over at Hillcrest Country Club. I was with my wife and said: "Groucho, you know my wife?"

He answered: "Yes, I know your wife, but does your wife know you? And how about that sexy starlet, does she know her?"

It was the same old Groucho, even if it did take a little explaining at home.

You have to group George Burns and Jack Benny together. They were lifetime pals, and Burns could break up Benny with one of Benny's own pauses.

One night we are all at a party—Kirk Douglas's house, I recall. All the stars were entertaining. Judy Garland, in her prime, knocked everybody dead with just a pickup band behind her. No one could follow her. When the entertainment was over, Benny came up to George and asked for a light for his cigarette. George gave him a box of matches and then turned to the band and asked for a fanfare and a couple of rim shots on the drums. Then he turned to the assembled stars and announced: "Ladies and gentlemen, Jack Benny will now do his famous cigarette bit." Then Burns walked away, leaving Benny looking like a dummy, saying: "What cigarette bit?"

Jack was a lovable guy. No one ever said a bad word about Benny. That's because he loved only the simple things.

One day a bunch of us were sitting at the comics' roundtable at Hillcrest, when Benny came in fresh from signing a new $3 million contract with CBS. Everybody was waiting breathlessly for the details.

Jack turned to his pals and said: "You know, if you only drive thirty miles an hour up Pico Boulevard, you can make it from CBS to here without hitting a red light." That was all he had to say.

Once he and I had lunch at Romanoff's. He did twenty minutes on how wonderful it felt to have a clean pair of socks. He said that in his vaudeville days, his greatest memory was playing San Francisco, where you could always get a girl.

"My happiest days," he recalled, "were putting on a pair of clean socks and then getting a blow job."

George Burns is the most outrageous storyteller of all time.

I have seen him hold a room spellbound as he tells a show business story. Sometimes they are so touching they make people cry, especially the one about the hoofer who always wore yellow shoes in his act. He was a terrific hoofer and the curtain always went down to great applause.

"The guy had a great gimmick," George said. "As the curtain dropped, his yellow shoes took the spotlight outside the curtain. The audience yelled, screamed, and cheered as the spotlight lingered on those yellow shoes.

"The hoofer always stepped out of the shoes and went into the wings so he could bask in that applause.

"One night, he stepped out of the shoes and went back towards the wings and collapsed of a fatal heart attack. He died as the audience was still applauding his shoes.

"Isn't that a great show business story?"

As everybody was brushing away a tear, George turned to me and said: "The whole goddam thing is a lie. I made it all up."

I first met Milton Berle in 1933, and in a strange way. I was a freshman at the University of Notre Dame, and the Chicago World's Fair was on. At the fair, the big attraction was Sally Rand and her fan dance. In the Loop, the big attraction was a twenty-five-year-old comedian who had been booked for two weeks and had lasted for six months. He was a sensation; and everybody had to see him, including me.

I'm a good laugher, and I was sitting next to a woman who even outlaughed me. Milton was brash, irreverent, and hilarious. This woman was having such a good time that she even seemed to enjoy my having a good time. In fact, she kept poking me in the ribs whenever I didn't get the joke right away. Milton seemed to be playing to her. "Lady, what joke are you working on now?" Or: "I remember you from my show last year. I never forget a dress." If the material sounds familiar—Milton is still using it.

At the closing, Milton made a little speech to the audience and then asked his mother, Mrs. Sadie Berle—she later changed her name to Sandra after Milton became Mr. Television—to take a bow.

It was my seat companion. The lights went down, and she said to me, "I want you to meet my son, the comedian."

She took me backstage and introduced me. It was a big thrill for a college freshman. Milton was very gracious and says he remembers the incident vividly. I believe him because Milton has the most fabulous memory of anyone I know.

Once we were on TV, on the "Mike Douglas Show," in Philadelphia. Mike had put us up at the Warwick Hotel, and we were in the elevator on the way up to our floor when an elderly chambermaid accosted Milton; he hadn't been in the hotel in thirty years.

"Hello, Bridget," he said. "How nice to see you again. How's your family?"

The woman, whose name actually *was* Bridget, was flabbergasted that Milton could remember her after all these years. But that's Milton.

He's always handing out fifty dollars to someone from vaudeville who stops him on the street and recalls being on the same bill with him.

"Yeh," Milton will say, "it was Shea's Buffalo. The Avon comedy four, Willie, West, and McGinty, and Frank and Milt Britton and their band, were on the same bill— an all-comedy show." If you press him, he'll even name the manager of the theater.

Milton in person is totally unlike the brash comedian you see onstage. He'll get temperamental around showtime; it's his nerves showing. But it is all forgotten with the first laugh from the audience.

He was once the victim of a brutal TV play called "The

Comedian," in which Mickey Rooney gave one of the great all-time performances. But no one knows the background of why that play was written.

Milton was the king of television back in the fifties when *Cosmopolitan* magazine assigned a young, unknown writer by the name of Ernest Lehman to do an article on him.

Milton is the most cooperative star in the business with the press. He pulls no punches, and his answers are always honest—even when they are at his own expense. Lehman, who has since become one of the screen's top writers and producers and an Oscar winner, approached the Berle story the way *Time* magazine does with a cover piece: more psychoanalysis than reportage.

"Ernie was following me into the toilet. I couldn't shake him," Milton told me. "I was romancing Ruth in those days (Mrs. Berle), and one night I wanted to take her to El Morocco for a romantic dinner. I asked Ernie in a nice way not to tag along; told him this was the girl I was going to marry—you know, the whole two's company, three's a crowd shit. Ernie got furious. He said, 'You son-of-a-bitch, I'll fix you.' A few months later, there was no article on Berle, but Lehman had written a short story called 'The Comedian.' It was vicious."

It really was. Milton didn't deserve it. I don't think he's ever told that story to anyone but me. He's not a vindictive man. He lives by a simple philosophy. Whenever someone does him dirt, he just says, "Fuck 'em," and forgets it.

On a nightclub stage, Berle is the absolute master of timing and delivery. I have seen his act a thousand times; I know it better than he does. But I always find myself laughing just as hard as I did the first time. It's not what he says, it's the way he says it.

Owners in Las Vegas are always after him to change the act. He has, a couple of times, but those big yawks didn't come like they did with the old act. So he keeps returning to it. If he does a benefit, he will come up with bright, new material that lays people in the audience, but he won't use it in his act. Comics are basically insecure. They want to go with the surefire stuff when they are getting paid for it. It all goes back to Milton's days as a kid star in vaudeville. If the act didn't go over, the manager would fire you after the Monday matinee, and that meant you didn't eat much for a week.

You hear a lot about Milton's mother but seldom anything about his father, Moe Berlinger. "He was a Willy Loman of his time," says Milton. "He tried a lot of things but never succeeded in any of them."

Over the years, Milton has been accused of stealing other comedian's jokes. "The Thief of Badgags," Walter Winchell once dubbed him. But all comics steal from each other. What angered them about Berle was that he told them better than they did.

I have seen gags that I have originated myself for my column—I'm a frustrated gag writer—wind up in a comic's act and performed while I'm in the audience.

Years ago, when Harry Cohn, the tyrannical boss of Columbia Pictures, died, he had one of the biggest funerals in Hollywood history. I left the funeral with Producer Jerry Wald, who commented on the huge turnout. I said, not with any pride—because I liked Harry: "You give the public what it wants, and it will show up."

The next day the line was in a Hollywood trade paper column, with Wald saying it. A couple of nights later, Red Skelton had picked it up and used it on his TV show. Today Skelton is generally credited with the line. It just proves a point—that every joke is in the public domain.

One thing Milton does not have is phony humility—for which I am ever grateful. For nearly thirty years as a Hollywood writer, I have attended awards ceremonies and heard more horseshit uttered by more industry figures than any other man in the business except Jack L. Warner. Humility is OK if it comes from St. Francis of Assisi, but not from actors and producers.

Thank God for Milton. One night the Television Academy honored him for his great contribution to the industry, which he almost singlehandedly took out of the wrestling business.

In accepting, Milton said: "People say I owe a lot to television because TV made me a star—but the fact is that I was a star long before television. What TV made me is unemployed.

"Today wherever I go, I hear people saying, 'Look—there goes Uncle What's His Name?'

"Usually when one is honored like this, they find themselves without words. I've got more words than *Gone With the Wind*. But it's a night I'll remember—at least until ten or eleven o'clock tomorrow morning."

Good for Milton. Humble is the name of an oil company.

4

My Gawd!
That Crazy Comedian Is
at the Controls

DANNY KAYE called one day and said: "Can you be out at Van Nuys Airport in a half hour? Clay Lacy and I are taking the Lear Jet to Dallas for a golf tournament."

Since I live only a short distance from the airport, I was there in no time. I sat back in the jet, my seat belt fastened and a scotch in my hand, as we taxied toward the runway. I didn't notice at first that Danny was in the pilot's seat and Clay, a commercial airline pilot, was in the co-pilot's seat.

Suddenly we were going down that runway like a shot out of hell, and Danny was doing all the work. Clay was talking on the radio.

It's a damn funny feeling. You're about to take off in a jet and a comic is flying it. Danny was a pilot, I knew, but I had never heard of him flying anything but Pipers or Beechcrafts. This was the big time. But I usually relax in an airplane, and when I saw how well Danny was handling it, I relaxed fully.

He was all business at those controls, no comedy. I soon found out that Danny had had a lesson in flying the jet. This was his second. But he is such a good pilot that he had it completely mastered.

Over New Mexico, we even did a few barrel rolls—or rather I rolled while Danny did them. We were going to some kind of airline pilot's golf tournament in Dallas.

Danny had the operation of the plane down so well that

he decided to dive down on the golf course the way the military pilots do and buzz the golfers. That was a thrill, too. It was something that I hadn't done since World War II, and I loved it.

Not many months after, Danny had checked himself out in the big commercial jets. Right now he's qualified to get a job with any airline—except he's too rich, and some people are too squeamish to have a comic at the controls. Not me. I'll fly anyplace with Danny—anytime.

5

Shecky Greene—the Comic, Not the Horse

SHECKY GREENE—the comic, not the horse—is the King of Las Vegas, but, except for appearances on talk shows, he is not generally known around the country. He's the comic's comic, the gambler's comic, and the drinker's comic. But, unfortunately for the rest of the nation, the horse that ran in the 1973 Kentucky Derby—Shecky Greene—is better known than the guy for whom it was named.

It's a pity because Shecky Greene the comic is brilliant. Not since the late Joe E. Lewis has there been a saloon comic like Shecky. The lack of TV exposure has hurt Shecky's national image. And, surprisingly, his absence from the national TV scene is of his own choosing.

"I really don't want a TV series. I think I'm too hard to categorize."

And that is a revealing self-appraisal.

Shecky is a better mimic than Sammy Davis; he sings better than three-fourths of the singers who make their living at it; he is a superb dramatic actor, and, above all, the most creative comedian in the business.

A good question: Where does Shecky fit?

Las Vegas, that's where.

For more than twenty of his forty-five years, Shecky has been a top draw in Vegas—the darling of the high rollers. His contract with the MGM Grand Hotel is worth $1 million per year. Few performers, outside of Sinatra, do better up there.

Some say that Shecky's extraordinary after hours exploits are the reason he has never made it big nationally. When Shecky drinks, he turns Las Vegas into Dodge City of 100 years ago. One explosive night, he rambled through the ornate Caesars Palace, knocking statues of Roman emperors and gods right and left off their pedestals. And then, getting into his car, he drove through the huge fountains in front of Caesars yelling, "No spray wax, please."

Shecky is no alcoholic. He's just a guy who gets wild when he drinks. Maybe it's a throwback to his boyhood in Chicago, but he sees red when he sees a cop. He loves fighting cops.

"The result is," says Shecky, "I have my own drive-in cell at the Clark County Jail."

The funny thing is that the cops all love Shecky. They put up with more things he does than anyone else, but eventually they have to haul him away for both their own and his safety.

Bob Hope is Shecky's number one fan. Hope says that if a cop instead of a jockey had ridden Shecky Greene, the horse would have won the Kentucky Derby.

Shecky goes on the wagon periodically. That once happened after some friends with whom he was dining in San Francisco told him of a shortcut back to his hotel.

"I didn't realize until too late that the shortcut was off a cliff. And someone at the restaurant had spilled a bottle of red wine on me. The ambulance attendants thought my whole gut was cut wide open."

Fortunately, all Shecky got from the shortcut was a bruised shoulder. He made his show at Harrah's in Reno that night.

And sometimes Shecky's reputation gets him in trouble even when he's innocent. Once he was dining in a New York restaurant with his manager, Irving Schacht. Three girls came up to Shecky and said how much they had admired him on the "Tom Jones Show." Shecky thanked them, and one of the girls said: "We all prefer Englebert Humperdinck." Strictly as a gag, Shecky replied: "Humperdinck's a fink."

"Now all of a sudden this one girl starts crying," Shecky recalls. "I tried to quiet her but she wouldn't be quiet, so

I resumed my dinner. All of a sudden about eighteen squad cars drive up with sirens blazing.

" 'There must be one hell of a fire around here,' said Irving Schacht.

"At that, the restaurant is filled with cops, all of them yelling, 'OK, which one is Shecky Greene?'

"I identified myself, and one cop wanted to throw the handcuffs on me.

"Irving said, 'Now why do you want to do that for?'

"The one cop with the crying girl says, 'How come you hit this girl?'

"The maitre d' chimes in, 'He didn't hit nobody.' And the bartender says, 'I ain't saying nothing. Last week I opened my mouth to the cops, and the next night, the guys come in and beat me up.'

"And then I ask, 'How come you brought along so many cops?'

"The cop answers, 'We know all about Shecky Greene fighting cops.'

"I asked, 'Where did you hear about me?'

"The cop answered, 'On the Johnny Carson, Mike Douglas, and Merv Griffin shows.'

"So I wound up down at the station house making bail for something I didn't do."

One night in Miami Beach, Shecky had better luck. Frank Sinatra saved his life, or so he gags onstage.

"Five guys are beating me up in front of the Fontainebleau and Frank, standing on the curb, says, 'That's enough.' "

His act is completely unpredictable. No two shows are ever alike. It's a kind of controlled lunacy, very reminiscent of the late, great movie comedian Hugh Herbert. Shecky is a great admirer of Herbert and does a marvelous imitation of him.

In person, Shecky is a warm, kind-hearted man, and it shows onstage. He inspires warmth from his audience and does every dialect skillfully. For instance, he tells a story in Chinese so expertly that you think you are actually understanding it. Then, midway, he stops for the punch line: "You've heard this before?"

On graduating from Chicago's Senn High School, he

found himself in the middle of World War II aboard the carrier *Bon Homme Richard,* in South Pacific combat. Shecky's battle station was the soda fountain in ship's service.

"The bombs would be falling all around and I'd be yellin' below: 'Ya want chocolate and sprinkles, too?' "

Stationed aboard the same ship at the same time was another great creative comedian—U.S. Marine Jonathan Winters. Both young comics learned to drink in the service.

"When you're at sea for months, a sailor or a marine has to get drunk to release his tensions," says Shecky.

Bob Hope thinks Shecky should get more TV exposure. He sees some of the Jackie Gleason appeal in him.

"They both have the same hobby—booze," says Bob.

Sometimes a natural comedian makes his fame in another field. Steve Lawrence is a case in point.

One of the nation's finest singers, Steve is a natural comedian—although the general public doesn't know it. Nightclub audiences at Caesars Palace know it when he trades quips with his favorite straightwoman—Eydie Gorme.

But Steve's finest line came the first time he was ever introduced to Linda Lovelace.

After the introductions, Steve casually asked the star of *Deep Throat* what she was doing currently.

"Nothing," said Linda.

"Don't worry, honey," said Steve. "I know a lot of other cocksuckers out of work too."

6

Dean Martin:
He Drinks Moderately—
Old Moderately

PEOPLE ALWAYS ARE ASKING ME if Dean Martin is drunk all the time—or if it's just an act. The answer is: Dean drinks, but he's not drunk all the time. He's not as heavy a drinker as he would have you think. Frank Sinatra spills more than Dean drinks. But Dean *does* drink; he goes around with a perpetual glow on. But I have known Dean since 1946, and I must confess that I have never seen him falling-down drunk.

It's true that he was walking home early that morning of the disastrous Sylmar earthquake and later said he didn't notice any shaking. It's also true that he will go into a McDonalds and ask for the wine list. But no, he is not a heavy drinker.

Dean is, however, a very complex man. He won't ride in an elevator, but he thinks nothing of flying at 35,000 feet in a jet.

He is a very kind, easygoing man, but he has no compassion. That's because of another phobia: he has a big thing about illness and death. Once his former wife Jeannie was seriously ill in Cedars of Lebanon for more than a month. Dean never once visited her. That bothered everybody but Jeannie, who understood his phobias.

When his brother Bill, his mother Angela, and his father Guy died, I would get the same instructions from Jeannie: don't mention the time of the funeral. "Dean is afraid there will be a lot of Italians there, crying over the coffin. He couldn't take it," she warned.

In person and on television, he is so relaxed that even Perry Como looks nervous beside him. Yet Dean has had an ulcer for years. He couldn't find his way to Oxnard, yet he is the largest single landowner in Ventura County, the rich farmland just north of Los Angeles County on the Pacific coast. He did his television show with just a dress rehearsal, fought to do it without any rehearsal at all.

He pays a big publicity firm $20,000 a year and seldom, if ever, gives an interview or seeks publicity in any way. When he does, it is usually for NBC-TV publicity people, whom he doesn't have to pay a cent.

The elevator phobia is so pronounced that he walks up eight flights to his dentist. I know, because we both go to the same dentist.

He is an excellent golfer, almost like a pro, but he always plays with guys who can take money from him. Fletcher Jones, one of Los Angeles' biggest auto dealers, used to make more money off Dean than he did selling cars. After Dean gets fed up playing with the same guy, who always seems to play just a little bit better, he changes his country club.

He started at Lakeside and put all the children of some of the Lakeside hustlers through college; then he switched to Riviera and did the same. For years he played Bel-Air, and now he's back to Riviera. Some of the guys he plays with could take money away from Arnold Palmer—and have. It's kind of sadistic, the way Dean plays golf, but he's rich enough to afford it.

He surrounds himself with gofers—the show business term for the parasitical guy who goes for sandwiches or ice. They all run scared and keep everybody away from him—except women, whom they sometimes supply. I should say *supplied* because Dean's marriage to Cathy Hawn seems at this writing to be a happy one.

In the last days with Jeannie, Dean had so many girl friends that he made Warren Beatty look like a fag. Have to tell you one amusing incident. Dean and I get along so well that the gofers don't bother with me. I am one of the few—press or otherwise—who have access to him when I want it.

One day I went over to Columbia pictures to visit Dean

when he was making a Matt Helm movie with all those gorgeous Matt Helm girls. His dressing room door was closed. One of the gofers gave me a look that told me Dean was in the midst of something good between camera setups. A good friend would never interrupt that.

Soon the door opened and Dean invited me in. With him was a gorgeous young girl. You could tell by the way Dean fondled this sweet young thing that they were more than just friends. We chatted a little bit, and soon there was a knock on the door. It was the teacher supplied by the Los Angeles Board of Education for all actresses under 18. It was time for Dean's girl friend's school lesson.

When the girl left, Dean commented: "That girl needs no lessons."

7

Jonathan Winters,
Comedy's Master of Mayhem

JONATHAN WINTERS, one of the most inventive comics ever, hasn't had a drink in more than fifteen years. I don't see much of him anymore, but in his drinking days, Jonnie and I were drinking buddies. Some of his greatest routines have never been seen on television.

Jonnie admits that he was an alcoholic at eighteen. A long period of drinking sent him to what he calls the zoo —his own name for the psycho ward. "It was a mental breakdown, not the booze, that actually put me in the psycho ward." He had stopped drinking just before he landed in the funny farm. "Coffee did it. Instead of booze, I was drinking twenty-five to forty cups of coffee a day and wondering why I never slept."

This happened at age thirty-four. Jonnie hasn't had a drink since. He's pushing fifty now—and still as funny as ever, when he's getting paid for it.

In the old drinking days, he was funny all the time. In bars, on street corners, any place a fan stopped him and asked for a routine. In short, he was always on.

I first met Jonnie one night at NBC when Steve Allen brought his old "Tonight Show" out to Hollywood. There was a party at NBC, and this rotund fellow sat down next to me and had a drink or two. We became great friends. At first I thought he was an NBC press agent from New York who was just naturally funny. Then Steve, a genius at discovering bright new talent, told me who he was. At this time, in the early fifties, Jonnie had made only one TV appearance, on the Sunday afternoon show "Omnibus."

Steve had caught it and immediately signed him for "Tonight," which was the springboard for Don Knotts, Louis Nye, Steve Lawrence, Eydie Gorme, Bill (Jose Jimenez) Dana, and many others.

Jonnie and I became instant drinking buddies. I remember that first night we wound up at the mountaintop home of Frederick William Wile, Jr., an NBC executive. Both of us went swimming, although it was a chilly 38 degrees outside in the winter air. Next day we met for lunch at the Vine Street Derby—a lunch that started innocently enough with a dozen or so screwdrivers.

Then Jonnie got talking about his hometown—I think it was Mansfield, Ohio—and the girl he had lost in high school to the guy with the big car, now the town's leading mortician. As often happens with drinkers, they get telephonitis. I suggested that we get a phone at our table and put in a call to Mansfield, and I would tell the undertaker's wife that she had blown the glamorous world of show business for life in a small town in an embalming parlor. Jonnie would be big out here.

That conversation never took place—the mortician answered the phone, and upon hearing that voice, the demon that is ever present in Winters's humor took over. He became Elwood P. Suggs, his famous small town, midwestern character. "My brother LeRoy came here from Boise, Idaho, to visit with us for a spell and Sunday a week he up and died. I'd like you boys to do a job on him."

There was a horrendous pause on the other end of the line. Finally, the mortician said: "When did you say he died?"

"Sunday a week," said Elwood.

Another pause in Ohio, and the mortician said: "My God, man. What have you been doing with the body? That's ten days."

"Well," said Elwood, "we stood him up on the front porch. It worked fine because the temperature was around zero. No need to pay for cold storage. Then some of them brat kids in the neighborhood started picking at his eyeballs. One kid was kinda nice, though. Put a softball in his hand. But when that thaw hit yesterday, LeRoy started looking a little fleshy. That's why I decided to call you boys."

Another pause on the line, and the mortician said:

"Are you sure this isn't Jonnie Winters? You always were like this, Jonnie, even in high school."

Click, and the phone hung up.

That same luncheon, Jonnie told me his idol among the comics was Red Skelton. Since Red was one of my dearest friends, in a matter of seconds I had him on the phone. "Bring him up," said Red. "I saw him on 'Omnibus.' I'd like to meet him."

Jonnie and I went up to Red's house in Bel-Air. It was filled with comics—Herb Shriner, Milton Berle, and a few others. Winters was flying high by this time. For five hours straight, he did every one of his routines until these great comics fell exhausted from laughing.

It was such a night that I wound up in bed in a little anteroom off the entry hall, on the only cot in the room, and there on the floor, asleep with an unlit cigar in his mouth, was Skelton in a sleeping bag. This scene is funny because Red's mansion must have had about twelve or fifteen luxurious bedrooms in it, and this room was little more than a maid's closet.

In the morning my first worry was for Jonnie. I felt responsible for him. Red kept looking at my shorts; they had rosebuds on them. Almost 20 years later he will still do a routine on my shorts, which, I must confess, did look a little feminine. Anyway, we didn't have to worry about Jonnie long. The phone rang. It was Winters. He had spent the whole night climbing up and down mountainsides, trying to get out of Bel-Air.

Red answered the phone and told him: "Don't worry. The guy I bought the house from still calls me periodically and asks how in the hell he can get out of Bel-Air."

This is a joke that will play big on the Bel-Air circuit. Bel-Air is a place I always get lost in, and I've been going there weekly for thirty years.

But I'll never forget how brilliant Jonnie was in front of those comedians—and how hard they laughed. Among the routines he did that night was the famous takeoff on

Shane, complete with all sound effects. I call it a takeoff on the movie, but Jonnie refers to it as "The Dalton Boys."

The Daltons are stealing all the cattle and terrorizing the widow Flickert and her small boy. Jonnie plays all parts and then he switches to the Sir Galahad gunfighter of the old west, who's just like Alan Ladd in *Shane.* The gunfighter listens plaintively to the misfortunes of the widow and her son and then rides off fearlessly to confront the Daltons.

The switch, of course, is pure Winters macabre. The gunfighter joins the Daltons and helps steal more of the widow's cattle, scaring hell out of her and her son in the process.

And then he did his John Wayne *Sands of Iwo Jima* bit, which is a classic. Jonnie, as an enlisted Marine, saw a lot of combat in the South Pacific while still a teenager.

In this routine, he is Lt. Duke Wayne, giving a pep talk to his men just before they leave the LST to go into the small boats for the suicidal landing. It's a stirring speech that would make any Marine die gloriously for the corps. It ends with this line: "I had hoped to be with you boys today, but unfortunately . . ."

Yeh, Jonnie was a card in those days, as we used to say back in Lock Haven, Pennsylvania.

I remember once coming out of the Brown Derby with him after dinner. Two fans stopped him on the street and told him how much they admired him. For forty-five minutes, Jonnie stood on Vine Street and did every routine they asked for. Another time, we went into a bar after already having a little too much to drink. The bartender refused to serve us. "You meatheads are all alike," said Jonnie to the bartender. "I know your type. You beat the draft in the war and you got it in for veterans. Well, I fought for bastards like you out in the South Pacific, and I'm not going to let you get away with it."

I didn't know that Jonnie carried props in his pocket, but all of a sudden he pulled a toy hand grenade out and started biting the pin like the combat veteran he was.

Now I was standing right next to Jonnie. I didn't think it was a toy and neither did the bartender, who literally dove under the bar. So did half the patrons. I was so stunned that like the other half, I froze in my tracks. Only Jonnie knew it was a toy. He accomplished his joke, and off we went to another bar.

Probably the turning point in Jonnie's social behavior came when he was arrested and hauled off to the psycho ward in San Francisco. Down in Fisherman's Wharf, he had boarded the old three-masted sailing schooner moored there as a tourist attraction. Jonnie, unlike the other tourists, started climbing up the rigging, shouting: "Ahoy, me buckos, Man of War off the starboard." Police and firemen hauled him down. As the police took him away, he raged: "This boat is a fake. It's got an outboard motor on it." Had Jonnie pulled this stunt in Hollywood, no one would have paid any heed. People would just have thought of it as Winters's weird sense of humor.

After a few months' rest in a San Francisco hospital, Jonnie went back on the road. Then he came to Hollywood and opened at a club on the Sunset Strip called the Crescendo. President Eisenhower was in town that night, and I was working but I was through by the midnight show. I took along Merriman Smith, Stan Tretick, and a few others of the White House Press Corps.

Jonnie came out and was hilariously funny for five minutes and then abruptly left the stage. I went back to his dressing room to see what was the matter. I found him jumping up and down. He didn't seem to recognize anybody there. I left and rejoined my friends at the table. Jonnie never came back onstage.

As we left the club we viewed an astonishing sight. There was Jonnie out in the middle of Sunset Boulevard, directing traffic. We maneuvered him out of that precarious spot and back into the club. Someone got his wife, who was living back East, on the phone. She was in town the next day and took Jonnie to another psycho ward. He said later: "I couldn't even get my best friends to believe that it was a mental breakdown. They all thought it was the booze. They didn't know what working in nightclubs did to me. I couldn't work up there and watch all those people drinking. It just got to me."

A few more weeks in the hospital and Jonnie was back on the TV talk shows, funnier than ever. That was 1959. Jonnie hasn't had a drink since. And I can't recall having seen him working a nightclub either. I recently talked with his wife over in Hawaii about all those days and commented: "He's just as funny without the sauce." "Funnier," said Mrs. Winters.

8

Welcome to Naked City

FRENCHIE ALLEN, the wife of Marty, called one day and said: "I've got you booked to judge a beauty contest in a nudist camp."

Frenchie, who once managed the Concord Hotel in the Catskills, is my unofficial manager. She also booked Marty as a judge in the same contest, which was Miss Nude World and was to be held at a place called Naked City, Indiana. It really was a nudist camp out in the middle of the Indiana farmlands, not far from Gary.

So one August day, Marty and I took off for O'Hare Airport in Chicago, where a helicopter was to meet us and take us to Naked City. I almost wrote Naked Titty, which is a Freudian slip if ever there was one. Naked City has its own heliport and we were dropped down in the middle of the camp. As we alighted, a sweet, little old lady—who had to be eighty, if she was a day—came up to greet us. She was stark naked and gray all over.

"Welcome to Naked City," she smiled. Neither Marty nor I could bring ourselves to lower our eyes. We were scanning the blue skies as we thanked her. Who wants to look at someone in the nude who could be your own grandmother?

It was the first visit to a nudist camp for both of us. First thing I noticed was a guy with a pot belly, pushing a lawn mower in front of his mobile home. His balls were dangling down near his knees. "Milton Berle would be castrated in this camp," I said to Marty, who broke up.

The little old lady took us to the camp's headquarters. A particularly sexy looking girl, completely nude, stopped us. Marty Allen, I have found, is one of the most instantly recognizable of stars. She soon found out that we were to be judges. She put her arms around me and said, pointing to a trailer, "That's where I'm staying. If you don't have any place to sleep, come on over."

The little old lady pulled us away and scolded her. "No fooling around with the judges," she said. It turned out the girl was Miss Italy, and she was determined to win at any cost.

Inside the headquarters, a particularly gorgeous secretary, who was wearing only a thin belt around her midsection, was sitting at a typewriter. She must have had a forty-two inch bust that drooped down to the keys. As Marty pointed out, "She erased everything she wrote."

The secretary asked us some questions. It had been a long trip, and Marty and I simultaneously asked her where the men's room was. As she pointed, her magnificent breasts jumped. Marty and I went off in different directions.

It turned out that we, being judges, were barred from staying at the nudist camp. So it was back into the helicopter, which, in a matter of minutes, dropped us in the parking lot of a Holiday Inn in the middle of nowhere. It was surrounded by cornfields as far as the eye could see. A major interstate highway ran past it, which explained the location. Marty and I both figured we had nothing to look forward to in this desolate spot but sleep. We went to our rooms, showered, and arranged to meet downstairs for dinner.

Now even we had not known where we were going to stay when we left Los Angeles International Airport that morning. But as we walked past the cashier's cage into the restaurant, the phone rang.

"Wanna bet that's Frenchie?" asked Marty.

The cashier answered the phone and handed it to Marty. "Yes, Frenchie," said Marty. How she ever found us, we will never know, but that's Frenchie. She knows how to use a phone better than Alexander Graham Bell.

After a quiet dinner, interrupted by some tourists asking Marty for autographs, the manager invited us to visit the motel's discotheque. You won't believe this. This discotheque was like Las Vegas on a Saturday night. It was the swingingest place imaginable. It seemed as if every young girl for miles around had descended on the place, and we danced with them all. You couldn't believe you were out in the middle of a cornfield in Indiana.

At one point a grandmother type with too much to drink walked by our table and suddenly realized that a familiar face from television was sitting there. She actually peed in her pants on the spot. It was the goddamndest thing I have ever seen. She just stood there—as transfixed as we were—and let a torrent drop on the floor. I told Marty that I hadn't heard of that reaction since Rudolph Valentino. We both moved our chairs back as a busboy came over with a mop. The woman naturally was embarrassed, so we invited her to sit down for a drink. Little did we know that she would have eight drinks before the security guard took her upstairs to let her sleep it off.

Next day was the actual contest. Professor Irwin Corey, the world's foremost expert, was the third judge. Everybody was nude except the paying customers—and us. Dick Drost, who runs the camp, sells tickets at fifteen dollars a head, and there must have been 15,000 people there. He's got a gold mine. And here Marty and I got nothing except expenses.

There were about 50 girls in the contest and they were quite beautiful. The first prize was $10,000. Poor Miss Scotland was a light-skinned redhead who got a terrible sunburn during the contest. A half hour more and she would have collapsed. I noticed that the photographers covering the contest were mostly nude. One guy wore only a hat with a press card in it—just like a Jimmy Cagney movie.

Marty and I were a little hurt that no one had asked us to take off our clothes. You get a funny feeling, being dressed among nudists. It makes you feel out of place. I told Marty that if I took my clothes off, everybody would know it was my first day in camp. Professor Irwin Corey, who is as nuts in person as he is on TV, worked topless.

Contest over, we had a plane to catch. The helicopter was busy, so the gorgeous secretary put on a sexy body suit and a chauffeur's cap and drove us to O'Hare Airport in a big Cadillac upholstered in flaming pink. I don't know whether it was the pink upholstery or the sexy chauffeur, but there were a lot of stares from other cars on the interstate.

We had been looking at this secretary for days in the nude. Somehow, when she opened the door at the airport, she took on a new sex appeal. That short, leotard-like body suit made her ravenously sexy looking.

There's some kind of a moral there.

9

Who Would Rather Be
Henny Youngman?

ASK ME WHO my favorite movie tycoon is and I'll say Jack L. Warner, a frustrated comic.

Jack and I have hit it off ever since I first started covering Hollywood. I'm a great laugher. It was Jack Benny who once said: "Jack Warner would sooner do Henry Youngman's act than make a great picture." It's true.

On the opening day of *Giant*, Warners tossed a big luncheon. I took Elizabeth Taylor to the lunch because, believe it or not, she had never been on the Warners lot before that day. She had never even met Jack Warner. People think everybody in Hollywood knows everybody else. Not so.

At the luncheon, I'm sitting with Elizabeth and Director George Stevens, and J.L. comes to the table and says: "Jim, I have never met our lovely star."

I introduced the two. Now you would expect the usual studio head to go into flowery words of welcome and all the usual horseshit. Do you know what Jack said to Elizabeth, who looked gorgeous that day, as always? "Some people may like a moon to make love," said J.L. "I like a double bed." Elizabeth looked at me quizzically. I was laughing, so she laughed too. It was a typical Jack Warner line.

Warner, as befits his preeminence in the industry, often was called upon to make speeches at solemn industry affairs. At least they were solemn until Jack got to the podium. Hollywood is a town that takes itself much too seriously. Guys like Jack Warner make it the Gilbert and Sullivan operetta it really is.

A fellow, by the name of Bill Rice, in the Warner's publicity department used to write all of Warner's speeches. Bill was a nervous type, and it was an ordeal to watch him during the week he wrote one of J.L.'s speeches. There were more revisions than there were for a presidential speech. Bill would take a comma out there and put another line someplace else, on orders from Warner's office. Come night of the speech, and Jack would invariably throw the speech away with some line like "Who wants to hear this shit?" Mercifully, Rice usually was not present, else he would have slit his throat long ago.

When *My Fair Lady* opened on Broadway in the middle fifties, a multimillionaire oilman named Tex Feldman wanted to throw a special New Year's Eve party for his wife, who had fallen in love with the Lerner-Loewe classic.

Tex hired the big party hall at Romanoff's and brought in decorators—he may have hired Cecil Beaton—to redo the room to match the famous Ascot setting of *My Fair Lady*. It cost him $100,000 for that little chore, and probably another $100,000 for the food, champagne, and caviar. I was invited and so was Jack L. Warner.

In the course of the evening, I was carrying on a very animated conversation with Natalie Wood, when all of a sudden I felt a hand feeling my ass quite amorously.

I turned around to see who the culprit was. It was J.L.—standing with his back to me and groping blindly but meaningfully.

"J.L.," I said, "I didn't know you cared."

You should have seen the look he gave me. "Goddamn it, Jim. I thought you were a broad."

I told the story around, and a few days later, J.L. called and said: "Keep that quiet. All my male employees are starting to walk on the other side of the street when I come on the lot."

J.L. is involved in one of my favorite sneak preview stories. In the silent era, Paramount made a big hit: *Beau Geste,* starring Ronald Colman and William Powell. Immediately J.L. assigned writers to come up with a similar Foreign Legion story. In the leading feminine role, he cast Irene Rich.

Now, as you all know, *Beau Geste* is a tragedy, and Warner's version was meant to be. J.L. took the film out on a sneak preview, and the audience laughed in all the serious places. This would have caused any other studio tycoon to scrap the movie then and there. Not J.L. He said: "Fuck 'em. If they want a comedy, they'll get a comedy."

So he took the picture and recut it so that it moved at jet speed. Then he scrapped all the original dialogue and called in one of his gag writers, Jimmy Starr, who had written comedy titles for Mack Sennett.

Now remember, these were the silent days. Nothing had to be reshot. Titles were just cards inserted between the shots of the action. Jimmy came up with hilarious gag titles. When the picture was sneaked again, it became one of Warner's hit comedies. That was fifty years ago, and I don't believe that Irene Rich has forgiven J.L. to this day. After all, she had made her reputation as a serious actress.

The Warner Brothers, of course, are responsible for the talkie revolution financed by J.L.'s favorite actor—Rin Tin Tin: "The only actor I have ever known who never complained about his dressing room," said J.L.

But Rin Tin Tin the box office star was not the original World War One German dog that you read about in those days. J.L. signed the original war dog and his trainer without the huge German shepherd being present.

Came first day of shooting, and J.L. showed up on the set: Rin Tin Tin promptly bit the head of the studio in the ass.

"Fire the goddamn mutt," said J.L.

It was Rin Tin Tin's son who took over.

Once Madame Chiang Kai-shek and a group of Chinese dignitaries, including the Chinese ambassador to the United States, visited Warner's. J.L. tossed them a luncheon befitting visiting heads of state. Everything about it was in exquisite taste, supervised by Richard Gully, a gentleman of the old British school. Then Jack got up to address the group. He looked at the sea of Oriental faces, and he became Henny Youngman: "Looking over this gathering today reminds me that I forgot to send out my laundry."

10

Henny
(A guy goes into a psychiatrist's office)
Youngman

THE PHONE RINGS. Maybe it's from Atlanta, Miami Beach, or New York City. Never a word of greeting. The voice says: "A guy goes into a psychiatrist's office . . ." The opening varies according to the joke, but I always know who it is: the one and only Henny Youngman.

The first time I met Henny was many years ago at the Hollywood Brown Derby. He sat down in the booth.

"I just got arrested in Beverly Hills," said Youngman.

Like the perfect straight man, I replied, with great alarm: "Why?"

"I was driving an American-made car."

He is truly the king of the one-liners. His whole life is one one-liner after another. It's the toughest form of comedy. Henny lives or dies—as does his career—when he throws that one-liner at the audience. Often he has to make a comeback every thirty seconds. His friend Milton Berle says: "Henny is only funny when he's dying up there, which is often enough to keep him going for fifty years."

But there's another joke side of Henny you seldom hear about—the practical joker.

Youngman comes to town and invites me to have lunch with him at the Copa Room of Linny's delicatessen in Beverly Hills. Only in Beverly Hills would a delicatessen have a Copa Room. The Copa Room has only one employee—bartender Irving Case, whom I always call Maitre D' Irving. It has a private entrance off Beverly Drive, but

Youngman, this day, wants to go through the main deli, where he stops at the meat counter. He buys a half pound of corned beef and sticks the package in his side pocket. This doesn't surprise me because nothing surprises me about Youngman.

We go into the Copa Room through the back entrance in the main delicatessen. Irving takes our orders. Henny orders a corned-beef sandwich. Still I am not surprised.

The corned-beef sandwich comes. Irving turns away to serve another customer. Youngman reaches into his side pocket, takes out the half pound of corned beef, and slips it between the two slices of rye bread.

It makes the biggest sandwich you ever saw—a good six inches thick. Henny lifts the sandwich to his mouth and yells: "Irving!" Maitre D' Irving turns and gazes in shock at Youngman's sandwich. "For once, Irving," says Henny, "you have given me a decent corned-beef sandwich."

Henny is still in a playful mood. He insists that we walk back to the Beverly Wilshire Hotel, only a few blocks. Fine. It's a gorgeous Southern California day in February, with the sun shining like August. We take a few steps and Henny hails a cab. As I say, nothing surprises me about Henny. The cab pulls up to the curb and, out of another pocket, Henny pulls a card that reads "Off Duty" and keeps walking.

We reach Wilshire Boulevard and run into Jan Murray, a devoted family man among comics. The two of them toss a few lines at one another. Finally, Henny reaches into his wallet and says to Jan: "Would you like to see my pride and joy?"

Jan, figuring it's Henny's grandchildren, beams yes. Henny shows him another card on which are two boxes of detergent respectively named Pride and Joy. Corny, but Youngman. Who would have him any other way?

It is World War II, and there are long lines and longer waits for dining-car service on trains. Henny is riding west with Harry Brand, director of publicity for 20th Century-Fox. They are on the famed Super Chief, but the lines are still long.

The train stops in Albuquerque, where it's met by a

bunch of Indians. Henny gets off the train, presumably to buy some Indian souvenirs. Harry stays on.

The train pulls out of Albuquerque and Harry and Henny get in line for the dining car. The train is just pulling into Gallup, New Mexico, some 90 or 100 miles west of Albuquerque, and Henny and Harry finally get their seats in the dining car.

The two start to eat as the conductor comes up to the table and hands Harry a telegram, datelined Albuquerque. It reads: "Harry, please pass me the salt. Love. Henny."

Sometimes, as once happened before World War II, Henny is the victim of a practical joke.

It was Henny's first trip to Hollywood. He had been signed to play himself in some long forgotten movie. As soon as he hit town, he called an old friend, Harry Crane, the comedy writer.

"Harry," said Henny, "how about taking me to some of those wild Hollywood parties with all the starlets?" Harry, the way all of us have done a thousand times, explained that there is no such thing, that people out here are hard-working and homecooking, not to mention early-rising. But Henny had read too many scandal magazines.

"He kept bugging the ass off me," recalls Harry. "Finally one day I call him. 'Henny, You're in luck. I got you an invite to the Starlets Annual Nudist banquet. These are all the young actresses in town who belong to a nudist colony.' "

Henny got excited—almost as excited as his wife, Sadie, will get when she reads this. Crane gave Henny the address of a huge mansion in Bel-Air and told him to be there at eight sharp—not a minute earlier nor a minute later. As Crane recalls: "I knew there was going to be a big black tie dinner this night, with every important tycoon, producer, and director in town there. I knew the host, and I told him I would provide him the greatest entertainment in show business. Just don't ask questions." The next step was to hire a butler type from Central Casting, as part of the act.

Youngman showed up at the house right on time. He rang the bell, and a stark-naked butler answered the door.

"Right this way, Mr. Youngman," said the butler. "I'll show you where to disrobe."

Henny was led to a side room where he took off all his clothes. The butler then pointed to a door and said: "The rest of the guests are in there."

Henny, stark naked and smoking a cigar, opened the door and looked down from a landing upon one of the most distinguished gatherings in Hollywood history—Louis B. Mayer, Sam Goldwyn, and a few other tycoons sat there, dressed to the teeth—in a complete state of shock. A couple of the wives screamed.

Youngman recalls that the cigar fell out of his mouth onto the expensive carpet. Since he couldn't come up with a suitable one-liner, he did the only thing he could—made a fast exit, picking up his clothes on the way. None of the guests—not even the host—had expected such entertainment. Henny Youngman was the talk of the town for many days afterwards. By coincidence, he didn't make another movie until long after World War II.

The only thing in Hollywood history that ever topped Youngman's nude entrance happened only a few months afterward, this time quite by chance. It has nothing to do with Henny, but it involved a marvelous one-liner.

One of MGM's biggest male stars decided, on the spur of the moment, to surprise his famous actress wife on her birthday. When the male star finished shooting for the day, he invited some of the couple's cronies from the studio out to his home to provide the surprise. Clark Gable, who told this to me, was among the cronies.

The male star brought the gang into the house and hid them at the foot of the stairs. Then he shouted to his wife: "I got something special for your birthday."

She soon appeared and provided her own surprise. Bare-ass naked at the top of the stairs, she yelled: "I hope it's a fuck because I'm ready!"

A few of the guests uttered faint cries of "Surprise," but nobody was able to top what they had just seen and heard.

PART II

The Tycoons

*Jack L. Warner belongs here,
but he would rather be
listed under comics.*

11

I Saw Too Much of
Howard Hughes

WHEN HOWARD HUGHES debunked the Clifford Irving book hoax on that famous telephone press conference, everyone asked how I was able to recognize his voice so readily while all the others checked him with catch questions.

First, I was the only one of that televised panel who had ever known Hughes as a friend. Several had talked to him at aviation press conferences; one admitted that he had seen him in a telephone booth once; another admitted that he had never seen him.

But one reporter does not a press conference make.

Anyway, my story was different. I saw too much of Howard. In fact, in one week he called me on the phone 200 times. No wonder I recognized his voice. It is forever etched on my memory.

When people first learn of my escapades with Howard, they are always somewhat shocked by my appraisal of him. They are amazed when I paint him as charming, affable, extremely well-mannered, humorous, and not nearly as eccentric as legend would have you believe.

But that's the Howard Hughes I know, and since I am one of the few people—including the $500,000 a year executives on his payroll—who have spent any time with him in the last twenty-five years, it's an accurate, if rare, evaluation of him. Howard and I were friends during what might be called the only frivolous period of his life—as a movie tycoon. He was not that hard to see in those days, if you were nocturnal, as he was.

Howard's stay in Las Vegas of a few years ago was not his first in the Nevada resort. He had lived there in the early fifties, long before he bought up the town and half the state of Nevada. He has always liked Vegas because the air is pure and it keeps the same hours he does. When he would finish work, he would wander around the Las Vegas Strip. A favorite stopping place, early in the morning, was the old El Rancho Vegas, where he could buy a sandwich and chat with a waiter or a bartender, though he seldom, if ever, took a drink. He never gambled.

None of the tourists—the great majority of the population of Las Vegas—ever knew who he was, although he mingled with them. Howard liked anonymity, and Las Vegas is loaded with it.

I remember one hot summer morning when I was en route to Los Angeles after a cross-country drive. I pulled into the parking lot of the El Rancho to grab a fast cup of coffee before hitting the Mojave Desert. It was about 4 A.M. The children were all asleep in the car except daughter Carol, about fourteen at the time.

I walked out of the coffee shop with a tall, slim fellow with black hair and black mustache. He wore a slouch felt hat and a business suit. He needed a shave, and his clothes looked as if he had slept in them. His costume definitely was not Las Vegas casual. There was an excuse for his unkempt appearance, he told me. He had been working for 48 hours without sleep, and now he was going back to his penthouse suite at the Flamingo to hit the sack.

I got into my car. He got into his—a much cheaper model than mine, incidentally. We waved good-bye to each other.

As I sat down in the front seat, Carol asked, "Dad, who was that bum you were talking to? Did he try to hit you for some money?"

"That," I said, "was no bum. That's Howard Hughes."

Howard, in those days, would chat affably and then, in parting, make an inevitable request: "Jim, please don't write that you saw me."

I never did because I wasn't a gossip columnist in those days and there was no need to write anything for the AP about chance encounters in casinos or parking lots. But there came a time when I had to write plenty about Howard for the Associated Press. And that's how I got to see much of The Man.

The Man, incidentally, is how all of Hughes's top aides refer to their boss. Often I would get calls from one of Howard's Mormons—he prefers hiring members of that sect because of their nonalcoholic tenets—and they would begin: "The Man wants to call you around 10 P.M. tonight. Where can he reach you?"

I would tell them, and the calls from The Man always came through punctually.

By way of background, here's how my Howard Hughes series for AP was spawned. Along about late 1953, Hughes, as head of RKO Studios in Hollywood, got into trouble with the Roman Catholic Legion of Decency over a Jane Russell movie called *French Line.*

It was considered shocking in those days. Compared with the filth on today's market, it was about as sexy as Shirley Temple in *Little Miss Marker.*

But the legion rated it a C—for condemned, the worst. The only thing I remember about the movie is Kim Novak, who made her debut playing a girl in the chorus.

Defying the legion's edict that he cut certain scenes from the movie, Howard opened *French Line* in St. Louis. Only Hughes, who would later best the Mafia in Las Vegas, dared take on the Catholic Church in those days.

The very next day, my boss called me into the office and said: "The Cardinal (James Francis Cardinal McIntyre) called me last night about Hughes. I think we should do an in-depth profile on him now that he's in the headlines. Call Dick Davis over at Carl Byoir and Associates and arrange an interview with Howard."

He was being naive, of course, since at least 1,000 reporters had tried without success to arrange interviews with Hughes.

Discreetly, I told the boss: "You don't call Howard. He calls you. I suggest that we start the series on what I already know and then play it by ear."

It was a gamble but it paid off. For a week or so, I researched and wrote five articles covering everything from his remarkable contribution to aviation to his numerous girl friends. I knew all the girls, and they all loved to talk about Howard, except one—Jean Peters.

The research on Hughes's role in pioneering the aircraft industry in this country was fascinating. Probably no other pioneer, and this includes Lindbergh, ever did as much as Howard. In 1954, there was not a plane in the air that didn't have some Hughes design component. In 1938, Hughes designed a plane and piloted it and its crew around the world in a record-breaking ninety-one hours. So remarkable was this plane that the Japanese stole the design; it became the famed Zero of World War II. The Lockheed Lightning, the first twin-boom fighter, as well as the mighty Constellation, were Hughes-designed. He's an engineering genius, so much so that he even invented the uplift bra for a Jane Russell movie. On that matter, he once commented to me: "It was very simple. Just an application of basic engineering principles."

The series told of his early days in Houston as the son of the man who invented the famous rock-bit oil-well drill that chewed through flint as easily as mud. Howard's inheritance from his father at age nineteen always has been greatly exaggerated. Some reports at the time had it as high as $17 million. Actually it was only $650,000, a figure I got by writing the probate clerk in Houston; Howard was quite impressed that I was on the button. That's still a good figure for an inheritance, but today's Hughes fortune, around $2.5 billion, is a tribute to Howard's genius of management.

The series also told of his early visits to Hollywood, where he first came as guest of his famous author-uncle, Rupert Hughes, and later he produced some of the all-time classic movies—*Hell's Angels, Scarface, The Front Page,* and others. No matter what he did, he excelled.

Even as a golfer, he was listed as a scratch handicap player in those long-ago days. Willie Hunter, the old Scottish pro at Riviera Country Club, where Howard often played, used to tell of the time Howard came into the pro shop after firing a 68, a fancy score then and even now, as the pros who make the Los Angeles Open will tell you. It is one of the nation's toughest courses.

"Willie," asked Howard. "I'm thinking of entering the

National Amateur this year. Do you think I have a chance to beat Bobby Jones?"

"No," said Willie. "Not a chance."

Willie said that was the last time Hughes ever picked up his golf sticks. He was too much the perfectionist to place second. That was nearly fifty years ago. Over at Lakeside Golf Club in Hollywood, where Hughes is still a member, his check for dues comes in on time each month. Although it's been half a century since he has set foot in the place, his name is still on a locker.

My series was very readable, even without Hughes. We had a winner going. When it was mailed to AP headquarters in New York, the decision was made to move it immediately. I learned about this not from the AP, where it should have come from, but from Dick Davis, a man from Hughes's public relations firm. Hughes was so powerful that he had obtained a copy of my series even before it reached the West Coast on the AP wire. Davis said Howard wanted to talk to me, and as he talked he quoted my own words back to me. I was impressed.

The next day, Sunday, brought the first of that week's 200 calls from Hughes. He wanted to know where he could reach me. By coincidence, that night I was to be the guest of Producer Jerry Wald, then in charge of his own RKO production set-up, at the Screen Directors Guild's Annual Awards Dinner. Jerry had been moaning to me about how impossible it was to see his boss, Hughes, so that he could get his pictures off the ground. He was partnered with Norman Krasna at the time; the combination is thought to have been the composite for Sammy Glick in Budd Schulberg's great Hollywood novel *What Makes Sammy Run?* They were known around Hollywood as "The Whiz Kids," but they slowed down after some frustrating experiences with Hughes.

Before I left for the dinner, one of the Mormons had informed me that The Man wanted to call me that night. I told him where I would be and at what table. Midway through the dinner, the maitre d' came to the RKO table and announced that Mr. Howard Hughes was on the phone. There was a lot of instant and collective gulping. "He wants to talk with Mr. Bacon," the maitre d' added. It's doubtful if any of the high-paid talent at the table had ever seen the boss, let alone received a phone call from him. As I left to take the call, I could see that they were impressed.

On the phone, Howard told me that he had seen the rest of the articles and that he wanted urgently to talk with me in person. Fine. Next day was Monday, and he would let me know where and when. When I returned to the table, Wald kept pumping me: Was it a gag? Or was it really Howard who called? I assured him that it was no gag.

Soon the whole room—which included the ruling gentry of Hollywood—was abuzz with my phone call. L.B. Mayer, Jack L. Warner, even Clark Gable were among those who asked me about the call. Naturally, I was enjoying every minute of this instant fame among world-famous people.

The next day brought one of those torrential California rains—the kind that wash houses down canyons. Mid-afternoon, with the rain still pouring, the Mormon called: "The Man wants to see you at Clover Field in Santa Monica." He gave explicit instructions, including the gate number. I drove out there, barely able to see in the rain. At the gate, a man greeted me and pointed to a car parked nearby. "Will you please follow that car?" he instructed politely.

Trailing the car, I soon found myself driving down a runway where a huge Constellation was parked. It was Howard's personal plane. Next to the big plane sat a small Chevrolet—the stripped-down model with stick shift and no extras that dealers often advertised in those days for $1,995. No more. At the wheel was Howard. As he invited me to sit down next to him, I noted that the Chevy had linoleum instead of carpeting on the floor. Howard could have bought Rolls Royces by the fleet but never did. After all, if you're Howard Hughes who have you got to impress? Davis and Bill Utley, another public relations man, were in the backseat.

Howard very charmingly apologized for the unorthodox meeting place, explaining that he wanted to be near his plane in case the weather unexpectedly cleared. We talked for three hours, sitting there in a rain that could only be compared to a waterfall.

It could have been a tense meeting, between a man who shunned publicity like the plague and a reporter who had given him too much. The first article in the series had already appeared in print that day among the AP's 8,000 member outlets throughout the world.

Howard said that he had investigated my boss and his friendship with Cardinal McIntyre and, in a nice way, added that he thought himself the victim of a hatchet job because of his fight with the Catholic Legion of Decency. I told him that had not been my intent. I asked him if he thought the articles he had already read were fair.

"Yes," he said, "they are. I'm not blaming you in any way. You have to do what your boss says, I understand that."

I was somewhat nonplussed at Howard's attitude and told him so. "I'd like to have it said about me," I said, "that I was a genius who had contributed probably more than any other one man to the development of aviation in this country."

He admitted that it was all very complimentary but insisted that he didn't want any publicity, good or bad, about himself. He indicated to the two men in the backseat. "I pay them big money to keep my name out of the paper." Then he smiled: "I'll tell you why I don't want publicity. Every time something is written about me, some minority stockholder who owns 100 shares of RKO files a suit. I've had these guys come to court with stories like this pasted on cardboard. And then the lawyers question me paragraph by paragraph. The reason I shun publicity is because I haven't got the time to go to court and still run a business. There's nothing I hate worse than litigation.

"RKO represents about 5 percent of my holdings, and it takes up 95 percent of my time because there is something about the movie business, even the corporate end, that invites publicity and lawsuits. That's why I hide out. I could be badgered to death by agents, executives, and stockholders. It's getting that we don't have a studio anymore. Our contract list is five actors and 135 lawyers."

When you hear it from The Man's own lips, his hermitlike eccentricities don't seem half as odd.

Howard wanted things changed on some upcoming articles, since he realized even he couldn't stop publication. One particularly human paragraph he wanted eliminated completely. I couldn't understand why. It read: "Though sometimes called ruthless in business deals, he has a gentle side. Once his car hit a mongrel dog. He sped it to a vet and spared no expense or worry until it was taken care of."

The story, which I got from an eyewitness, had only one error. Another car had struck the dog. The rest was accurate: Howard, following, had stopped and taken the dog to a veterinarian, who got out of bed when he found out who brought in the patient. Howard did not leave the vet's office until he got word that the stray dog would be all right.

"Why in hell, Howard," I asked, "would you be ashamed to see that story in print? It's human interest. It reveals a side of you unknown to the general public."

He replied, "Well, how do you think the employees at Hughes Aircraft would feel if they knew that their boss was out on the street picking up mongrel dogs at all hours of the morning?"

"They'd love you for it," I said.

Next we went from dogs to beautiful women. One paragraph quoted a beautiful young Hollywood actress who had a reputation for being the only virgin in town, because of a zealous blockingback mother who ran interference for her. It related how she received her first kiss and her first mink coat from Howard. Hughes laughed as he gave his version:

"This girl's own mother called me and said she wanted her daughter to have a date with me. 'She's clean. I guarantee it,' the mother said. I not only didn't have a date with her, I didn't give her a mink coat."

"Well," I replied, "the girl lied to me then, because that is exactly what she told me. And her mother was sitting right beside her."

Hughes, still smiling, said that it was harmless enough to say that he dated her, but that the mink coat bit already had caused him trouble. "Jean Peters read it and called and asked: 'How come you never gave me a mink coat?' "

I asked Howard how he got out of that one. "I told her

I couldn't stand to see little animals killed and referred her to the story about the mongrel dog."

Then we discussed Howard's other girl friends. To any woman in the movies, Howard represented what Mt. Everest is to a mountain climber. All the stars from Billie Dove in silent movies to Lana Turner in the talkies thought they were the one who could hook him. I remarked that I held him in considerable awe, the way he juggled those girls—he sometimes had twenty on the string at a time. And none seemed to be jealous of the others. I also gave him a little advice to the lovelorn.

"Howard," I said, as we sat there in that little car. "If I were you, I'd marry Jean Peters. She's beautiful and she's as secretive as you are. She's the only one of your girl friends who refused to contribute to this series. Some, like Terry Moore and Debra Paget, I couldn't shut up."

Howard reflected soberly for a moment and commented: "Come to think of it, you're right."

A few years later, he heeded my advice but gave the exclusive story to his oldest friend in Hollywood—Louella Parsons. I understood that. Louella, a dear friend of mine, called me a few moments after her story hit the streets. As a fellow newspaperman, I understood that, too.

"Jimmy," she said in that famous voice, "Howard told me to tell you that he took your advice and asked that I call you."

I thanked her and then said: "Louella, how come you buried such a page-one banner headline story deep in your column in the *Examiner*?"

Louella then revealed that Howard dictated the play under threat of issuing a formal denial if it came out as anything other than a mere column item. "I begged him to let me make it the lead of my column," she said. "He wouldn't hear of it, so what else could I do? I know Howard well enough to know that if he says he will do something, he will do it. If you want to make a news story out of it, go ahead. You have my word that it's true. I have kept my word with Howard."

No sooner had Louella hung up than an urgent message came over the wire from AP, New York: "Parsons, *Journal-American*, has Howard Hughes marrying Jean Peters. Unsays where. *Daily News* asks ours soonest."

As the Hughes expert, the message was thrown to me. I replied, without mentioning Louella, that I knew the story was true and that I could write a story saying so flatly without quoting any source. The conservative AP would have none of that.

For several days nothing appeared in print except Louella's item. True to her word, she didn't try to expand on it; it was the price she had to pay for getting an exclusive story. Her rival, Hedda Hopper, called me and said the *Los Angeles Times* was pressuring her for a story but that she couldn't confirm it. I told Hedda I knew the story was true but didn't tell her how I knew. Then, all of a sudden, AP New York ran a story, giving the *New York Daily News* as its source, reporting the wedding of Howard and Jean at an undisclosed place. The *News* story had a Hollywood dateline and was by-lined by Florabel Muir, the *News*'s veteran Los Angeles correspondent. Florabel had quoted a friend as her source.

I called Florabel and said: "I know who your 'friend' is."

She answered: "I know damn well you do. It was Louella, who else?"

Louella, God bless her, was too good a newspaperwoman to bury that story inside—even if she had to give it to a rival. I had already told her that the AP had turned down my version.

To this day, no one has ever been able to find out where that marriage took place. There was quite a lot of speculation that Howard bought himself an island in the Caribbean, got married there, and then sealed the records forevermore.

Years later, in Portofino, Italy, I learned something that might give a clue to the locale of the marriage. Gina Lollobrigida, an old Hughes girl friend, told me that Hughes wanted to marry her once.

"He brought me over to America and kept me in a hotel for a month where I couldn't do anything but eat. Then one day he took me up in his plane and said that the pilot of a plane has the same powers as a captain of an ocean liner. We could be married right then and there up in the sky, with Howard as the priest and the groom both.

"He was very convincing, but I kept saying: 'Howard, I am already married.' And so we landed, and he never asked me again."

No matter what, neither Howard nor Jean will ever tell. C'est la vie!

Howard, greatest of all living legends, knows all the stories about himself. He called most of them untrue, ridiculous, and harmless, and he laughed about them. But he was upset over the others, particularly the comics' continual gags about his wearing tennis shoes with a tuxedo. Sitting in his Chevy in the rain, he looked down at his plain black shoes—more Thom McAn than Gucci— and said: "The only time I ever remember wearing tennis shoes was when I used to play tennis."

Remembering the Willy Hunter golf story, I commented: "I suppose you gave up tennis when someone told you you couldn't beat Bill Tilden at Wimbledon." He laughed.

Some of Howard's versions of the legends are better than the legends themselves. For instance, one Hollywood story had Howard visiting RKO studios at midnight shortly after he bought it and uttering the single command: "Paint it"—then never entering the studio again.

Not true, said Howard. "All the years I owned RKO, I never once set foot inside the place."

Actually, what had happened was that he had driven down Gower Street one night past the studio and had observed to an aide that it needed a coat of paint. It was promptly painted.

Another famous Hollywood story of that era had Hughes personally restyling Mona Freeman's hair for a movie called *Angel Face*. She was one of his girl friends at the time. Here's another Hughes legend by the wayside. Howard told me:

"This girl was sitting around her house sulking one day with nothing better to do, so she cut off all her hair— right in the middle of a movie. Here we had money invested in her, and she had a crew cut. There were discussions, and I simply ordered that the hairdressing department style a wig so that we could match the earlier shots."

Robert Mitchum, sometimes given to exaggeration, got a lot of circulation with a story of a meeting with Howard, then Mitch's boss at RKO. To hear Mitch tell it, when the meeting had progressed past the dinner hour, Mitchum said he was hungry for a good hamburger.

"Hughes said he knew a place that made the best hamburgers in the country," recalls Mitch. "I thought it was around the corner, but we drove down to Santa Monica, boarded Hughes's plane, flew to Tucson, taxied up to a a hamburger stand at the edge of the airport."

Howard thought this hilarious but added: "I've never even had Mitchum in a plane." At that he looked at the rain and his big plane on the runway.

"I guess I won't get that baby in the air tonight."

"Where were you going?" I asked.

"I thought we might fly down to Tucson for a couple of hamburgers," he laughed.

Later, we did.

He did confirm another Mitchum story, however. Mitchum had once told me how Hughes had him in three pictures back-to-back: "Finally, it was all over, and I just had to get out of town. I piled Chris and Jim in our camper and told Dorothy (his wife) that I was taking the boys fishing for a week or two. I didn't tell her where I was going because I really didn't know myself. We drove and drove until we were someplace where they had never heard of me, Howard Hughes, or RKO—the Snake River in Idaho. Man, it was peaceful. And the trout were biting.

"One night the boys and I were sitting around the camp fire and I was thinking how great it was to be lost, when a forest ranger drives up in a jeep. He said there was an emergency phone call for me in his fire tower about twenty miles down the road—the only phone for a hundred miles or more."

Mitch, fearful that something was wrong at home, didn't even recall that he had told no one where he was. At the tower, he placed the call via the forest service network to the operator in Los Angeles. On the other end of the line came Hughes; he wanted Mitchum back in town to start another picture.

I asked Hughes how he ever found Mitch in that wilderness, one of the few remaining primitive areas in the United States. "It was easy," said Howard. And, for him, it probably was.

Our session in the car over, we parted on a very friendly note. Once more he apologized for bringing me out in the rain. I drove away thinking that living legends can be fun.

It so happened that I was invited that same night to a party over at Ciro's given by Darryl F. Zanuck for his daughter Susan. As I walked in the door, I was greeted by Terry Moore, a Hughes flame at the time.

"You've been out talking with Howard, haven't you?" she said.

News travels fast in Hollywood: I had come directly from Clover Field to Ciro's—a half hour trip at most.

Along about midnight, Zanuck, feeling no pain, came onstage to thank his guests for coming to the party. As he talked, he kept glancing skyward at trapeze equipment still hanging there. It had been used earlier in the evening by one of the acts. Suddenly he tore off his coat, shirt, and undershirt and announced: "I used to be pretty damn good at chinning myself one-handed. Let's see if I can still do it."

Clifton Webb, Mrs. Zanuck, and a few others of us, knowing what he was going to do, tried to talk him off stage, but Darryl would have none of our entreaties. He grabbed the bar and pulled and pulled and pulled, but never quite made that one-armed chin. I sat there thinking—first, three hours in a parked car with Hughes and, now, watching one of the biggest names in Hollywood history up on a stage trying a one-armed chin trick. It was a night to remember.

But the next night was even more incredible. All day long the calls came from the Mormons and some from Hughes. Once he asked me to stand by while he changed phones. "Ah, that's better," he explained. "I'm sitting in a bathtub now and your voice is more distinct. You know, I have quite a hearing problem and the phone has to be just in the right place for me to hear right."

Howard was still worrying about a hatchet job. Always polite, he kept hammering away on that subject. I assured him that such would not be the case if I had anything to do with it. He wanted to talk with my boss and I told him I would try to arrange a meeting. The time was set for late afternoon at the Paul Hesse photography studio on the Sunset Strip. Paul did a lot of still work for Howard in his search for beautiful women to place under contract at RKO.

To sidestep, it was Howard who first discovered Marilyn Monroe when she was working as a riveter at Lockheed out in Burbank. A cheesecake picture of her appeared in a house organ, and Hughes immediately ordered a photographer to shoot more stills of her. That was the end of her marriage to a Van Nuys cop and the beginning of her fabulous career.

I relayed Hughes's desire to my boss who turned whiter than usual. "You know," he said, "there's been some guy trailing me for a couple nights and parking his car in front of my house. I don't like it." I told him that he had nothing to fear from Hughes, that he was actually a very nice guy. I also told him about Howard's fears that he was being railroaded in print.

At this, the boss got very paternal and put his hand on my shoulder the way they do at retirement parties, just before they give you the gold watch. "I realize the harassment you have undergone from Hughes," he said, "but I want you to know that I think you are handling it magnificently. I have complete confidence in you. I don't want to talk with Hughes. You tell him that you have complete authority to speak for me and the AP in all things." I showed up alone at Hesse's studio and relayed the boss's exact words to Hughes. "In other words," said Howard, "he said: 'Let's you and him fight.' "

This session, as it turned out, would be our longest— about ten or twelve hours. He had the fifth article of the series in his hand. How he got it is still a mystery. It had just moved on the wire when I left the office a half hour earlier. But any guy who could find Mitchum in the Snake River country shouldn't have any trouble getting a teletype copy off an AP printer.

This particular chapter dealt with the women in his life. It had them all—Ginger Rogers, Elizabeth Taylor, Katharine Hepburn, Yvonne de Carlo, Lana Turner, Ava Gardner, Cyd Charisse, Faith Domergue, Mitzi Gaynor, Joan Fontaine, and all the others I have already mentioned—plus some more. He was more concerned with this story than any of the others. He was still affable, still polite, but damned more serious about getting it changed or killed.

I had used one expression in quoting one of the women anonymously. I had written, "Let's hear from another veteran star, a paid-up member of the Hughes Alumni Association."

Howard got a little indignant about the use of the word "paid-up" here. I explained that my intent was to indicate that she was an ex-girl friend, no longer in contention, which was exactly the truth.

"But it makes her sound like a whore."

"OK," I agreed. "I'll see that it is deleted." After all, it was a poor choice of words on my part.

Then he took the story, paragraph by paragraph, arguing, editing, and occasionally writing in what he would like it to say. I still have that edited copy, much of it in Howard's own handwriting. It makes for an interesting commentary on the man. One paragraph, describing Hughes's women in general, read: "All fit a familiar pattern: When Hughes dated them they were young, beautiful and usually unsophisticated." He crossed out *unsophisticated*.

"When in the hell were Katharine Hepburn or Joan Fontaine ever unsophisticated?"

Touché! (But I *had* said *usually*.)

He came to a Lana Turner anecdote and laughed uproariously. He didn't touch it because, he admitted, it was true. It gives an insight into the Hughes humor. The story read: "A favorite story involves Lana Turner. When Hughes told her marriage was out, she is reported to have pouted: 'But, Howie, I have all our silk sheets monogrammed *HH*.' "

Hughes's supposed reply shows either a great sense of humor or unusual thrift:

"Why don't you marry Huntington Hartford?"

There was a paragraph calling Jean Peters the most loyal of all Hughes's girl friends. He read it but didn't touch it.

Then came several paragraphs calling Terry Moore currently number one in Hughes's affections. They told of a time when I was at Terry's house and Hughes called her four times within an hour. With the last call, she had hung up with the words: "Sorry, Howard, I hear my date at the front door now." The date was there, and Terry introduced us. He was Bob Kenaston, son of Billie Dove, first of Hughes's old flames in Hollywood.

He crossed out all of those paragraphs, especially the reference to young Kenaston.

He circled a paragraph which quoted chorus girls saying, "He dazzles you with gifts." The next paragraph read: "That may explain why some of Hughes's girl friends drive Cadillacs on $80 a week salaries as chorines. Hughes drives a 1950 Chevrolet. Often sleeps in it."

When Hughes got through editing it the way he would have liked it to read, it went something like this: "Some of Hughes's girl friends drive Cadillacs. Hughes drives a 1950 Chevrolet. He would sleep in it if he felt like it."

The AP copy, except for minor exceptions, wasn't changed in print, but he sure gave it the old college try. In some newspapers, he was actually powerful enough to get it killed completely. In its place, he personally wrote a rather dull treatise on the ultimate wedding of television and the movies, then considered mortal enemies. The piece, a collector's item, was years ahead of its time, but it certainly lacked the sex appeal of my original copy. Hughes wrote the substitute without byline, for which he apologized the next day.

"No need," said I. "I read your piece and I want to thank you for not putting my byline on it."

One of the most embarrassing moments of my life came during this marathon session with Hughes, when I moved into a new house with a new phone number.

Several times during the meetings, when Howard would say something he felt should be immortalized in print, he asked why I wasn't writing it down. I told him I never took notes because I felt it inhibited the subject being interviewed, and also that I had perfect recall. Finally, I said that I worked on the theory that if you didn't remember it, it wasn't worth remembering. It still bothered him no end.

Fade. Dissolve. And it's dinnertime. Howard said: "How about steak over at Dave Chasen's?"

Great, but first I must call home to say that I would be eating out. The phone was by Howard's chair, and he handed it to me. I started dialing and then suddenly stopped. I didn't know my new number. How could I? I dialed information and asked for the number of the James Bacon residence.

"Oh, boy!" stormed Howard. "What am I dealing with here? A reporter who says he doesn't need to take notes, that he remembers everything, and then he has to dial information for his own phone number. Oh, boy!" It was useless to explain.

Howard and I drove over to Chasen's in his stripped-down Chevy. I recall wondering, on the way over, why such an introverted man would want to eat at a celebrity hangout. I also figured that it wouldn't hurt my status around town to be seen dining in Chasen's with Hollywood's most legendary power.

As we arrived at Chasen's, Howard drove directly onto the parking lot instead of up to the front door and the valet attendant. It was the first time I had ever entered through the kitchen, but there was a reason: We weren't going any further. There, in the midst of the pots and pans and gas ranges, directly in the path of the scurrying waiters and captains, was a beautiful table for two, already set up. There were flowers on the table, and soon the steaks were served. They were delicious. I had a bottle of Pouilly-Fuisse, 1952, I believe. Howard drank nothing. The service was, if possible, even more impeccable than it always is out front.

Howard explained that he had called ahead. "I can't hear very well, and it's much quieter in the kitchen than in the main dining room with all those actors trying to out-talk each other." I had to agree. All in all, it was a memorable night.

Howard's frequent reference to his hearing problems may be an important key to the Hughes mystique. It's not too unusual to find hard-of-hearing people overly introverted and crowd shy. It's understandable that one would want to avoid a leftout feeling in public. Hughes's general behavior, called eccentric by most, didn't seem so after my experiences with him. His whole life is dedicated to running his businesses. His only hobby is playing Monopoly with real buildings. He's a perfectionist to end all perfectionists. The golf story is the best example of that. And he's a genius. And all real geniuses value privacy more than anything else.

I only saw Howard once after that night, and that was by accident. Some months later, Hughes Aircraft demonstrated a new jet-powered helicopter at its Culver City plant. Many aircraft executives were there, along with TV cameramen, newsmen, aviation trade magazine writers, and the merely curious. On the way, I noticed a solitary figure sitting alone in a car, far off the runway where most of the action took place. It was Howard. I waved at him. He waved back and then drove off. The jet helicopter was his baby, and he wanted to see it take its first steps.

Over the years, I have heard indirectly from Howard via some of the men working close to him.

Once, during the TWA stock squabble, the AP in New York said it would like to send a writer from its New York bureau to interview Hughes. The request was relayed to Hughes by an aide. In due time, Howard's reply came back: "If anybody interviews me, it will be Jim Bacon. No one else. When I'm ready for an interview, I'll get in touch with him."

So far he hasn't, but I sure appreciate his plug. As of this writing, I am the last newsman ever to talk with Hughes and one of the few who ever did so intimately.

Incredible man. There's been no one else like him in our time.

12

Often Broke but Never Poor

MILLIONAIRES ARE BORN—not self-made, as everyone thinks. I mean those who are born to live like millionaires. Take Sam Spiegel for instance. Sam's life-style—yacht and the whole works—is like that of an Iranian shah. And back in 1949, when he didn't have the money he does now, he lived the same way. I was invited to Sam's house for New Year's Eve that year. It was one of the most lavish parties I ever attended. And I used to be on Marion Davies's guest list, so I know lavish when I see it.

Sam was known as S.P. Eagle in those days, a name change that once prompted Darryl F. Zanuck to send Sam a wire signed D.Z. Nuck. The party was first-cabin deluxe, all the way: Iranian caviar at twenty-five dollars an ounce was stashed in huge silver bowls like oatmeal. Dom Perignon was the champagne, and it flowed like the Feather River water project.

The party was held in a huge tent in back of Sam's palatial movieland estate. Two, not one, bands played continous music for dancing. Chateaubriand in rich, rare strips was the entrée. Everybody who was anybody in Hollywood was there in black tie and sequins. Then came an uninvited guest—the party pooper to end all party poopers: He was the guy from the finance company, and he presented Sam with a writ and repossessed his Cadillac in the driveway.

It would have embarrassed the rest of us to death. Not Sam. He merely shrugged and ordered the waiters to bring more caviar and to fill the champagne glasses. And he did it with such aplomb that you had to admire his style.

Fortunately *The Bridge on the River Kwai* made so

many millions for Sam that he now can live the way he always did, and without fear of bill collectors.

Jackie Gleason, spawned in an Irish ghetto in Brooklyn, is to the manor born.

Back in the early days of television, around 1948 or 1949, Jackie came to Hollywood to do the first thirteen episodes of "The Life of Riley." Bill Bendix had created the part of Riley on radio, but his RKO movie contract forbade him to do TV—hence Jackie. I doubt if Jackie was getting more than $300 a week for those episodes, but you would never know it from his life-style. Every night he used to go into the old Villa Capri and throw a party for his pals. When the tab came, Jackie signed it.

He and owner Patsy D'Amore were longtime pals from New York. At the end of thirteen weeks, Jackie went back to New York. Patsy was holding about $5,000 in tabs. To Patsy's credit, he never dunned Jackie. "He's agonna pay some day," said Patsy, with considerable optimism.

A few years passed and Jackie Gleason became the biggest thing on television. He signed an $8 million contract with CBS. Finally, after many weeks of the Gleason show in New York, Jackie returned to Hollywood. First place he hit was the old Villa Capri. He didn't bring a big party with him, just a few friends. With all the spaghetti and the Soave Bertani, the tab came to about fifty dollars. Patsy never said a word about the other tab, and neither did Jackie.

Came time to pay the bill, Jackie grabbed the check, took a look at it, and then brought out his checkbook. He wrote out a check for $6,000 and handed it to Patsy. "I'm a big tipper, pal," said Jackie, who then made his exit as the Poor Soul. He always exits like that when he knows he can't top himself. I looked at Patsy, who was looking at the check and smiling.

For years, Toots Shor always gave Jackie signing privileges in his famous bar. I was there one night with Jackie when he was between paying jobs. He was the host—a big man with the pen. As any patron will tell you, Toots's place always was a great place to drink, but as for food, forget it.

As Jackie and I and a few friends were eating and drinking this night, Gleason took a taste of his main dish. He called Toots over. "I can't eat this shit," said Jackie. "And, furthermore, I'd like to turn in my fountain pen."

Mike Todd was another born millionaire. When he had it, he spent it like a drunken sailor. When he didn't have it, he spent it the same way. In fact, the title of this chapter came from one of Mike's favorite sayings—"Often broke but never poor."

During the making of *Around the World in 80 Days,* I am with Mike in a projection room at MGM, where Victor Young is scoring the movie. Into the gathering comes a typical Rotarian type carrying a briefcase. He's an insurance man. He and Mike get into a long discussion about cashing in a few insurance policies and borrowing on a few others. Mike signs a few papers, and the insurance man writes out a check and leaves. Mike turns to Victor and yells: "Tell your musicians they get paid today."

Mike financed that movie on a day-to-day basis. Thank God, it hit big, even though he didn't live long to enjoy his prosperity.

All the time Mike was conning people or cashing in insurance policies, he was living like a king with Elizabeth Taylor. Hardly a day went by that he didn't buy her an expensive bauble. And here's something that will surprise a lot of people: When Mike Todd first went after Elizabeth, he wasn't the least bit in love with her.

Ernie Anderson, who was one of Mike's many press agents at the time, told me that Mike had confided to him once: "I've got a movie to make. I'm going to romance Elizabeth Taylor to publicize it."

And he did. But Elizabeth is very easy to fall in love with, and, before long, Mike had fallen head over heels for his publicity romance.

13

How to Enjoy Paris
on Only $10,000 a Night

ASIDE FROM HOWARD HUGHES, the most fabulous character I ever met was Baby Pignatari, the Howard Hughes of Brazil. When Baby swings, no one can touch him—not even Frank Sinatra. Last I heard, he had mellowed somewhat and was running his vast industrial empire from São Paulo. But I became a friend of Baby during his frivolous years. Such frivolity.

One night on the town in Paris is forever etched in my memory. Both Baby and I happened to be staying at the George V. I was in a room. Baby, as befits a billionaire, had a whole apartment. But we used the same lobby, and that's where we ran into each other. Baby insisted that I come up to his apartment for a drink. With him was our mutual friend Richard Gully, a member of an aristocratic English family—he is first cousin to Anthony Eden, both being grandsons of a Viceroy of India. Richard, as younger brother, could not inherit his family's title, so off he went to the United States to become, of all things, a Hollywood press agent—and a super one at that. He was Jack L. Warner's right arm for years. Richard, at this time in 1958, was working for Baby as a public relations man.

So the three of us went to Baby's apartment, where we drank Dom Perignon, 1955. (For some reason, Dom Perignon seems to figure in a lot of my mad escapades.) After a few magnums were killed, we were joined by two beautiful girls—one a Dior model and the other a Parisian socialite. These were prearranged dates for Baby and Richard. Richard, taking it upon himself to get me a date, suggested Agnes Laurent, a beautiful French actress who was considered the rival of Brigitte Bardot. Fine.

Richard got on the phone and called Agnes at a theater where she was doing a play. In flawless French, this proper Britisher told her how we were going to dinner and how by the time dinner was over, her play would be finished. She could join us back at the hotel. Agnes agreed. I assumed at the time that Richard knew her. He had never met her. He just told her there was a very important journalist from Hollywood he wanted her to go out with. He added that I wrote for 8,000 newspapers around the world. That apparently was the magic word.

Next stop was the cashier's window of the George V. Baby took out $10,000 worth of traveler's checks from his safe deposit vault.

"Do you think this is enough?" he asked me.

"Are you kidding?" I said. "That's enough to take us around the world." I didn't know Baby well at that time or I would never have made such a foolish statement.

We next went into the bar of the George V for a drink or two to get us on our way. As we went in, I heard someone yell at me. It was Darryl F. Zanuck, having a drink with his flame of the moment—Juliette Greco, the darling of the Paris Left Bank in those days. I waved back. Darryl did a double take when he saw who I was with. He obviously didn't know Baby, but Baby bore a striking resemblance to one of 20th Century-Fox's biggest stars—Victor Mature.

We had a few rounds of drinks, amid hilarity, and then the gorgeous Dior model turned to me and said, "Who is that horrible man over there with the mustache? He keeps showing me his hotel keys when his girl friend isn't looking. He must think I am a whore."

It was Zanuck. I told the girl that he was one of the most powerful studio tycoons in Hollywood and if she wanted to be a star, here was the chance to make her move. She wasn't interested. Zanuck persisted with the hotel key byplay. Finally, I went over to Darryl and said, "Forget it. She's Baby Pignatari's girl friend. He can buy Fox out of petty cash."

Darryl was impressed, and he then devoted full attention

to Juliette. This was a strange relationship because, of all the times I was ever around Darryl and Juliette, she did nothing but insult and belittle him. If anyone at Fox had done this, their heads would have been off. But Darryl apparently enjoyed every minute of it. Come to think of it, it must have been a refreshing change from all those years of hearing everybody yes you.

It came time for dinner in an elegant restaurant called Laurent. The food was superb, and Baby prepared the dessert himself. He ordered a bowl of whole, ripe peaches at the beginning of the meal, along with several bottles of Chateau Lafite Rothschild, 1955, which he used to marinate the peaches during the meal. You have not eaten peaches until you have had them soaked in Lafite Rothschild.

Baby cashed a $1,000 traveler's check for the dinner and passed out lavish tips all around—$100 to the waiters and the captain. You have never seen such bowing, especially when he refused the change from the $1,000 check. The dinner, in those days, couldn't have cost more than $100 for the five of us. What Baby had done was leave a 900 percent tip.

Next stop was back to the George V bar, where Agnes Laurent was waiting for us. I was amazed to see Richard introduce himself to her for the first time and then introduce her to me. I said, "God, how did you ever talk her into this?"

Richard shrugged. "It was easy. French is a much more romantic language."

Baby, by this time, was swinging pretty well. He took one look at Agnes, and I could see this gorgeous girl might not wind up with me. Baby said, "Let's all go to Jimmy's." He tried to get Agnes into his chauffeur-driven Rolls Royce. She was more interested in my 8,000 newspapers than in this wild Brazilian and insisted on driving her own car, a tiny Renault. Baby was not to be thwarted. He said he would ride with her. This switch didn't bother me because it meant that I wound up with the Dior model. And after all, Baby was the host.

Baby, well over six feet tall, climbed into the tiny car and immediately, from the backseat, the biggest Great Dane

I had ever seen jumped up and started licking his face. The two cars drove side-by-side across town to Jimmy's. I can't begin to describe the scene in Agnes's car. Baby's head almost going through the top and this huge dog licking him at every stop sign. It's a scene only Cary Grant, in his prime, could have played.

At Jimmy's, the maitre d' and captains hugged and kissed Baby as he came in. He had been there many times before. The Cuban band started playing Brazilian sambas. They all knew Baby. Soon he was on the bongo drums, and I was playing the maracas in the band. The whole joint was swinging. I gave up the maracas and did a torrid Latin dance with the Dior model, who was a superb dancer. Agnes, who wasn't drinking much, seemed confused as to how she had gotten mixed up with this crazy group. Baby then organized something I hadn't seen since World War II—a conga line. By this time, it was well past midnight.

Someone suggested we next go to Le Elephant Blanc, which in those days was the Parisian El Morocco, somewhat sedate compared with the swinging Jimmy's. This bothered Baby, but not for long. He called the manager over and handed out a few $1,000 traveler's checks. Baby then called his chauffeur and told him to get some taxicabs. Jimmy's Cuban band was going with us.

This entourage descended on Le Elephant Blanc, which was filled with jaded jet-setters. It looked more like the Slumber Room at Forest Lawn than a Parisian nightclub. But Baby changed all that. He bought off the Mickey Mouse band that was on the bandstand, and soon the hot Latin music took over. In a matter of minutes, Le Elephant Blanc was an elegant version of Jimmy's.

About this time, Agnes Laurent turned to me, somewhat hysterically, and said that she was taking her Great Dane and leaving. I told her the night was still young. She said: "That's what I'm afraid of." And she left.

Baby didn't even miss her. He was deliriously happy. Baby hates dignity of any sort, and Le Elephant Blanc no longer was sedate. Finally, about 5 A.M., the Cuban band literally blew itself out. The tables were empty. The nightclub was deserted. In fact, only our party remained—the Unholy Five. Richard and his socialite girl friend were all for calling it a night. And they did. Now it was Baby, the model, and me.

"Let's go to Scheherazade," said Baby.

The chauffeur interrupted: "I think it's closed at this time of day."

It was about 5:30 A.M., but Baby insisted that we go anyway.

Now Scheherazade was a famous Parisian landmark. It was the locale for a famous Ingrid Bergman movie *Arc de Triomphe*. The nightclub was better than the movie. When we drove up, the place was in darkness, except for a tiny beam of light showing under the front door. Baby got out of the Rolls and pounded on the door, calling the owner by name in Italian.

The manager, recognizing his famous customer, opened the place. He poured us champagne and soon was on the phone. Within minutes, it seemed, the place was back in business with waiters and wild Gypsy violinists.

Baby, like a scene out of an Erich Von Stroheim movie, finished his champagne and smashed his glass against the wall. Soon we were all doing it. The owner didn't mind. His computer brain was tabulating everything. By this time, it was bright dawn. Baby peeled off the traveler's checks and distributed them all around. One particularly wild Gypsy fiddler came up to me with several $100 checks in his hand. "Are you American?" he asked.

"Yes," I said.

"I used to play fiddle with Ace Brigode and his Virginians on WLW, Cincinnati," said the fiddler. "I came over here on a cruise ship orchestra and have been a Gypsy fiddler ever since. Your friend is a big tipper, n'est-ce pas?"

It was breakfast time and we all headed for Calvados, a little restaurant across the street from the George V. It was bacon and egg time. Also more champagne, which is really the only decent breakfast beverage—much better than coffee. Came the tab, Baby reached into his pocket. The traveler's checks were all gone—the whole $10,000.

I paid the tab. We walked back to the hotel. Baby wanted some more champagne, and I told him I had some in my room. So Baby, the Dior model, and I went there and drank more champagne. Soon Baby and the Dior model fell asleep on my bed.

A knock came on my door. It was Lynn Unkefer, a press agent for 20th Century-Fox. I had completely forgotten that I was due to go to London in an hour. I packed in fifteen minutes and jumped into the limousine. Soon I was headed for London. Richard Gully later told me Baby had come to have great respect for me. No one had ever stayed that long with him. No one, in fact, had ever drunk him under the table.

I have great respect for Baby. No one else has ever spent $10,000 on me on a night to be remembered in Paris.

14

The Romance
That Gave Harry Cohn
a Heart Attack

THE YEAR WAS 1958, long before the Black Revolution of the sixties, and I was playing golf with Jack Keller, Jerry Lewis's press agent.

"You won't believe this," said Jack, as he hit one about 250 yards off the first tee at what was then the Knollwood Country Club. "Jerry's filling in for Sammy Davis up at the Sands Hotel in Vegas tonight and Sunday, because Sammy told Jerry he's going back to Chicago and ask his girl friend's parents for her hand in marriage. You won't believe who the girl friend is." I couldn't swing a club because of curiosity. "Kim Novak!" Keller practically shouted.

"Kim Novak?" I yelled back. A couple other golfers wondered what the hell was going on at the first tee.

I found out that Kim was in Chicago, too. It meant a page-one story in every newspaper in the world. Here was the screen's big box office sex symbol going to marry a black man. Nothing like this had happened since Jack Johnson.

I knew that Sammy, who weighs 120 pounds—100 of it cock—had banged many of the white actresses around town. He told me so himself, and I could tell from the look in the actresses' eyes that it was true. There's a certain smile that Superhump produces.

One very well known blonde actress—a Southerner, too —told me of Sammy's approach to a girl's liberal instincts.

"He really comes on," she said. "He says, 'I know it's dangerous for you to be seen with a black man. I'll leave right now if you say.'" And Sammy, a genius at playing Charley Humble, didn't have to ask. The actresses, with their liberal instincts touched, unzipped his fly. So it was with Kim, no doubt. But marriage?

In those days it was unthinkable. It was a page-one story all right, but only on one condition. These words had to come from Kim, not Sammy. The march on Selma hadn't happened yet.

I never finished the round of golf. I got on the phone to Kim's family home in Austin, on the west side of Chicago. For two days the phone rang and rang, with no answer. I later found out that the family—and Sammy—had gone to Aurora, Illinois, a suburb, to visit other relatives. I didn't give up on the story because it was the weekend, and it would have been too late anyway for the Sunday morning papers and there are no Sunday evening papers. I kept dialing, hoping to reach someone for a Monday P.M. break.

Finally, on a Monday night, the phone was answered in Austin. It was Kim's father. I asked for Kim. The father told me she was on the City of Los Angeles, the Union Pacific train that was due in Los Angeles Union depot at 9 A.M. Tuesday. Mr. Novak, a railroader, even gave me the car number and its location on the long train.

I asked him about Sammy. Yes, Sammy had spent the weekend with them. The whole family thought him a wonderful person, but that's all he would say. "Ask Kim when she gets off the train," said her father.

When I reached her father, it was about 9 P.M. Monday. Sammy, I found out, was back onstage at the Sands. The City of Los Angeles was due to stop in Las Vegas at 2 A.M., when Sammy's midnight show would be over. I called a friend in Vegas, since there was no way I could get up there that late unless I drove those desert roads like an Italian Grand Prix driver. The last plane had left. I didn't tell the friend why I wanted him to check the City of Los Angeles at 2 A.M.—just let me know if Sammy Davis got on the train.

About 2:15 A.M., the friend called back. Yes, Sammy

had indeed boarded the train, and it had pulled out with him still aboard. Great. There was the story. When Kim and Sammy got off the train at Union Station, I would be waiting. With the two of them, how could they deny it?

I was working for the Associated Press in those days and had filled in my bosses on what I was doing. I was told it was a story only if Kim confirmed it, regardless of what Sammy said. Had I been a gossip columnist as I am now, it would have been the lead of the column since I was the only reporter in town who knew what was going on.

Promptly at 8:30 A.M., a half hour before arrival, I was at Union Station, way down the platform, because I knew which car Kim was on. It's a long platform, a quarter mile at least. I looked down and spotted a delegation of four from Columbia Pictures—Muriel Roberts, Kim's press agent; Norma Cassell, her business manager; and two executives from the studio; plus a limousine driver. They didn't see me, and I made sure they wouldn't. I hid behind a concrete pillar. When the train pulled in, I was at Kim's car—last on the track—as she alighted. She was astonished to see me.

"Where's Sammy?" I asked.

I must say she handled herself coolly.

"Sammy who?"

I told her as fast as I could why I was there. Yes, she had seen Sammy in Chicago, but he was doing a benefit there and she had taken her family to see him. "I think he is a marvelous entertainer. And my folks, who had never seen him before, loved him. But marriage to Sammy Davis? You gotta be kidding."

She knew I knew she was lying, but it's a game stars and the press play all the time. She denied it. And that was it. No story.

I grabbed her makeup case and we walked down the long platform practically into the arms of a horrified Muriel Roberts. "What are you doing here?" she practically screamed at me.

"Kim and I got married last night in Las Vegas," I said and walked away.

This all took place about 9:30 A.M. By coincidence, I

was due to meet Bing Crosby at his Holmby Hills home at 10:30. I drove there, and Bing and I went into the study. Kathy, Bing's pretty and young wife, served us coffee and, as she was pouring, the housekeeper came in and announced: "Mr. Harry Cohn's on the phone." Bing started to get up and Kathy, a Columbia contract actress, also made a move. The housekeeper stopped them. "He wants to talk to Mr. Bacon." Must say Bing and Kathy were impressed, although they had no idea of what the call was about.

When I got to the phone, Al Horwits, director of publicity at Columbia, said: "The boss wants to talk with you." Harry got on the phone and in his typically genteel way, said: "I hear you met our Miss Novak at the train today."

"Yep," I answered. I knew what he was getting at, so I continued. "There's no story. She denied the whole thing."

Harry said, "Jesus Christ. That's good news."

End of conversation, and I went back to Bing, never telling him why Cohn had run me down at the Crosby home. Bing's only comment was: "I got new respect for you, getting calls from Harry Cohn in my house."

This was Tuesday. That next weekend Sammy Davis, feeling no pain, jumped up on the stage at the Las Vegas Silver Slipper and grabbed Loray White, who was as astonished as the audience. Grabbing the microphone, Sammy told her, "I want you to be my wife."

Loray, a very beautiful black dancer, didn't know what to say, but she apparently said yes because, before the week was out, she and Sammy Davis were wed. Six months later, after their divorce, I talked with Loray. She told me that Sammy and she never once went to bed during their marriage, not even on their wedding night. "He gave me a check for $25,000 and that was it. Crazy?" Crazy, yes, to anyone who was looking at the gorgeous Loray in those days.

Today Sammy will talk about his romance with Kim, but he is mum when it comes to his impromptu proposal to Loray and the subsequent wedding.

A Las Vegas friend, with mob connections, later told me what happened. He also told me that Sammy had ridden in Kim's compartment from Las Vegas only to San Bernardino that night, thus clearing up the mystery of why Sammy didn't get off the train in Los Angeles.

"Harry Cohn knew someone big in the Chicago Syndicate who owed Harry a favor. Harry made a call and explained that he wanted Sammy Davis married to a black girl as soon as possible. He didn't care how it was done, except that he specified no mayhem. Two boys from Chicago got off a plane and somehow got Sammy into a rented car and drove him about thirty miles out of Las Vegas, into the desert."

In those days, Las Vegas was an open city among the Mafia families. No rough stuff in the city limits, so as not to give Las Vegas a bad name.

My friend continued: "They took Sammy out of the car. He was already terrified by this time because he thought they were going to kill him. One of the guys picked up a sharp branch from the ground and held it in front of Sammy's face. He said, 'You got one eye missing, you want to try for two? Stay away from Kim Novak for good and marry a colored girl as soon as possible. I don't care who, just so she's black. Understand?' " Sammy, of course, understood.

It wasn't many weeks after that that Harry Cohn was dead of a heart attack.

As I say, Sammy's always been mum about his wedding to Loray White. Kim, who said she was treated like "a piece of meat in a butcher shop" by Cohn, had staged a rebellion.

I had known Kim almost from the first day she arrived in town. I was introduced to her by Milton Stein. Milton, a little bald guy with glasses, was not anyone's idea of Don Juan, but until he died, he could come up with more beautiful girls than anyone I have ever known, Warren Beatty included.

Kim, then known as Marilyn Novak, was due to have a meeting with Max Arnow, head of casting and new talent at Columbia, at 2 P.M. the day we all had lunch in the Naples Restaurant, same place where Milton, Marilyn Monroe, and I had met five years earlier. I got the same vibrations with Kim that I did with Marilyn. Somehow, my instincts told me that I was sitting with a girl who was going to make it big. Kim had the same animal sex appeal Marilyn had. And she had the looks and the body to go with it. We had a fun lunch. It was no interview because this girl hadn't done anything yet except come West, demonstrating refrigerators for appliance salesmen.

I went back to my office wanting to write something about her but not knowing quite what. She just wasn't big enough for the AP trunk wire. Then the phone rang. It was Harry Cohn, in his typical gruff way, saying: "Jim, you want to be a big man in this town?" I naturally answered yes. "Then write a story about Marilyn Novak— I think we'll call her Kim; too goddamn many Marilyns around—and say that within one year she will be queen of the Columbia lot. You can quote me all you want, but don't use my name. But I guarantee that she will be queen of this lot in a year, maybe a whole lot sooner. OK?"

Well, I wrote the story because I knew how powerful Harry was. And if he said it, he meant it.

One of the questions I asked him on the phone was the obvious one. "What about Rita Hayworth? She's the queen now."

Harry said, "Fuck Rita Hayworth. She's finished here. Do you know what that horse's ass of a husband did [crooner Dick Haymes]? He pulled her out of *Joseph and His Brethren,* and I have already got $400,000 hard cash invested in this movie that will have to be scrapped. That son-of-a-bitch Haymes came into my office with a beard and said: 'Unless I play Joseph, then my wife's out of the picture.'

"I told him to take his fucking wife and go back to Argentina. I would make a big star out of the next girl who walked into my office, whoever in the hell she is. Well, Max Arnow walked in with Kim Novak. She was the next girl through the door."

Harry was true to his word. Within a year, Kim was queen of the lot. Her first picture was *Pushover,* which had another long forgotten title relating more to its star, Fred MacMurray. Harry changed the title to accent Kim's lesser role as a prostitute.

George Lait, then director of publicity for Columbia, was ordered to give the big buildup to Kim. She had walked into the office of Doc Shurr, Bob Hope's agent, in Beverly Hills. Doc, who had a keen eye for beauty, signed her and arranged the appointment with Max Arnow. It was strictly routine. Too routine for the publicity buildup Harry Cohn wanted. George Lait called in Bob Yeager, his most imaginative press agent, and told him to talk to Kim and to come up with a gimmick story announcing Columbia's new find.

Yeager asked Kim a few questions about what she liked to do. She thought a moment and said, "I like to bicycle."

That ended the interview. The next day, the world press printed a Columbia publicity release that announced how Columbia's newest star was discovered by famed agent Louis (Doc) Shurr, who had spotted her, clad only in shorts, pedaling a bicycle through Beverly Hills.

Kim, soon to be queen, got the royal treatment. When she was made up, it was not just any makeup man. Benny Lane, head of makeup for the studio, took personal charge. Cameramen spent extra hours every day lighting Kim. In a way, she was manufactured, but could Cohn have done it with anyone but Kim? I doubt it.

This chapter could be very interesting to actresses Jody Lawrence, Lucy Marlowe, Diane Foster, Jana Mason, and Betsy Palmer, all of whom were signed about the same time as Kim. What if one of them had walked next through that door? Or maybe Kim wasn't the next one through the door. Maybe she was last and Harry had the same vibes about her as I did earlier that day at Naples Restaurant.

Kim got good roles in important pictures. She played a dizzy blonde with Jack Lemmon and Judy Holliday in *Phfft*, the story of a divorce. Kim was brilliant in the movie.

"I was new in town, too," Lemmon recalls, "but when I went to the sneak preview of that movie, I couldn't take my eyes off Kim on that screen, even when I was in the scene with her. She was brilliant, and the damndest thing —she didn't know she was being funny when she made the movie. I think it's a classic comedy performance." It was.

When you can steal a comedy from Jack and Judy, it's not petty larceny.

Muriel Roberts, the press agent whom I terrified five years later at the Union Depot, was assigned practically full time to Kim's publicity. It was Muriel who came up with Kim's famous lavender look. Her whole house was done in lavender. She wore lavender dresses, tinted her finger nails lavender, even her hair. Kim went along with what was a good publicity gimmick, but years later, when she had retired to the Big Sur, she told me, "I hate purple now. And I hated it then."

Cohn bought the Broadway hit *Picnic* and cast Kim in the main feminine role of the young girl. Director Josh Logan balked. He felt that the role required a much more experienced actress. Janice Rule had played it on Broadway.

Cohn, with his usual gruffness, told Logan: "Kim's in the picture. You don't like her, we can always get another director. But she stays." She was quite good in the movie. More than any other, it made her a big star, a reigning Sex Goddess of the Silver Screen.

The Eddy Duchin Story with Tyrone Power, *Pal Joey* with Frank Sinatra—Kim got the best. So much so that when her own salary was only $200 a week, Otto Preminger had to pay Cohn $100,000 to let her do *Man with the Golden Arm* with Sinatra. In those days, that was top dollar for a loan-out.

Over the years, Kim has often mentioned that first story I wrote about her. It was the first story ever.

"How did you know that I was going to be Queen of the Columbia lot?" she has asked me a dozen times.

Now she knows.

Harry once bitched to me when he was having a contract squabble with Kim. "There's no gratitude in this business. What the hell does she know? I could have taken a two-bit whore and made her a star just as I did Kim. She's goddamn lucky, but she doesn't know it. Lives in that big house up there in Bel-Air. How in the hell do you think she got it? I gave it to her, that's how."

Cohn was exaggerating. He was probably the most powerful studio boss in town, except for L.B. Mayer, but he couldn't have made a star out of just anyone. The public still makes stars. And the public made Kim—with a little help from Harry Cohn.

Often I am asked what is the difference between a star and an ordinary, competent actor or actress. It's very simple. The public falls in love with the stars. It merely applauds the good work of the good actor.

15

Dore Isn't Izzy Anymore

THE VOICE ON THE OTHER END of the phone was the great Louis B. Mayer himself. He was sobbing.

"Jim," he cried. "How could you do such a thing? You, a good Catholic!"

Then, more sobbing. The sobs didn't bother me because everyone in Hollywood knew that L.B. always cried when he wanted something from somebody. Still, it was the first time the MGM lion had ever whimpered instead of roared at me.

"After all I've done for your church," he continued. "How could you take the word of that Nazi bastard?"

"But L.B.," I interrupted, "he's Jewish the same as you."

"Yes, but he's a Nazi Jew. They're the worst kind."

On and on he raved between sobs. In retrospect, it reads like a crazy conversation for a multimillionaire tycoon—the most powerful one in the history of Hollywood—to have with a columnist. Truthfully, I didn't think so at the time. That sort of thing was commonplace then, even more so now. The whole town always has been a Gilbert and Sullivan operetta and, fortunately, I have always viewed it as such. Insecurity is one of the few shortcomings I've missed.

But to explain that weird phone conversation, we have to go back to the day that Izzy Freeman, one of the more or less insignificant subjects of King Mayer's Kingdom of MGM, changed his name to Dore Freeman. Had Izzy not made this change, Mayer, perhaps, might have bowed out of MGM some twenty-seven years after he founded it with little fanfare. This is doubtful but possible. A terse "resignation" notice, planted in the trade and consumer press by the MGM publicity department, would have stated that Mayer, weary of the horrendous problems of running the town's biggest studio, wanted the much easier job of independent production. Hollywood, being the Jewish community it is, would have read the announcement and commented, "At his age, he's entitled."

But Izzy had changed his name. And, when Louis B. Mayer announced on June 23, 1951, that he was quitting the studio he once could brag contained "more stars than there are in Heaven," Hollywood knew that he, the King, had been toppled. Long live Dore Schary, the new King!

A palace revolution had succeeded. It was *What Makes Sammy Run?* with real characters—only with a twist. Mayer, who was dethroned, had more of the Sammy Glick qualities than Schary, who did the overthrowing.

But back to Izzy or, more properly, Dore Freeman.

Isadore Freeman came to Hollywood from New York with only one mark of distinction. He was Joan Crawford's greatest fan—and still is. The walls of his little apartment are plastered with stills of Joan from every one of her movies. He saw all her movies a dozen times; wrote her loving letters almost daily, and, when he talked, it was only to praise the beauty, the talent, and the grace of his beloved Miss Crawford.

Joan couldn't help but be impressed and grateful. She was so grateful, in fact, that she asked L.B. if there wasn't a job in Culver City for such a devoted fan. So Izzy came to town and went to work in the photo department at MGM publicity. This, to Izzy, was the same as going to Heaven. Maybe even better.

He was still working there the last time I visited MGM, but, with the way things are, MGM's severe austerity program may have forced a layoff. Last I heard, he had retired early.

Everybody who knows Izzy likes him. He's pleasant, unobtrusive, and much sharper than I am sure his superiors ever realized. Had he come to the studio almost any other way, he probably would be a producer. But people who write fan letters are victims of a rigid Hollywood caste system. It's the one Horatio Alger story the town won't buy. Izzy always knew what was going on around the big lot but, unlike others who have advanced, he was too grateful and too loyal to put the knowledge to his own advantage. In short, he's a nice guy. And you know what Leo Durocher said about nice guys.

So it happened, one day when I was at MGM en route to an interview with Producer Gottfried Reinhardt, son of the immortal Max, that I bumped into Izzy.

"Hello, Izzy," said I, as I had done time and time before.

"It's Dore," said Izzy politely. "I changed my name." He changed it, he said, in honor of Dore Schary, who— I thought along with everybody else—was number two on the lot.

"Isn't that a little risky?" I asked. "Why not change it to Louis B. Freeman?"

"No," answered the new Dore. "I think it's better that I change it to Dore."

Then he walked off, leaving me slightly bewildered and very suspicious. I tried to rationalize that the change from Isadore to Dore was a logical one. Perhaps Dore Schary had been born Isadore Schary.

Mayer himself had brought Dore Schary to MGM in 1948—just as Mayer himself had brought Izzy Freeman to MGM. Schary had come to the studio on a three-year contract, hailed as the new Irving Thalberg. His contract stipulated that he was to be the head of production, with the title of vice-president. He would be answerable to Mayer, who was vice-president in charge of the studio, and to Nicholas Schenck, president of Loews, Inc., the parent company. Schenck, in New York, was the overall nominal boss, but over the years he had pretty much let Mayer run the Hollywood end.

The teaming of Schary and Mayer at MGM was the original Odd Couple. Schary was the bright young intellectual with ultraliberal political leanings—an Adlai Stevenson Democrat. Mayer was a Cal Coolidge Republican—so far to the right that he had disinherited his own daughter, Mrs. Edith Goetz, because she and her producer husband, Bill, had voted for Franklin Delano Roosevelt. It was Mayer who took George Murphy out of the song and dance ranks and nurtured him in politics until George became the conservative Republican senior United States senator from the state of California.

But what did politics have to do with making good pictures? Nothing, of course. Still, Izzy's abrupt name change was puzzling. What did he know?

I walked out the studio gate and over to the Thalberg building, the palace of the MGM kingdom. As luck would have it, first person I bumped into was Mayer emerging. L.B. then was in his Catholic phase. Some people thought he might even convert. He was chummy with the archbishop and had recently married a Catholic widow as his second wife. Since L.B. knew me as an alumnus of Notre Dame University, we were friends. Had I graduated from Southern Methodist, he wouldn't have given me the time of day. I recall how he told me that a parish priest out in the San Gabriel Valley had asked him to deliver the commencement address at a parochial school. And he was thrilled to do it.

All of this took place in the spring of 1951. We chatted amiably about things Catholic. With Izzy's name change fresh on my mind, I brought up Schary's name.

"A great humanitarian," said L.B. And then he asked what brought me out to the studio. I told him that I was en route to Gottfried Reinhardt's office for an interview.

"A great American," said L.B. "Why don't you use my office? It's much bigger, and I won't be using it." And then he was off.

As I say, nothing surprises me in Hollywood, so I thought little of Reinhardt being called a great American, even though he was born in Berlin. Schary didn't rate that accolade because he was a Democrat, which to Mayer was almost tantamount to being *un*-American.

As I went into the Thalberg building, I thought it would be kind of nice to take Mayer up on the use of his office. It was *the* office in the building. Offices, as most everyone in town knew, were rated by bathroom fixtures in the Thalberg building, sometimes known as "The Iron Lung." A producer or director of a low-budget picture might have to use the men's room down the corridor. A status executive had his own toilet and washbasin. Schary, as number two man, had all this and a shower. Mayer had both a shower and bath. It was a caste system of plumbing, much more rigid than the key to the executive washroom on Madison Avenue.

I reached Reinhardt's office, which had a washbasin. His secretary was apologetic: "Mr. Bacon, I just missed you at your office. Mr. Reinhardt wants to meet with you at Romanoff's for lunch. Is that all right?" It was more than all right, of course.

Off to Romanoff's and the affable Reinhardt, who was always talkative. This is a trait common to most sons of famous fathers. As Frank Sinatra, Jr. was to tell me years later, it's tough being the son of a living legend.

It was a pleasant lunch during which Gottfried told me of all the problems and hopes in bringing the Civil War classic *Red Badge of Courage* to the screen. He had hired an outside press agent because much of the publicity on the Stephen Crane classic had gone to John Huston, the director. And, as Gottfried pointed out, it was he, as producer, who had first brought the property to Huston's attention.

As the Havana cigars were passed around with the brandy, I tossed this at Gottfried: "I don't see how a producer of your stature can work with all the conflict going on between Dore and L.B."

Reinhardt, assuming that I was privy to court secrets, never paused for breath as he spilled all: "I fought two Civil Wars. The one in the picture and the one between Schary and Mayer. I would order six hundred Union army uniforms from wardrobe—Schary would okay it, Mayer would countermand it. Every damn detail of the picture, no matter how routine, touched off a crisis. Even Nick Schenck is in the act. Christ, you would think I was making *Ben Hur* instead of a picture for one million two. Dore wants the movie, L.B. never wanted it. He said it was a popgun war in a nuclear age. He said the script didn't have heart."

Reinhardt's outside press agent was with us. He never made a move to get his client off the subject. Had the interview been held, as scheduled, in the studio office, an MGM publicity man would have been kicking furiously under the table at Gottfried's leg and trying desperately to get the interview off on another tack.

But Gottfried was over in Beverly Hills, worlds away from Culver City. God could not listen in here. On and on and on he went. Obviously this was something that he wanted to get off his chest. It was therapy, after a year of frustration, to tell all this to a writer for the Associated Press whose worldwide syndication included many papers in his native Germany, where he was known mostly as Max's boy.

I listened amazed and fascinated. Lots of people had speculated about trouble between Mayer and Schary, but that was par for any studio in town. The MGM publicity department, if it knew trouble existed, had done a magnificent job of keeping it quiet. But here it was—and no off-the-record edict. I had a scoop and couldn't get to my typewriter fast enough.

I submitted the story to the boss, a conservative don't-rock-the-boat sort of editor who was, worse, a professional Catholic and one of Mayer's new religious friends.

"The story is too trady," he pontificated. "The public is only interested in stars. Who cares about producers, except the trade?"

I argued that Mayer was, in effect, a bigger star than most of the people he hired. For years, he had been listed as the highest-salaried executive in the nation. He also was a star on the sports pages. The Mayer racing stable was among the finest in the world. And what about its merit as a major story on the financial pages—a palace revolution brewing in a corporate kingdom?

No use. I had shown enterprise, a cardinal sin in a wire service that is geared to mediocrity. The story went into the wastebasket. But it was still in my head. A few months later, I was assigned to write a weekly Hollywood column, which was considered to be such an innocuous type of journalism that even the boss didn't read it.

Condensing what had been a major news story into a few paragraphs, I used the information in the column. The Los Angeles papers didn't pick it up, but it did get good play around the country. Not one paper lifted the information onto its financial section. Was the boss right, after all? Or—and many years of experience later proved me right on this—was the presentation wrong? Had this story moved on the AP's A-wire, it would have made front pages. Coming as it did on a weekly Hollywood column, it was a throwaway, a kiss-off.

But one man read it in some midwestern town paper like Youngstown or Fort Wayne. That man was Mayer. And that's how the telephone conversation at the beginning of this chapter originated.

L.B. Mayer, who once had called Gottfried Reinhardt a great American, now was on the phone calling him "a Nazi bastard." Here was the vengeful boss who had blacklisted stars, made world famous screen idols tremble at the nuances in his voice, and ruined careers with mere memos. Here he was crying over the telephone.

"Do you think I worry about a pinko?" sobbed Mayer in that phone conversation. Schary, of course, was no pinko, but anyone who had voted against Alf Landon in 1936 had to be pink in Mayer's estimation. "Believe me, I'll be here long after Dore Schary and all the other pricks around him. I've had them sniping at me before. Where in the hell are they now?

"Let Schary make his goddamn message pictures. When I want to send a message, I'll call Western Union. The pictures made by Irving Thalberg and me had heart. They entertained. They made MGM the greatest studio in the history of Hollywood. Let Schary play up to the Schwarzas and the pinkos. See where it gets him. Do you know what the most successful movies ever made were? Andy Hardy! Clean, wholesome and with heart. Not one goddamn message in them. As for Schary, fuck him!"

And then L.B. hung up. Whenever he mentioned the word *heart* in the conversation, you could actually hear his fist pounding his chest. It was an incredible sound over the phone.

And as for the reference to Western Union and messages, it was the first time I ever heard it used. Years later, when Mayer no longer was in power, other producers in town used to utter the same quote with a gentle hint that it should be carved on the face of Mt. Rushmore over their names.

Mayer's phone conversation convinced me that my information was on the button and that it was only a matter of time until the whole thing erupted. Naturally, I had more to go on than the change of Izzy Freeman's name to Dore Freeman. The trouble between Mayer and Schary had started long before the Civil War movie. It first began during filming of *Intruder in the Dust,* the William Faulkner story that dealt with a near lynching in Mississippi.

Schary wanted Juan Hernandez, the black man of the script, to be proud and defiant, displaying a militancy among blacks that would have been twenty-five years ahead of its time. Mayer, of course, wanted Hernandez to be Uncle Tom. Schary won this victory.

Next came *Battleground,* a script that Schary had brought over from RKO, where he had been studio boss under Howard Hughes. Mayer said that it was a lousy title and that no one wanted to see a war picture so soon after the big war. Mayer was doubly wrong, because *Battleground* turned out to be one of the biggest hits of Schary's tenure at MGM. Schary's prestige soared with Nick Schenck and the New York home office.

It was the beginning of the end, and more was to come. Schary resurrected *Quo Vadis,* which Mayer's men had been trying to make for years with no success. Mayer thought the new script lousy. Schary called it excellent. Then came the most crushing blow of all. Schary wanted to leave the final decision up to Schenck. No one—not even Thalberg—had ever gone over Mayer's head before. Surprisingly, Schenck sided with Schary.

The fight was one long palace revolution, and it looked like Schary was going to pull the coup. Schenck tried to stall the showdown by offering to come out to the coast and become the peacemaker and soothe Mayer. L.B. told him if he did, he'd take a poke at him. And he would have. L.B., when tears failed, had been known to throw punches.

On June 23, 1951, the story that shocked Hollywood broke. Louis B. Mayer was quitting the studio he had helped found. No one believed that Mayer really quit, although that was the technical wording. Once again it was the old Hollywood story—two Hannibals and only one

Alp. Schenck had chosen the younger Schary over the aging Mayer. It was hard to imagine MGM without Mayer, but there it was.

There are many in Hollywood who say that it was Thalberg, not Mayer, who made MGM the great studio it was in Hollywood's Golden Era. True, Thalberg was the creative genius who could take a stinker back to the cutting room, order a few more scenes reshot, and come up with a winner. But Irving could never have functioned in the Hollywood jungle without L.B. swinging the machete for him.

"I made it easy for Irving," L.B. once told me. "All I ever wanted Irving to worry about was what was up there on the screen. I loved him like the son I never had. I just wanted him to be Mr. Nice Guy. 'Irving,' I used to tell him, 'just be charming. I'll be the prick,'" And prick he was.

Dick Hanley, later Elizabeth Tayor's right arm, was Mayer's confidential secretary for eleven years. "He was the most evil man who ever lived," said Hanley. "He could destroy a big star, or a little secretary, all with the same delight."

Hanley worked eleven years straight without a vacation. Finally, when he took one to save his sanity, he returned to find that he had been fired. "And worse," adds Hanley. "I couldn't get a job anyplace in the movie industry for a year. L.B. had me blacklisted. I'd be selling ties in the May Company today if it hadn't been for Mike Todd, who wasn't the least bit scared by Mayer's power."

Hanley's blacklisting was nothing compared with that of Francis X. Bushman, who first came to the old Metro company in 1915 and, as Messala in the silent *Ben Hur*, launched Mayer and the new MGM in 1924. Bushman once told me an almost incredible story of how Mayer had blacklisted him in the industry for twenty-four years.

"I was doing a play in downtown Los Angeles," the screen's first matinee idol recalled. "It was just about the time when the talkies were taking over the town. And I was thankful for my stage voice and training.

"When my play opened I invited a number of people to be my guests at the play and later at a party. Louis, whom I considered to be a very dear friend, was included, of course. He came to the play but not to the party. I was concerned why and tried to get him on the phone the next day. His secretary brushed me off brusquely. And I got the same runaround for days afterwards.

"All of a sudden, when the movies were bringing stage actors out from New York by the trainload for the talkies, I found I couldn't get myself arrested in Hollywood. No one wanted to hire me. I couldn't figure what had happened. Finally, my agent gave me the bad news. And he quit me, too. Mayer had blacklisted me with every studio in town. And in those days, believe me, he was powerful enough to do it. I could only ask: 'Why? What the hell have I done to him?'

"No one seemed to know except Louis, and I couldn't get within a mile of him. For twenty-four years, I kept myself alive with radio soap operas because of Mayer's senseless blacklisting. And when he was out of MGM, I came back to work in Hollywood. But by then I could only play kindly old grandfathers."

What was behind the blacklisting? It took years for Bushman to uncover the reason.

"The whole thing was so ridiculous that it's funny," Bushman now says. "It shows the smallness of the man who did it.

"Going back to that party after my play opening, I had just that very day hired a new butler, who apparently knew nothing about the movie industry and cared even less. When Louis showed up at my home for the party, the butler asked his name so that he might properly introduce him. It made Louis furious to think that anyone would dare ask the name of the great Louis B. Mayer in his own bailiwick. The more furious Louis became, the more rude the butler became in turn. Louis finally grabbed his hat and coat and stormed out the door. He never came into the room where the party was.

"The butler, of course, never said a word to me about the incident. The whole thing cost me great mental anguish and God knows how many millions in dollars."

Judy Garland was another who felt the Mayer wrath in a different way. She once told me: "I was so overly pro-

My favorite shot of W. C. Fields, which Will Fowler sent as a Christmas card in 1968. "Humbug!" it says.

Sue Ann Langdon and Jackie Gleason on the famous train trip east. Sue Ann doesn't drink.

James Bacon and Jack Oakie like each other.

With Red Skelton at Perrino's—last refuge of the $1.50 cup of coffee.

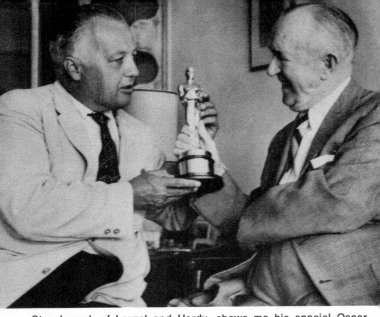

Stan Laurel, of Laurel and Hardy, shows me his special Oscar shortly before his death. (Associated Press)

George Burns, in younger days.

Bob Hope and Bing Crosby on the set of one of the "Road" pictures.

With Hope after a latrine trip at Da Nang, South Vietnam. Hope is almost never without a golf club.

Hope and me, with Zsa Zsa
Gabor, George Maharis
(right), and Mike Douglas (at
mike) at Baltimore telethon
for Susquehanna River flood
victims. Hope and I have been
without sleep for twenty-one
hours. He's eleven years older,
but see how fresh he looks.

Joanna Cameron, queen of the commercials (left), with Groucho Marx (rear), Marty Allen, the arcade owner, and Victoria Principal. Groucho won the trophy but let Marty hold it. (Peter C. Borsari)

A good group at Frank Sinatra's comeback at Caesar's Palace in Las Vegas. Foreground, Carroll O'Connor and Doris Bacon. I'm shaking hands with Jilly Rizzo (left) while Milton Berle plays to another table. Johnny Carson is with Sinatra. (Peter C. Borsari)

Frank Sinatra, Dean Martin, and publicist Jim Mahoney, in a trailer dressing room before a benefit. Sinatra says it is the only picture extant of me drinking a soft drink. Another unusual thing: I'm the only one drinking anything.

Listening to Howard Hughes on his famous televised and tele-phoned press conference denouncing the Clifford Irving biography as a hoax, with Marvin Miles of the *Los Angeles Times*.

A party at the home of Sammy Davis, Jr. (Peter C. Borsari)

Marilyn Monroe and I strike a couple of amorous poses.

With Gary Cooper on the set of *High Noon*.

With Marlon Brando in costume for *The Young Lions*.

With Lana Turner at a party for *Imitation of Life*.

With Cary Grant at a benefit at the Houston Astrodome.

With John (Big Duke) Wayne in a jovial mood after the first showing of *True Grit*, with Bob Goodfried of Paramount.

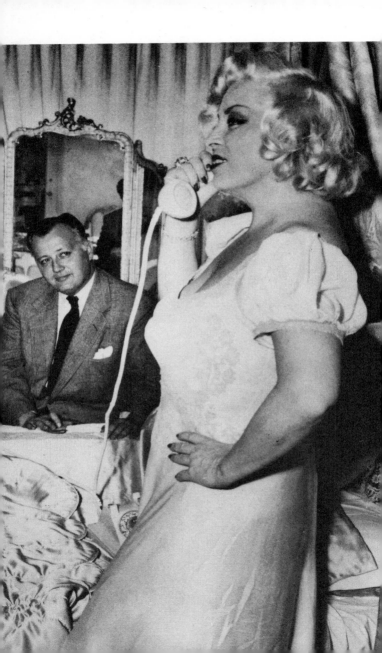

Opposite page; In Mae West's bedroom. Where else?

Here I am in dark glasses, with Frank Sinatra on a camel, as the Sands takes over the Dunes in Las Vegas. (Ulloms)

On a lunch break from *Harper,* with Paul Newman. This picture is a collector's item; it is one of the few times I have seen Paul off-stage without a beer. (Don Dorman)

By rail through Florida with Robert Redford for *The Candidate.*

Opposite page: With Elizabeth Taylor and Mike Todd in happier days (Earl Leaf); coming back from Mike Todd's funeral in Chicago with Elizabeth, her brother, and Mike, Jr. (right), on a Constellation provided by Howard Hughes. Right: With Richard Burton and little Liza Todd at the Puerto Vallarta airport, waiting for Elizabeth to arrive from Mexico City. (Wide World) Below: With Elizabeth and Eddie Fisher, reacting to an impertinent question about Debbie Reynolds (Joe Shere).

Sophia Loren autographed this "Dear Jim, I only have eyes fo you." I must be stupid or something, because I'm not getting th message.

Looking over sketches of *The Ten Commandments* with Cecil B DeMille.

A little horseplay with Peter Marshall of *"Hollywood Squares"* and George Kennedy. (Peter C. Borsari)

Richard Nixon, about to become president, in the 1968 campaign.

With Marion Davies, Hollywood's most famous party giver.

Opposite Page: Edward G. Robinson and I examine the prop electric chair used in *Black Tuesday*. "Little Caesar" flinched.

Hedda Hopper, with the producer Frank Ross (left) and Frank Sinatra, who just said a funny thing, at Le Pirat in Monaco.

Louella Parsons one New Year's Eve. In those days, columnists were friendly rivals. (Green & Tillisch)

With Raquel Welch on the set of one of her first movies, *Fantastic Voyage*. Even in a rubber suit, that body is something. Raquel's is nice, too.

Chastity, Sonny, and Cher with James Bacon the clown, at the circus. (Roy Cummings)

Laurence Olivier with Beebe Kline (left) and Doris Bacon. I was kidding him because Bogey always called him Oliver. (Rothschild)

Doris and me with Pope Tony Quinn at Cinecitta, Rome. Tony was so deep into his character that he made me kiss his ring three times.

With Bette Davis on location for some long forgotten movie.

I had just told James Stewart that he talked just like Rich Little. Notice the big laughs it got.

I was right there when Rita Hayworth and Dick Haymes got their marriage license. Later, at the wedding in the Sands, Rita's procession marched through the casino, and though she was the screen's reigning sex goddess, not a crapshooter looked up.

Liv Ullmann, with whom I worked in *40 Carats*.

With Milton Berle and the Lear Jet he chartered to plug his short-lived TV show. He quipped: "I know how you can end the war in Vietnam. Put it on ABC and it will be over in thirteen weeks."

Party after Liza Minnelli's opening at the Riviera Hotel in Las Vegas. From left: Frank Calcagnini, Jeannie Martin, the two of us, Olivia Hussey, and Dino Martin, Jr.

tected by Mr. Mayer and the studio that it was not until I was thirty years old and married twice that I stepped off a train in New York City without the studio meeting me. I felt as if I had really grown up for the first time."

Judy got Mayer's superpaternal treatment because she was big box office and, in those days, big-beamed. She was Mayer's idea of the All-American girl, the sweetheart of the All-American Andy Hardy.

Judy once confided that Mayer's method of licking her weight problem was to give her her own cook for the dressing room—a real status symbol even for MGM stars:

"She was nice and motherly. But, as I later learned, her main job was to mix Benzedrine into my food. In those days, it was the main appetite suppressant. And it made me fly higher than a kite. I was high-strung to begin with, and when I started taking this drug (a form of speed) I became a walking nervous breakdown.

"Mr. Mayer had a solution for this, too. He hauled me off to a funny farm in the middle of the night. It was considered quite chic in those days to be confined to a psychiatric clinic. I remember the big limousine with a couple of fellows from the studio pulling up to a big estate with iron gates. It was like Alfred Hitchcock remaking *Rebecca*. A couple of husky orderlies took over from the studio guards, and they said they were taking me across a big lawn to the psychiatrist's bungalow. He was waiting up for me.

"They literally dragged me across the lawn because I suddenly felt the funniest sensation that someone was grabbing at my ankles and pulling me back. I really began to think I was crazy. But they pulled me across the lawn as I stumbled like an idiot, screaming: 'They're grabbing my legs.' I told the story to the doctor, who listened patiently, said nothing, and then stabbed a needle into my arm.

"Next morning I woke up in a room with padded walls and bars on the window. I thought to myself 'Boy, I really am nuts.' Then I looked out the barred window at the lawn I had come across the night before. There, sprawled across the lawn—in disarray—was the villain who had grabbed at my ankles. We had come across a croquet field, and my feet had caught in the wickets, but the two burly guards just pulled me along, uprooting the wickets."

But didn't anyone at MGM ever say anything good about L.B.?

Lionel Barrymore once told me, as he sat in his wheelchair crippled with arthritis, that he would have killed himself long ago if it hadn't been for L.B.: "L.B. gets me $400 worth of cocaine a day to ease my pain. I don't know where he gets it. And I don't care. But I bless him every time it puts me to sleep."

PART III

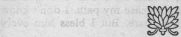

The Superstars

*Big Duke and Coop and
Elizabeth and Richard and
all the rest who sell tickets
for Jack L. Warner*

16

The Night I Made Love to Marilyn Monroe and Joe Schenck Didn't

I MAY SHOCK SOME PEOPLE with this chapter, especially a wife or two, but after a quarter-century or more I just had to tell somebody.

Marilyn Monroe and I had a love affair for a brief time. I loved her and she, in her actress way, was in love with me.

No born actress can ever truly love somebody, but I believe that Marilyn was as much in love with me as she was with Joe Di Maggio or Arthur Miller when she was married to them. And I can keep it quiet no longer, even though the critics will yell, "Kiss and tell," or "Crass."

Some people in those long ago Hollywood days suspected it. Maybe Marilyn told some. I never did. Marilyn often told me of her own amorous adventures, including the much publicized one with a virile president of the United States.

I knew Marilyn as well as any man could. We remained good friends until the day she died. It was not she who ended our brief fling. It was my own big mouth, with a line out of a corny soap opera.

Our affair started before Marilyn Monroe became Marilyn Monroe, movie star. She had the new name, but there was still a little of Norma Jean Baker around.

Sadly, I never knew Norma Jean Baker. No one did. Least of all Marilyn herself. Had some of us, like Di Maggio, JFK, and others, known Norma Jean a little better, Marilyn Monroe might be alive today. Marilyn Monroe was a goddess whose deity lasted roughly from

1950 to 1962. Marilyn could have coped with being a goddess. Norma Jean couldn't. Norma Jean was a frightened, lonely, and bewildered little girl. It was not Marilyn Monroe I saw sprawled nude on that wide mattress in the bedroom of the little Brentwood house early that tragic Sunday of August 5, 1962.

It was Norma Jean.

And when the coroner's staff threw that cheap cotton blanket over that beautiful face that was loved the world over, I knew that Norma Jean had found the peace that had eluded her for a brief lifetime. Marilyn Monroe would always live—and the proof is that there have been more books written about her than any other living superstar.

But no one ever writes about Norma Jean.

It was a sad Sunday—one of the saddest of my life. Reporters—I have been one for 40 years—are hard people, companions of disaster and tragedy. I'm not ashamed to admit that I cried that morning as they hauled Marilyn's body away in the coroner's station wagon.

I think it was the cheap blanket that did it. What an inglorious end to such a glorious career. And then, of course, I knew that the body would have to wind up at the county morgue unclaimed. Any police reporter knows that. And unclaimed it was until Di Maggio could get down to Hollywood fast from his home in San Francisco.

Joe, the second of her three husbands, had been married only ten months to Marilyn. My fling lasted three months at most, but while I cried, Joe acted.

Marilyn inspired that kind of love in some men. Over in Van Nuys, her first husband—a cop—reacted with typical underplay. His second wife was uptight about his early marriage to an international sex symbol.

And up in Woodbury, Connecticut, Arthur Miller, the Jewish Shakespeare, when asked if he had any comment on Marilyn's death, reacted like a prick. "I don't really," he said of the wife from whom he had been divorced less than a year. A few years later, he murdered her in his play *After the Fall.* But, in a way, who can blame Miller? He was cuckolded by Yves Montand while still married to Marilyn.

I say he reacted like a prick because the only time

Marilyn ever introduced him to me—after a warm and friendly kiss—he also acted like a prick. He refused to acknowledge the introduction or even shake hands.

I will say he's a hell of a playwright.

Marilyn and I first met in late 1948 or early 1949. She had finished a movie called *Ladies of the Chorus,* one of the all-time lousy movies—except for Marilyn. She was so exciting in the movie that it looked as if she had danced in from another picture. I told her so when I first met her at the old Naples Restaurant up the street from Columbia Pictures. Milton Stein, one of the legendary press agents of Hollywood, arranged the meeting and was present. She was still under contract to Columbia—her first six months option due.

It was an exciting lunch because here was a girl who had everything, plus excitement. Excitement—that's the key word in separating the stars from the actresses.

A few weeks later she called me, in tears. Columbia hadn't picked up her option, but that very afternoon she was going to see Groucho Marx for an audition for a new Marx Brothers movie called *Love Happy*. The next day she called me excitedly.

"There were three girls there and Groucho had us each walk away from him. I was the only one he asked to do it twice. Then he whispered in my ear: 'You have the prettiest ass in the business.' I'm sure he meant it in the nicest way."

A few days later, the Hollywood trade papers carried the news that Marilyn Monroe had been set for *Love Happy*.

Another phone call:

"I was only supposed to walk in the movie, but Groucho said he would write some special lines just for me." And if you know Groucho, that was Groucho talking.

Marilyn and I had lunch again—just the two of us—at a drive-in hamburger stand on Santa Monica Boulevard. She told me how she had gotten the Columbia contract because Joe Schenck had called up Harry Cohn, the boss of Columbia. I asked her how well she knew Schenck, who was the founder and board chairman of 20th Century-Fox.

"Very well," said Marilyn, with a kind of innocence that destroyed all cynicism on my part. Joe was pushing seventy in those days and, although a Sultan of Hollywood, was more of a shopper than a buyer of young women.

"Marilyn, you are going to be a big star," I said, and as we talked, I could see that Marilyn knew what she had and how to deploy it.

She was living at the Studio Club in those days, a sort of YWCA for starlets. She wasn't living there because of any fear of predatory males.

"It's the cheapest place in town," she said, matter-of-factly.

A few weeks passed and I went to a Hollywood party alone. Marilyn came alone, too. A girl friend had dropped her off, and I offered to drive her back to the Studio Club.

"Oh," she said, "I don't live there any more, but you can drop me off anyhow."

"Oh," said I, "where do you live?"

"Joe Schenck's guest house," she answered.

"Marilyn, I'll say it again. You are going to be a really big star."

Marilyn and I drove up to the big gate of the Schenck estate—some six acres in Holmby Hills. The house itself was so big that even the rooms had rooms. And the guest house would be luxurious in any suburb. It was nestled down some winding stairs, out of sight of the big house up on a hill. Years later, Tony Curtis was to own the same estate and same guest house. I once told him I had spent a few afternoons and nights in the guest house. Tony looked at me incredulously.

"Come on in," Marilyn said as she unlocked the door. "I have buckets of Dom Perignon all chilled. I was hoping I would see you tonight."

She may not have meant it, but she convinced me. Marilyn had a way of making men melt, making each feel as if he were the only man in her life. Few women have this quality.

We both went in and drank champagne and talked. She told me of how she had been under contract at Fox but that Darryl Zanuck, for some strange reason, hadn't liked her and she had been dropped.

"Even with Joe Schenck in your corner?" I asked.

"Joe pretty much lets Zanuck handle production. He never interferes. I didn't care because Joe called Harry Cohn and I got the second lead with Adele Jergens in *Ladies of the Chorus*. I was cut out of everything I was in at Fox."

With such potent backing, I was surprised that Columbia had dropped her and told her so.

"Well, I said the wrong thing to Harry," Marilyn said. "One Friday he came on the set and suggested that I come along with him on his yacht on a trip to Catalina. I said a dumb thing, I guess."

Marilyn, it turned out, had asked Harry if his wife were going along on the trip. It touched Harry's devotion to his family, something the Jewish patriarchs of the movies treasure.

"Harry flew into rage," said Marilyn. "He called me a 'goddamn cunt' and said when the picture was finished, he never wanted to see me on the lot again." As far as I know, Marilyn never again did set foot on the Columbia lot.

By this time we had uncorked a second bottle of Dom Perignon, courtesy of Joe Schenck's wine cellar.

I started imagining that I was Clark Gable, and, of course, Marilyn Monroe was Marilyn Monroe. Who else?

The talk started getting a little sexy. Marilyn had me rolling on the floor in explaining why she had moved into Schenck's guest house. She was not really his lover or concubine, just his good friend. In Marilyn's book, that meant an occasional friendly hump. After all, what are friends for? But what she had to go through was a scream. Joe, in those days, was a worn-out seventy or so. He had resorted to a special shot from a doctor that could get it up for a minute or two. It was revolutionary. In fact, I wish I knew where to get it today. Marilyn said it was a medical miracle that worked. She was living proof.

"It's all very complicated," she said. "Sometimes when the doctor comes, I have to synchronize my watch. That's why I'm living in the guest house. This stuff can't wait for a studio limousine to drive me across town."

As I said, the champagne turned me into Clark Gable, and soon Marilyn and I were lying on a couch passionately kissing each other, touching each other. It was heaven. Soon we were naked in bed, just about to make love, when there came violent knocking on the door.

I won't say that my life flashed before my eyes, but the legend of Joe Schenck's castration of a famous, virile star who fooled around with Joe's wife, Norma Talmadge, did.

Marilyn quickly put on a robe. I almost had cardiac arrest on the spot. What do you do in a situation like that? I'll tell you what you do. You do exactly what they do in every French bedroom farce. You grab your clothes and hide under the bed. Thank God, it was not Joe at the door.

"Mr. Schenck wants you up at the house right away," the man's voice said.

"OK," said Marilyn, "I'll be right up."

She came back in the bedroom and yelled for me. I crawled sheepishly out from under the bed. Somehow this really broke up Marilyn. In retrospect, it was kind of funny.

"This won't take long," said Marilyn as she sat down nude at her dressing table. With agonizing slowness, she started combing her hair and putting on makeup. Somehow I felt sorry for poor Joe, sitting up in his master bedroom counting the seconds until that stiff cock started drooping.

Finally, Marilyn threw on a dress—no underwear—and some shoes and left. She was back in minutes.

"Late again," she laughed as she opened another bottle of champagne. I asked her why she took so long to answer Joe's hurry-up call.

"I didn't want you to go in on a wet deck," she laughed.

Clark Gable? The King would have been proud of me that night. We never heard from Joe again. I sneaked out before it turned light and drove home. Before I left, Marilyn asked: "When will I see you again?"

"How about this afternoon?"

"OK, I'll be waiting. Maybe we will have another interview."

And we did—and for some months after that. Dom Perignon has to be the greatest aphrodisiac of all time.

Almost a decade later, a glamorous, sexy star—still living, so she shall be nameless—invited me up to her home, not far from the Schenck estate.

Once again a few bottles of Dom Perignon. And once again I imagined myself the King. It was the same scene, but we managed to get dressed before the star's husband came home. The only thing that saved me from castration that night was that the husband had as much scotch in him as we had champagne.

His wife calmly announced that I was interviewing her for the Associated Press. He had such a load on that he never realized it was well past midnight, an unlikely time for an interview. To this day, we are still friends. The star has since divorced him and gone on to other men and other things. Being a Hollywood columnist doesn't always pay that well, but you can't beat the fringe benefits.

But this is about Marilyn. I thought about getting a divorce and asking her to marry me, but the Irish Catholic conscience was too deep. I fell hard for Marilyn. I can understand Joe Di Maggio's love for her long after they split. She was one hell of a woman. You couldn't help but be in love with her.

Our little fling ended because I, like Marilyn with Harry Cohn, gave the wrong answer.

It was the cocktail hour on New Year's Eve, 1951, that Marilyn called. I know people will find this hard to believe, but some of the most beautiful women in the world don't get asked out on New Year's Eve.

"I don't want to stay at home alone on New Year's Eve, Jim. Can I go to a party with you?"

I bit my tongue after I said it, but it came out anyway.

"I'm all for it, but I don't think my wife would understand."

This is the kind of line you hear every day on soap operas. I said it and I'm sorry. Marilyn, in her little girl voice, said: "Oh, I understand."

I don't know whether she went out that New Year's Eve or not. I did, and I know my whole evening was ruined. I blew it and I knew it. It never affected our friendship but it ended our affair. She gravitated to others for advice: Sidney Skolsky, Milton Greene, Di Maggio, Frank Sinatra,

Arthur Miller, Peter Lawford, and some more. Funny thing about Marilyn, she always took the advice of the last person she talked with. It accounted for most of her indecision. And insecurity.

Over the years, we always laughed about my hiding under the bed that night. She had never heard the Joe Schenck castration story until I told her.

"If I had known," she said, "I would have hidden the gardener's shears."

Years later when she was making *Some Like It Hot*, she spotted me on the Goldwyn lot. She gave me an affectionate kiss and then, in a casual aside to Arthur Miller, she introduced me "as an old friend of Joe Schenck's," strictly an inside joke which Miller didn't appreciate. He didn't say a word, just glared. I have always thought him a prick since.

Probably the guy who did the most for Marilyn was Johnny Hyde, a top agent at the time. The most a tycoon like Schenck ever did was get her bits, bits that sometimes were cut out of the picture. Hyde, who was madly in love with her, built her career. Johnny was a little guy, like so many of the William Morris agents are. I don't know whether Marilyn loved him or not, but she knew enough by now to give the right answers.

Marilyn and I, intimate together, often talked about her bedroom calisthenics. She said she always used the same line with Johnny in bed: "Oh, Johnny, you're hurting me."

Once again, I knew she was going to be a star. I asked her how come she never used that line with me. "You're not a little guy," she said.

Johnny's major contribution to Marilyn's career was *The Asphalt Jungle*, a movie directed by John Huston. In it she played Louis Calhern's concubine. This movie, more than any other, launched Marilyn Monroe as an international personality. It's seldom that a small role can do this, but it did it for Marilyn.

By coincidence, I ran into Marilyn on the steps of the Thalberg Building at MGM the day Johnny had set for her audition with Huston and Producer Arthur Hornblow. I took one look at her and was flabbergasted. As everyone knows, Marilyn had the most beautiful breasts in town. What she had done was stuff her bra with cotton.

"Marilyn," I asked, "what the hell have you done to yourself? You look grotesque. You look like a filing cabinet with the top drawer pulled out."

I could see I had hurt her by my bluntness, so I kissed her on the cheek and apologized. But I argued just the same for her to get rid of the falsies.

"They're looking for a girl with big bazooms. Johnny told me to dress sexy."

I couldn't talk her out of it. She went to the audition, cotton and all. A few days later, I saw Huston up at Humphrey Bogart's house and mentioned the incident to him.

"Well," said John, "I reached into her sweater and pulled out the falsies and said, 'Marilyn, now we'll read for the part.' "

As soon as she had busted out in those brief scenes in The Asphalt Jungle, the whole town was talking about her. It was not a blockbusting picture but it was a classic movie of its day, a favorite on the Bel-Air circuit. That's the private projection rooms of the directors and producers. Marilyn's emergence was all the more noteworthy because she had shone in scenes with Calhern, one of the finest actors of stage or screen. I had seen Calhern, with his back to the camera, steal scenes—like a Jack Oakie or Victor McLaglen. But in The Asphalt Jungle, he was the victim this time.

A year or two later, he and I were talking about it at lunch in the MGM commissary. Louie said: "Jack Barrymore always used to say, 'Never do a scene with a kid or a dog.' After Asphalt Jungle, I amend that to include beautiful tits.' "

Hyde followed "Jungle" with a similar type scene in All About Eve, in which she played George Sanders's girl friend. Also a hard guy to steal scenes from. But Marilyn shone again in this blockbuster, which was later to become the Broadway musical hit Applause. And, with this picture, the Hollywood press corps fell in love with Marilyn. Soon the publicity department at Fox was deluged with requests for interviews and photo layouts of Marilyn.

Harry Brand, who ironically had been Joe Schenck's long-time press agent, even in the Fatty Arbuckle case, knew he had a phenomenon on his hands. Harry, at this time, was director of publicity at 20th Century-Fox. He assigned one of his staffers, Roy Craft, to be in charge of the Monroe publicity buildup. Over the years, Craft has been credited with inventing the bright quotes that came from Marilyn. Craft always denied it, saying that he just planted them. They all came from Marilyn. He was so right.

Roy wasn't around when I asked Marilyn if it was true that she always sunbathed in the nude and she answered: "Yes, because I like to feel brown all over."

Nor was he around when I asked her what she said to Joe Di Maggio after their first date. "Well, we didn't discuss baseball." Nor was he around years later, during *The Misfits,* when Hedda Hopper came up to Marilyn and me drinking at a bar at a Hollywood party. Hedda, who was about as subtle as a runaway freight train, demanded: "Marilyn, I hear you drink nothing but bullshots all day long."

Marilyn turned to me with that beautiful look of bewilderment and pleaded with her eyes for my help.

"That's bouillon and vodka, Marilyn," I helped.

"What a horrible thing to do to vodka," said Marilyn.

Hedda howled uproariously at that reply.

Craft did a good job of supervising the Monroe buildup. Maybe too good. One day he fled Hollywood, and last I heard he was editing a weekly paper in some hamlet in the state of Washington, where the biggest news of the week is the Rotary luncheon.

In the midst of all this buildup came a crisis—the famous nude calendar.

I had known about Marilyn's nude calendar almost from the day she posed for it on May 27, 1949. She had told me how hungry she was and she desperately needed the fifty dollars to pay her back rent—and to eat. She was very fond of photographer Tom Kelley and his wife because after the picture was shot the Kelleys took Marilyn out for some chili. Although it was late in the day, that chili was the first thing she had eaten all day.

Other columnists knew about the calendar, too. One of them, Harrison Carroll, a kindly man who was columnist for the *Los Angeles Herald-Express* and later for the

Herald-Examiner, agreed with me that to write about it would mean the end of a career for a lovable girl. Hollywood was still puritanical in those days. Nowadays it's easier to count the girls who haven't posed in the nude than those who have.

The calendar certainly was no secret. It hung in every garage and filling station in Los Angeles County. It was spotted one day by Aline Mosby, the Hollywood correspondent for United Press. Aline, being a woman, didn't feel the same about Marilyn as the men columnists did. She broke the story. The story caused a panic. Women's clubs and church groups issued statements right and left. But most of the chaos was in the executive offices of 20th Century-Fox. Everybody, especially Harry Brand, remembered the Fatty Arbuckle scandal.

In the midst of all this hullabaloo, I got a frantic call from Marilyn. She was in tears. That afternoon, she was to meet with Harry and Zanuck, and she was afraid of the morals clause in every studio contract. That meant that if the public morals were offended, the contract was void. What should she do?

"Marilyn," I said, "whatever you do, don't be contrite." She interrupted: "What does that mean?"

"Sorry," I said.

"Oh," said Marilyn.

After all, what was there to be sorry for? A beautiful, young girl was starving. She posed nude. Big deal. She didn't sell herself like a hooker, the way a few other stars around town had in their prestar days.

I wish I could say that I gave her the line that was quoted around the world. When she asked me what she should say, I could only advise: "Say something funny."

A few hours after the meeting with Zanuck and Brand, Jet Fore, a Fox press agent, came into my office at the AP with an official release from the studio on the nude calendar crisis. In it was this line. "When Marilyn was asked what she had on," she replied 'The radio.' "

That was pure Marilyn. No press agent could have dreamed it up. That single line squashed the whole mess. In fact, it accelerated everything in the other direction. What had been a crisis all of a sudden turned into a success. From disaster to triumph. Nothing could stop Marilyn now. Even the wire services took the calendar out of the garages and transmitted it on their photo networks. It became the most celebrated picture in the world.

Within a day or two, I saw Marilyn.

"Well, how did I do?"

"Marilyn," I said, "Bob Hope should hire you as one of his writers."

Familiarity with Marilyn had its drawbacks too. I often saw her at her worst. Marilyn Monroe was not a tidy person. Or rather, Norma Jean Baker was not a tidy person. Marilyn Monroe the movie star was fastidious.

I have always thought that Marilyn didn't commit suicide, although the coroner's office ruled that she did. Their official report said that she had often expressed a desire to end it all and was frequently depressed. An important factor in the findings was the unkempt condition of her person—dirty fingernails, uncombed, matted hair, etc. But, I had often seen Marilyn looking like that.

The first time was during pre-camera rehearsals for *The River of No Return* with Robert Mitchum. Stan Margulies the producer, then a publicist, asked me to do a story on Marilyn. We arranged to meet in her dressing room on the Fox lot. What we saw shocked both of us. I can tell you it set my love affair back six months.

Marilyn looked like Phyllis Diller doing her act. Her hair was in tangles. She had cold cream all over her face, and her eyebrows were smeared. She was the same old Marilyn in spirit but on the outside, she was Dracula's Daughter. I couldn't get out of there fast enough. Stan and I still talk about it to this day.

But that was the waif, Norma Jean. Not Marilyn.

Another time, during the making of *All About Eve*, Jet Fore and I went over to Marilyn's apartment for an interview. She opened the door and once more I was in a state of shock. Sweetly as always, she said: "Fix yourself a drink while I put on some makeup." That was 2 P.M.

Marilyn didn't come out of her bedroom until 6 P.M. By that time, Jet and I were so roaring drunk, we didn't know what she looked like. We couldn't see her. Jet took off. I woke up the next morning in bed with Marilyn. The phone was ringing off the hook. Marilyn answered it.

"Where did Jet go?" Marilyn asked me.

"How in the hell would I know?"

"It's his wife. She's worried because she says he always calls her by 6 A.M. when he's going to stay out all night."

Somehow this worried Marilyn and she couldn't see the humor in that line. It broke me up.

That four-hour wait in Marilyn's living room while she put on her makeup probably tells more about Marilyn Monroe than anything. Often, I had waited for Marilyn while she went through that ritual. It was almost a Jekyll and Hyde experience. Instead of the mad doctor, it was Norma Jean Baker transforming herself into Marilyn Monroe, movie star. Marilyn did it when she was a star. She did it when she was a virtual unknown. It's pathetic, in retrospect.

On *Clash By Night*, such professionals as Barbara Stanwyck, Robert Ryan, and Paul Douglas used to fume at her delays. But, sorry as Marilyn was, she couldn't help it. Years later, when she appeared with Laurence Olivier in *The Prince and the Showgirl,* he said the experience aged him ten years, although he liked Marilyn enormously.

Tony Curtis was not so gracious. After a hot smooching scene with her in *Some Like It Hot,* he said: "It's like kissing Hitler."

Director Billy Wilder: "After working with her all day, I feel like going home and beating up my wife."

Little Miss Come Lately, that was Marilyn all her life.

But really, it was all worth it. She may have added $1 million to the budget of *Some Like It Hot* but she also added $5 million to the profits. After all, you can get dozens of beautiful blondes to show up in makeup at 6 A.M. and be on the set ready to go at 9 A.M., but they are not Marilyn Monroe.

Marilyn—not Norma Jean—was a perfectionist.

She said she knew nothing about baseball, but after her marriage to Di Maggio, she often spoke a baseball language. I once was astounded to have her compare herself with a pitcher in a ball game. I doubt if she had ever seen a game.

"Everything rides on the ball you throw. It's you up there alone. You got to give it your best shot."

Marilyn had an uncanny knack for knowing when she

delivered her best shot. She knew that no one ever goes to see a movie because it came in under schedule. They go to get a reward, to be entertained. What if it did go $1 million over budget? The star is judged by what is up there on the screen, not by what is on the company books.

She once confessed to me that her greatest insecurities as an actress came when she worked with Olivier:

"Here was this greatest of all actors, with fifty years of theater behind him. And here was I, supposed to match him scene for scene, with no training at all. If it hadn't been for the Russian vodka, I don't think I could have finished the picture."

She did, and it was a terrific strain. To Olivier's credit, he was overly cooperative with her and worked hard with her on every scene. But imagine a girl out of foster homes, who became a movie star before she became an actress, in competition with the Muhammad Ali of acting? It explains how her acceleration of drugs and booze dates from that picture. Marilyn drove directors nuts. If she didn't like the way she did a scene, she didn't wait for the director to yell, "Cut." She broke up the scene herself by saying something like, "Damn" or "I loused that one up, didn't I?"

Fritz Lang, the famed German director, directed her in *Clash By Night,* and he almost went into a Germanic rage. I watched Marilyn spoil twenty-seven takes of a scene one day. She had only one line, but before she could deliver it about 20 other actors had to go through a whole series of intricate movements on a boat. Everybody was letter perfect in every take, but Marilyn could not remember that one line. Fritz then had a cue card printed— unheard of in those days. Still Marilyn muffed it. Finally she got it right, and Fritz yelled: "Thank God. Print it."

Later, in her dressing room, Marilyn confessed that she had muffed the line on purpose for all those takes: "I just didn't like the way the scene was going. When I liked it, I said the line perfectly."

Now this was not Marilyn Monroe, movie star, talking. This was Marilyn Monroe the actress, in her first major feature part. At this point, she was little more than a crea- ture of publicity. Marilyn was no dummy. She understood

the movie business, even then, better than anyone: "I
never intentionally mean to hurt anyone, but you can't be
too nice to people you work with, else they will trample
you to death."

Sound cynical, perhaps? It's really a fact of life in the
survival of a movie star.

The only other novice I've ever known who was so
savvy so early in her career was Barbra Streisand. When
Barbra made her first movie, *Funny Girl,* she was the perfectionist to end all perfectionists. She told Willy Wyler,
winner of three Oscars, how to direct; Oscar-winning cam-
erman Harry Stradling, Sr., what angles to shoot; and top
musical director Herb Ross what dances to choreograph.

She got a terrifically bad press from it, leaked by the
studio brass—an old trick for keeping stars in line. But
when *Funny Girl* came out, Barbra proved that she knew
what she was doing. She even got an Oscar her first time
at bat.

So it was with Marilyn.

She felt that until *Some Like It Hot* she had never had
a good movie on the screen. Some, when she relaxed her
bird-dogging, were disasters. No one knew this better than
Marilyn. She was always trying, always learning. Especially the latter, in the scholarly sense.

One day at lunch, in the old RKO commissary during
Clash By Night, my college education came up in conversation. I told her how I had gone to Notre Dame and
then later Syracuse and Harvard. I could have told her I
owned the studio and she wouldn't have been any more
impressed. She related, with sadness, how she had dropped
out of Van Nuys High School, in her first year, to marry
a cop.

"I've always regretted not getting an education," she
said.

We had a long discussion about how easy it is for one
to educate oneself. I even remember coming up with a
line that Marilyn took down in a notebook.

"Most college graduates," I said, "are little more than
educated fools."

All of a sudden, I found myself being interviewed. Marilyn had produced the notebook and pen from her purse

and was writing down everything I said. I suggested books for her to read: Shakespeare, Thomas Wolfe, even St. Thomas Aquinas. And then I named off some of Dr. Mortimer Adler's list of "Great Books." For weeks after that, she would report to me what books she had read. I have never known such a voracious reader among show business people except—and this will surprise you—Richard Burton and Marty Allen. Burton drinks because, in reality, he is an Oxford Don but finds that he is enslaved to acting because of the money. Marty, the bushy-haired comic, averages five to seven books a week—from best-sellers to great literature. Marilyn had the same thirst for knowledge. She may not have understood what she read half the time, but she gave them all the old college try.

There was a funny, and a little bit pathetic side, to all this.

I'll never forget that this particular luncheon at RKO was a prelude to a photo session with Marilyn in a bathing suit, by the pool of the Hollywood Roosevelt. Clarey Barbieaux, an RKO press agent who later went over the hill to the liquor business in Sherman Oaks, went with Marilyn and me to the Roosevelt.

As we were getting ready to shoot some cheesecake art, a little girl asked for her autograph. Marilyn asked the little girl's name so she could make the autograph personal. The girl's name was Barbara. Suddenly, Marilyn, who had been discussing Aristotle at lunch, turned to me and asked: "How do you spell Barbara?"

Yet that same night, she stayed up all night to read Thomas Wolfe's *Look Homeward, Angel*.

The first time she ever met Bobby Kennedy was at a party at Peter and Pat Kennedy Lawford's Santa Monica beach house. Marilyn, wearing horn-rimmed glasses, followed Bobby from room to room with notebook in hand, writing down all the remarks he made. It presents a little different picture than some the lurid tales you may have heard about Marilyn and Bobby, which I, for one, never believed.

It seemed like there was an eternal clash between Marilyn the scholar and Marilyn the international sex symbol. No one knew better than Marilyn what she had to offer to the males of the world. That's why she invented the no-bra look twenty years ahead of its time. In fact, she seldom wore anything under her dress in public—sometimes not even panties.

I once asked: "Marilyn, what if you get hit by a truck?" It didn't throw her for long.

"That's why all the truck drivers like me on the screen."

In 1953, she won the Photoplay Award as the most promising newcomer of the year. In those days fan magazines had great stature in the industry, *Photoplay* in particular. The magazine's awards ceremony then was on a social par with today's Academy Awards or the Golden Globes. It was a prestigious industry function, and the stars turned out in droves.

Marilyn, late as always, just got there in time to hear her name called by Dean Martin and Jerry Lewis, who were at their zaniest in those presplit days. When she wiggled through the audience to come up on the podium, her derrière looked like two puppies fighting under a silk sheet. Her dress was so tight that it must have been sprayed on —and nothing underneath, not even panties. It was low cut, and her famous breasts undulated. Martin and Lewis went crazy. So did the audience—but there were many dissenters.

The next day Joan Crawford, a star of the Golden Era, gave out a blistering interview to the wire services calling Marilyn's appearance a disgrace to the industry. In later years, such a blast from someone of Joan's stature would kill off the career of a Jayne Mansfield, but it only made Marilyn more colorful. Once again she had triumphed over righteous indignation.

Nothing was ever going to stop Marilyn Monroe. That night she could have shown up nude. With those blatant sex displays, she became another person. She lost all her insecurities when she was flaunting that magnificent body. She knew she excited men. More important, Marilyn Monroe lost Norma Jean Baker when she was exuding sex. It really was a Jekyll and Hyde complex.

I recall, after the award, getting up from the table to give Marilyn a congratulatory kiss. She kissed back in such a way that I will always remember it as the night I saved her being raped. I restrained myself.

Marilyn was almost drugged when she was in this state.

She became the greatest cock teaser I have ever known—
and she loved every minute of it.

I walked out of the hotel with her. As we came down
the driveway, Joe Di Maggio was waiting for her.

"You know Joe," she said. "He doesn't like crowds."

I left her, and she and Joe drove off.

Marilyn had been a blind date for Joe or, to be more
exact, Joe had been a blind date for Marilyn. Vince Ed-
wards had set up the date:

"Joe had been brooding over his divorce from Dorothy
Arnold, and he was giving all of his friends concern. I
thought Marilyn would be good for him. I arranged for
them to meet at the Villa Nova, an Italian restaurant on
the Sunset Strip. They hit like gangbusters."

I happened to run into Marilyn the very next day at
Fox commissary.

"I met the most wonderful man last night. So handsome
and so gentlemanly." I naturally asked who.

"Joe Di Maggio," she said.

"Joe Di Maggio?" I practically screamed.

"Why, is there something wrong with him?"

"He can't go to his left for a ground ball!" My joke
was lost on Marilyn, so I then went into Joe's fame as the
noblest Yankee since Babe Ruth.

"You mean Baby Ruth?" she said.

When I asked what she and Joe did on their first date,
that's when Marilyn came up with her great line: "Well,
we didn't discuss baseball."

From then on it was Joe all the way. Even after they
divorced, she often had dates with Joe. She really tried to
make that marriage work.

"Joe distrusts everybody in the movie business except
his buddy Frank Sinatra. We just live in two different
worlds. He spends all day in front of the TV set watching
some game or another." And then she made a pleading
request. "You know so much about sports. Why don't you
have dinner with us some night? You could help me bridge
show business and sports. It would mean so much."

I told her anytime, but divorce came before dinner. The
closest I got was the front yard—just in time to meet
famed lawyer Jerry Giesler coming out the door.

"I just served the divorce papers on Mr. Di Maggio, who is still inside the house with Marilyn. Joe accepted the papers very complacently and very decently," said Jerry. I asked him where Marilyn was. "She's upstairs in the bedroom, very upset." I asked him if it were not unusual for a newly divorced couple to be living under the same roof. "Jim, how long have you been around Hollywood? You know that anything is possible in this town."

As marriages go, it only lasted ten months. But as a love affair, it is neverending. It's the story of two people from different worlds who couldn't communicate while the game was on TV. How many couples do you know like that in this country?

Jerry shook his head. "It's a kind of crazy divorce, even for this town. They both seem to love each other. It's much better when they hate. Much better for the lawyers anyway."

Joe swung a big bat in the romantic leagues, too.

To the day she died, Marilyn always rated her other loves alongside her love for Di Maggio. She even had a couple romances with big stars, but she would often say, "He's no Di Maggio."

Marilyn would have loved Joe's gesture—still in force— of seeing that a fresh rose is always in her crypt at Westwood Memorial Park. But his adoration had a darker side: his intense jealousy, a common trait among Italian men. It's no secret that they are the most possessive of all males. Even after Joe and Marilyn had split, he was still jealous of her.

One night I went to the old Villa Capri restaurant for a little wine and spaghetti. Over at a nearby table, it looked like a Sons of Italy meeting—Sinatra, Di Maggio, and a few other paisanos. Hank Sanicola, Sinatra's manager and close friend in those days, was among the group. In newspaper accounts, he was always listed as Frank's bodyguard but, in fact, he was the most gentle of men. I didn't join the table, although I always have been a friend of Frank's, because I could see that Di Maggio was in a terrible mood. Sinatra was pleading with him about something, as if he was trying to keep him from doing something foolish.

Finally the group got up and left. Sanicola told me why:

"Joe thinks Marilyn is shacked up in an apartment with some makeup guy or some other guy who works on her pictures. He wants to break in on her, and Frank has been trying for hours to talk him out of it. But you know Joe. He's in a rage and he's not listening, even to Frank. So they're going over to the apartment."

It puzzled me. Why would a guy want to break up an affair of a wife who had already left him, and he her? But I wasn't a gossip columnist in those days and I couldn't see any story for the conservative AP, so I let it drop.

The police department had the whole thing on the report the next day. It was the famous "Wrong-Door Raid." Frank, Joe, and a few others had gone to the apartment house, kicked in a door, and scared the hell out of a spinster who was in bed asleep. Imagine waking up and seeing an enraged Di Maggio kicking down your door and then Frank Sinatra right beside him. I listened to her tell it in court later and it was one of the funniest courtroom scenes of all time. The woman told it with a perfect Jean (Edith Bunker) Stapleton delivery.

Frank, being Sicilian, never has admitted that he may have led Joe to the wrong door on purpose. I saw Marilyn a few days later and her comment—once again the Monroe wit—was: "Joe is such a gentleman. Who else but a gentleman would kick in the wrong door?" When Marilyn made *Let's Make Love* out at Fox with Yves Montand, she introduced him to me with this comment: "Doesn't he remind you of Joe?" Then Yves told us that although he had lived all his life in France, he had much Italian blood in him. Simone Signoret, Yves's Oscar-winning wife, was with him during the making of the film. So nothing much happened, maybe an occasional pat on the thigh or derrière which, to a Frenchman, is like a handshake.

It was long after this, and Miss Signoret had gone back to France. Marilyn's marriage to Arthur Miller was floundering, so she checked into the Beverly Hills Hotel bungalow not far from Yves's own. One night, after drinking a lot of vodka, Marilyn knocked on Yves's door, wearing only a mink coat. He invited her in and she took off the coat. "I fucked her. What else would a Frenchman do in such a circumstance?" Yves confided to a mutual friend.

A few days later, a waiter friend at the Beverly Hills Hotel told me that he had just served breakfast to Marilyn and Yves, both of whom were in partial undress. He even supplied the number of the bungalow. This was a story. If Marilyn Monroe was divorcing the country's best-known playwright, we had to find out.

Yves answered the phone. "Are you and Simone planning to get divorced? I understand that Marilyn Monroe is with you right now."

Bluntness is often a reporter's best way of getting a story, by throwing the guy on the other end completely off guard. But Yves had a counterattack I couldn't cope with. He started speaking the most rapid French I have ever heard. About the only thing I understood was that he was going back to Paris immediately.

Within minutes, I got a call from Pat Newcomb, Marilyn's press agent and one of the last people ever to see her alive. Pat explained that Marilyn indeed was in Yves's bungalow, but they were discussing doing another movie together. "They are just good friends," said Pat. What the hell else could she say? She and I both knew it was all horseshit, but that's the way the game is played in this town.

Hedda Hopper must have gotten the same tip because the next day the lead in her column was this ungallant quote from Yves: "Marilyn had a schoolgirl's crush on me. That's all. I love my wife." Oh, you French kid.

I happened to be in Paris a few weeks after this, visiting the Burtons on some picture. A Fox publicity man stationed there asked me if I would interview Montand, since *Let's Make Love* was due to open in Paris.

"Do you think he wants to talk with me?" I asked, somewhat incredulously.

"Sure," said the PR man. "I told him you were in town. He wants to see you. Besides, you have to see the fifteenth-century apartment they live in, on an island in the Seine. It's a story in itself."

To reach the Montand apartment, you had to enter through a bistro kitchen. Both Yves and Simone were there. She greeted me warmly, but Yves immediately lapsed into rapid-fire French. I had talked with Yves many times in Beverly Hills. His English was good, if a little halting. But there was no English today. I have never heard French spoken so rapidly. Finally, he left the room. Simone turned to me. "I must apologize for my husband speaking French to you. He's afraid you will ask him about Marilyn Monroe instead of the picture." That tells a lot about a French wife.

Yves returned to the room. Simone gave him a look. He started talking English. I didn't have to ask any questions; he brought up the subject of Marilyn Monroe himself. Or rather he let out a tirade against Hedda Hopper!

"That beetch. Even my wife gave me the hell when she read that I said that Marilyn had a schoolgirl crush on me. No Frenchman would ever make such a statement. Nevair have I used such an expression—a schoolgirl crush. Marilyn is tres charmante. A lovely girl. I am so sorree she is divorcing her husband, but I am not divorcing my wife. Nevair!"

Simone bestowed what I would call a Simone Signoret look and then said: "I became friendly with Marilyn when she and Yves were making the picture together. Some of this talk may hurt our friendship."

I figured it was a good time to leave, but not before telling her how much I liked her place. "I understand it was remodeled during the Renaissance," I said. Simone got the joke. I figured it was best to leave them laughing.

Some months later, I heard that Yves's plane from Paris had a five-hour layover at JFK Airport in New York. Marilyn, again with Dom Perignon and caviar, met him in a suite at the International Hotel near the airport, and helped ease the layover. The girl who made the reservation told me that. I have never seen Yves or Simone since, but it looks as if they survived that domestic crisis. Marilyn, not long after that, divorced Miller.

All of this took place about the time that Marilyn was giving her greatest performance on the screen in *The Misfits*, which was written by Miller. Clark Gable thought it was his, too, but he never lived to see it put together. I visited him on a Friday at Paramount, where they were doing some process shooting before winding up the movie that day.

"This script is sheer poetry," said Gable. "I have never before spoken such words on the screen." He was waiting as usual for Marilyn, and we got into a discussion about her.

"What the hell is that girl's problem?" said the King. "Goddamn it, I like her, but she's so damn unprofessional. I damn near went nuts up there in Reno waiting for her to show. You know me, I'm on the set before it's time to shoot, with all my lines learned. Christ, she wouldn't show up until after lunch some days, and then she would blow take after take. And Goddamn it, she's good in it, too."

I went into a defense of Marilyn, as I had so many times before, telling Gable about her insecure beginnings in foster homes, then all of a sudden being a movie star before she really knew how to act.

"Christ," said Gable. "I'm a movie star and I ain't learned how to act yet. It's got to be deeper than that. I know she's heavy into the booze and pills. Huston told me that. I think it's something wrong with the marriage. Too bad. I like Arthur, but this marriage ain't long for this world. Christ, I'm glad this picture is finishing. She damn near gave me a heart attack."

Then he asked me not to write anything about what we had discussed. When I had given him my promise, we talked about his impending fatherhood. Gable told me he wanted a son—a son he would never see, because the following Sunday he had a heart attack from which he would never recover.

Marilyn felt great remorse at Gable's death. She stepped up her consumption of booze and pills. Several times within the next year or two, she talked of a haunting fear that her delays on the set had put an undue strain on Gable's heart. I told her to forget it—that in his career he had worked with some of the greatest drinkers in the business—Spencer Tracy for one. "Some of those guys delayed shooting for a week, not a few hours. That wouldn't faze the King."

But she even expressed the same fears to Kay Gable, Clark's widow. Kay once told me that Marilyn certainly didn't help her husband's heart condition, but that whatever happened was unintentional. Marilyn was basically a very kind woman. I never knew her to be intentionally mean to anyone.

She couldn't help what she did. To the day she died, there was a constant fight within her between Norma Jean Baker the loner and Marilyn Monroe the movie star.

A weird thing happened not too long ago.

Those of you from the early days of television will remember Korla Pandit, the Hindu organist with the hypnotic eyes. He was big in the early fifties, just like "The Continental" or Milton Berle's *Texaco Star Theater*. Korla was a good organist but apparently a better hypnotist. There was at least one recorded case of his putting a woman to sleep beside her TV set.

A couple of years ago I heard from him in Las Vegas, where he had been working both as an organist and a hypnotist. Most of his hypnotic business was for a private clientele—to lose weight, cut out cigarettes, that sort of thing.

One day, a cocktail waitress at the Union Plaza Hotel came to him about a weight problem. He put her under hypnosis and a strange thing happened. Her whole personality changed, and she insisted she was Marilyn Monroe. This sort of thing had never happened to Korla before. In fact, it scared him just a little. The girl was in her twenties; probably she had been just a child when Marilyn died.

Korla had never known Marilyn. He knew that I had and asked me if I would listen to this girl under the sleep. He even brought her down from Las Vegas one afternoon. In the poolhouse of a Beverly Hills home, I chatted with the girl for an hour or so. Other than seeing a Marilyn Monroe movie on television, she had had no contact with her. Her personality was different, her speech different, the quality of her voice different. Other than having blonde hair, there was no evident connection with Marilyn Monroe.

Korla put her under.

The transformation was astounding. She assumed Marilyn's breathless little girl voice. Her mannerisms were Marilyn's. I could see how this must have terrified Korla. We talked about many things in Marilyn's life. She had a good grasp on facts. Then I startèd questioning her about that last night in the Brentwood house in which Marilyn died.

"He gave me scotch to drink. I knew there was something in it, but I drank it anyway. I don't know why I did. Then everything got blurry. That's all I remember."

I tried for ten or fifteen minutes to get the name of the man who fixed the drink.

"Don't make me say it. He's still alive. I'm afraid of him."

All of this was said in Marilyn's voice. I looked at Korla—and also at a friend of Korla's who had witnessed it all—and said:

"This is so damn eerie. I don't think I want to know. Wake her up."

17

The Time an Ulcer Won
the Academy Award

WHENEVER THERE IS TALK about Hollywood's classic westerns, the name *High Noon* always comes up. But did you know that when *High Noon* was first sneaked in Riverside, it was one of the great disasters of all time? It was so bad that even the producer, Stanley Kramer, wanted to forget about it.

I know because I saw that first sneak. The picture was way too long because the director had a crush on a new actress by the name of Grace Kelly. About half the picture was close-ups of Grace. She may not have known that Fred Zinnemann was in love with her but that's the word of Elmo Williams, now a producer, in those days a cutter. Elmo won the Oscar for editing *High Noon*.

The original version stressed the love story between Grace and Gary Cooper—a co-plot with the tale of the killers arriving in town to kill the brave sheriff. But those close-ups of the future princess were too much. Incidentally, whenever you see a preponderance of close-ups in a movie you can always be sure that the director is in love with the star.

It was a depressed bunch who came back from that sneak in Riverside. One other major fault of the movie was Cooper's ulcer. It kept burping in key scenes. I had been on the set at the Columbia ranch in 1951 during the making of the movie. Coop told me then his ulcer had been giving him unusual trouble.

"Jesus, I don't know whether I'll make it through the picture," he said one day over a glass of tequila at the China Trader, a restaurant near the ranch in Burbank.

As I say, Kramer was so disgusted that he was all for writing off the movie. You would be amazed to learn how many movies made are never released. Elmo the cutter begged to have one weekend with the movie, a request that was granted.

"I worked night and day for a whole weekend cutting that movie. I took out most of the love story and about 99 percent of the close-ups of Grace," Elmo recalls. "I confined the action of the movie to the actual hour of high noon. There were shots of the town clock. I inserted more, ticking off the time.

"As the picture was cut, I could see that Coop's ulcer, a liability in the love scenes, was a huge asset in the suspense. Three killers were out to kill Coop and he was getting no help from the townspeople. It was a terrifying situation and the burp only accented his terror.

"Toward the end of the weekend, I knew I had a good movie. I also had a short movie. There was no exposition of the plot. I hit upon the idea of putting a song in front and over the titles. It had never been done before. I tested it with a recording of Vaughan Monroe singing 'Ghost Riders in the Sky.' That was just temporary until I could get a song in there. On Monday I talked with composers Ned Washington and Dimitri Tiomkin and told them that I needed a song that would both set the mood and also tell the plot before the picture got started. They came up with "The Ballad of High Noon."

Now, if you listen to that song even today, you don't have to see the movie to know what it's all about. The whole plot is in the song. Elmo said that he knew just the right voice to sing it—that of the old cowboy star Tex Ritter, who wasn't doing too well at that time. Tex jumped at the chance to sing the song.

George Glass, who was a member of the Kramer company at the time, says that it was Kramer who inserted the close-ups of Cooper and his ulcer and the town clock. "Stanley took over the final editing," says George, "giving the movie the sense of urgency that made it, especially the inserts of the town clock."

And Carl Foreman, the writer, says that Coop's not accepting credit for his acting was due to "Coop's characteristic modesty." It's true that Coop would downgrade even an Oscar, but I saw him right after he won it and this was his aside to me: "First time in the history of the Academy an ulcer ever won an Oscar."

As for the editing, I believe Elmo's version. After all, he won the Oscar that year. And the other editors who do the voting know who did the work. I am sure that Kramer oversaw Elmo's work and heartily approved. Who wouldn't approve a cutter who had turned disaster into triumph?

Whatever happened, it is still one hell of a picture. And now you know why studios have sneak previews. Only the audience can make a hit.

18

Marlon Brando— World's Highest-paid Geek

IN 1951, I was over at Warner's one day talking with Marlon Brando. He was making *Streetcar Named Desire*.

"I will discuss anything with you except my personal life," said Marlon, with a pontification I had heard many times before and a thousand times since from actors.

I said nothing. So then Marlon went into a detailed account of his personal life, one so raunchy that no one could possibly have printed it in those days. He talked about fucking a girl in the ass with butter, and even made a slight reference to a friendly romp with a goat back on the farm in Nebraska.

It was interesting, but I didn't think much about it until more than twenty years later when I saw *Last Tango in Paris*, in which Marlon pretty much improvised the sex scenes. Then I realized that I had been through this picture before, in Marlon's own words back there in 1951.

It's Marlon's perverse sense of humor.

Along about that same time he had a pet raccoon that he took with him everyplace, which leads me into a good story.

Liberace was in all his glory in those days titillating all the little old ladies on television and in concert. At his concerts, Liberace always held a receiving line afterwards, smiling and greeting his fans. In the line one day he was stunned to see Brando, holding his raccoon. Liberace kept looking over the little old ladies' shoulders at the strange sight—the only male in line. Came Brando's turn, and Liberace gave him his warmest smile—even more radiant than the one given the little old ladies—and was astonished when Brando asked, "I wonder if you can tell me where I can get my raccoon fucked in this town?" and walked away, leaving Lee in bewilderment, not knowing whether to laugh or cry. A couple of the little old ladies were horrified at hearing such language from a superstar, even then. But that's Marlon.

During the making of *The Godfather,* he, Jimmy Caan, Robert Duvall, and some of the other stars delighted in mooning. Mooning is a Hollywood game wherein a star— or actor—will drop his pants and show his ass to a friend in the most unlikely place. Actors are playful people, like bad little boys. These ruthless gangland killers of the movie did this in such improbable places as the backseat of a limousine on New York City streets. God knows how many pedestrians saw a bare ass in a limousine window and didn't realize it was one of the most famous in the world.

In fact, when Duvall announced Shelley Winters's name at the Oscars later that year, he burst out laughing. Shelley was infuriated because she thought she was getting the "Sonny Tufts?" routine. Not so. Just as Duvall announced Shelley's name, he spotted Jimmy Caan in the black-tie audience. "I thought sure as hell he was going to moon me right then and there," said Duvall. "That's why I busted out laughing." Shelley still doesn't believe it.

Marlon Brando has won two Oscars—for *On the Waterfront* and *The Godfather*—but he lost out to Humphrey Bogart and *The African Queen* despite what many consider Brando's finest performance in "Streetcar." It was such a landmark movie that he was a favorite to win. Even Bogey thought so.

I called up Marlon the day of the Oscars to find out if he would attend.

"No," he said, "but I'm sending a cabdriver to bring it home in case I do. Do you want his badge number?" Then he explained why he wouldn't show. "When I played Stanley Kowalski on the stage, I went to some awards dinner (probably the Tonys) and fully expected to win. I didn't. It hurt me for a moment, and then I thought: 'Fuck 'em. I'm only in this business for the money anyhow.' "

Once, as I was discussing Brando with Brando, he turned serious and asked: "Do you know what a geek is?" I did, but he answered himself. "A geek is the lowest form of show business. He is the guy in the carnival who bites the heads off live chickens and gets paid off in cheap whiskey or wine. Press agents have made me a geek who gets paid hundreds of thousands of dollars instead of cheap booze."

Then he laughed.

"I don't give a damn. Every time somebody writes about my torn T-shirt, it's money in the bank. When you reporters are up at midnight thinking up some new phrase that will still mean slob, I'll be over on the Riviera with some beautiful doll dropping grapes in my mouth."

And how true that was.

The late Wally Cox was a boyhood chum of Marlon's when they both lived in Barrington, Illinois. "My most vivid memory of Marlon was that he was always tying me to a tree and leaving me," Wally once recalled to me. "My mother took me over to play with him and then jerked me home quick. She said Marlon was too rough for me."

You wonder how Marlon got to be the great actor he is—and many in the business think he's the greatest. I've always had my own theory, something that I noticed the first time I ever met Marlon, when he was doing a movie called *The Men*, even before "Streetcar." He was the first actor I had ever met who listened to what I had to say. He never interrupted or looked around while I talked. Makes you wonder if that isn't a key to good acting. Watch Marlon on the screen. He always appears to be listening to the other actor's dialogue. Then he speaks deliberately. End of acting lesson.

Marlon got a bum rap for *Mutiny on the Bounty,* mostly because of a damaging piece in *The Saturday Evening Post* called "The Mutiny of Marlon Brando," which laid the blame for the staggering $25 million cost of the movie on Marlon's shoulders. Marlon told me:

"I had a press agent for six months in my career—Bill Blowitz—and later I found out that he had fed the writer of that piece all the misinformation while I was paying him to publicize me. That's why I no longer have a press agent.

"Sure, I staged my own rebellion on the picture, but it was an artistic rebellion—the only kind an actor can stage. There is one simple fact—MGM sent a full company to Tahiti at a cost of $32,000 a day at a time when neither the script nor the ship itself was finished. When the ship (costing $750,000) finally arrived, we were in the midst of the monsoon season. These decisions were not mine. Several top executives who made those decisions were fired from MGM. I wasn't. There's a lesson to be learned there."

In recent years, Brando has been vindicated on the huge overbudget of "Mutiny." It was strictly script and front office mistakes that caused it . . . and a costly dose of clap.

Now, any male who goes to Tahiti and shacks up with some of those brown-skinned native girls is likely to get a dose of clap. It's a hazard that is never mentioned in the travel folders. But there's an awful lot of fucking going on in Tahiti. It's always been that way.

It was a particularly tough strain, sometimes known as the Asian clap. It took massive doses of penicillin. Most of the crew got cured easily enough, but an overzealous doctor dealing with Brando's case wanted to make doubly sure. So he gave Marlon a double-double dose of penicillin.

It wasn't long before Marlon's balls were reaching the ground. There was even a rumor that he had elephantiasis. Not so. Just too much penicillin. That's the word from one of his buddies in the crew. "The doctor was so overwhelmed with treating an international star like Marlon that he just got overgenerous," said the buddy. That cost a lot of time on the picture, but that wasn't Marlon's fault either.

Lewis Milestone made a particularly damaging charge about Marlon during the movie. "Before he would take direction," said Milestone, "he would ask why. Then when the scene was being shot he put earplugs in so he wouldn't hear my direction." What Milestone, director of *All Quiet on the Western Front*, didn't know is that Marlon always wears earplugs when he acts.

"Acting is an illusion," says Marlon, "a form of histrionic sleight-of-hand, and in order to carry it off well an actor must have intense concentration. Before I go into a scene,

I study it, almost psychoanalyze it. Then I discuss it with the director, then rehearse it. When actual shooting commences, I put in earplugs to screen out the extraneous noises off the set that inevitably prick at one's concentration." End of another acting lesson.

Marlon, as the world knows, is a man who cares about causes. Some say he runs all John Wayne movies backwards in his projection room. That way the Indians always win. But he is sincerely interested in Indians, Chicanos, blacks, Vietnamese, and anyone else he feels is oppressed. There is nothing phony about it.

Not long ago he got some bad press because he gave the Indian cause some acreage he owned. The land had a $300,000 mortgage. A Los Angeles TV station made a big thing about Marlon being an Indian giver. Had they investigated a little further, they would have found that people who make huge sums always have a mortgage because interest payments are a tax shelter. Secondly, I never heard the station report the fact that came from Marlon's lawyer that the morgage would be paid in full by Marlon before turning over deed to the acreage. Maybe Marlon should have hired another press agent.

Marlon gets so immersed in his causes that it affects him emotionally. His old mentor, Elia Kazan, wanted Marlon for *The Arrangement*. It was at a time when Marlon's career was at its lowest ebb. It was the time before *The Godfather*, when he had had about ten flops in a row. The reunion of the team that had made *A Streetcar Named Desire* and *On the Waterfront* was looked upon in the industry as the salvation of the great acting talent that was Brando.

Then, all of a sudden, Kirk Douglas was announced for the movie. I asked Kazan why.

"Well, when I approached Marlon, it was right after the assassination of Martin Luther King, with whom Marlon had marched in many Civil Rights marches. Dr. King's death had so emotionally affected him that he actually was supine, unable to even talk about the picture. He just wasn't up to it. So I forgot about it. We'll get together again someday."

And that will be a movie.

19

Cary Grant—
Everybody's Favorite
but His Wives'

CARY GRANT, with the possible exception of Errol Flynn, is the most charming superstar I have ever known. No one is more handsome. No one is kinder or more thoughtful. But, like all superstars, he has his peculiarities.

For years the Plaza in New York listed English muffins plurally on the menu but, when you ordered them, you got only three halves. Now this irked Cary's English thriftiness. The Plaza, as you may know, charges a fortune for meals ordered from room service. When Cary was served three halves of muffins, he immediately asked the Puerto Rican waiter why. The waiter had no answer.

Cary got on the phone to room service and demanded to know why, when the menu clearly stated muffins in the plural, he only got "a muffin and a hawf."

Room service referred him to the assistant manager in charge of food and beverage. He didn't know. "We've always served three slices (halves) ever since I've had this job," said the assistant. Cary then went to the managing director of the hotel, who said he would gladly send up another muffin half but that he couldn't answer why three had been served in the first place.

Cary's next call went to Conrad Hilton's home in Beverly Hills, where he was informed that the famed hotelman was in Istanbul. By this time, a good hour had transpired but Cary finally got hold of Hilton in Istanbul. His coffee was cold, his muffins soggy. Hilton had the answer right off the top of his head. An efficiency expert had long ago discovered that 90 percent of all guests ate only three halves, leaving the fourth on their plates. The efficiency expert then ordered that the muffin cutters in the kitchen should toss the fourth half into a container, for use with eggs benedict.

This infuriated Cary, who told Hilton that the menu was fraudulent. It should list English muffins as "a muffin and a hawf, not *muffins*." Hilton, who then owned the hotel, issued a directive that henceforth all four halves should be served with orders of English muffins. It had cost Cary about $100 in phone calls, but he believes it was worth it.

Not long after he told me the story, I purposely changed another hotel reservation to the Plaza and ordered English muffins, which I can take or leave. Sure enough, there were four halves. I ate only three.

Once, in the South of France, Cary was making a movie for Alfred Hitchcock called *To Catch a Thief,* with Grace Kelly. This was long before Grace became the princess of this realm. One Sunday Aristotle Onassis invited Cary and guests to have lunch with him on the Onassis yacht moored in Monte Carlo harbor. It's a huge yacht, and Ari, as we all called him, had a lot of guests aboard. Grace, as was often her wont, wore horn-rimmed glasses and said little during the lunch. In those days, she was quite reserved, even shy. Lunch over, Ari took Cary aside and invited him back any time. "And please," the billionaire said, nodding towards Grace, "bring your secretary along with you."

On that same yacht, Betsy Drake, who is extremely shy, came up with the best ad-lib line ever. It even broke up Cary, who was married to her at the time. In the salon area was a huge bar with the most interesting barstools imaginable. Onassis took great pride in explaining that the stools were covered with the skin of a whale's penis. Now Betsy, who had not opened her mouth the whole meal, came up with this line: "You mean this is Moby's dick?"

Isn't that a classic?

I've known quite a few of Cary's wives. They still are fond of him, but they all give identical reasons as to why they left him.

Virginia Cherrill, Betsy, Barbara Hutton, and Dyan

Cannon all have told me their stories. All essentially say the same thing—that Cary killed them with kindness. Always considerate and thoughtful, he just was too dominant a personality for his wives.

"Cary was just too charming," Betsy told me, shortly after leaving him. "I loved him—and I still do—but you can't imagine what a joy it is to be in my own apartment and cook dinner all by myself. I never could do that in Cary's house." Ten years later, Dyan gave an interview to a woman's magazine and repeated almost the same words. Barbara Hutton still relies on Cary for expert advice. He was the only one of her husbands who never took any money from her.

Cary is the all time master of screen comedy—the hardest thing to do—but he makes it look so easy that he has never won an Academy Award. Until Cary quit the movies to become an executive with Fabergé, Vincent Price voted each year for Cary, no matter what picture he was in. "And I will keep voting until he wins," said the suave Vincent.

The great actors always make it look too easy. That's why a lot of them go unsung. Can you believe that Henry Fonda has never won an Oscar or that Edward G. Robinson died without even a nomination? The same goes for John Barrymore and Greta Garbo; they never won either.

It's not generally known, but Cary Grant got into the movies as a contract threat to Gary Cooper, then the hot star at Paramount. Cary had been a stilt walker in vaudeville when Adolph Zukor brought him to Hollywood at a time when Cooper had balked on his contract renewal and had threatened to go off on safari to Africa. Zukor knew he meant it, and he knew he had the wherewithal—because Cooper was the lover of Countess Dorothy di Frasso, who was loaded.

Finally Cooper got what he wanted—he became the first star in movie history to get a percentage deal on his pictures. Cary, his threat, was a lost soul on the lot. He had done a lot of tests but little more than a bit in an actual movie. Then the unerring eye of Mae West spotted him on the lot. Mae was about to do her first starring movie, the screen version of her Broadway hit *Diamond Lil*. "He was the best-looking man I had seen since I came to Hollywood," Mae recalls. "I said, 'If he can talk, he's my leading man.' "

The Paramount brass tried to talk her out of using the untested Cary, but Mae was in the driver's seat. Ever since her debut in *Night After Night,* exhibitors had been clamoring for more Mae West movies. "That guy plays the leading man," Mae insisted. And Cary did. It was Cary to whom Mae uttered that famous line that became a part of the language of the thirties: "C'mon up and see me sometime."

Paramount had fought making the movie on the argument that *Diamond Lil* was a period piece—the Gay Nineties—and that the public wasn't ready for it. But Mae argued that she would set a trend, and she did. The only concession she made was to allow Paramount to change the title to *She Done Him Wrong.*

It was a classic movie, and it launched one of Hollywood's greatest superstars—Cary Grant.

20

Who Killed
Johnny Stompanato?

It happened on April 4—Good Friday—1958, but even today most people don't believe that Cheryl Crane, then the sixteen-year-old daughter of Lana Turner, killed Johnny Stompanato, her mother's lover.

I had a unique look at that tragedy—not at the actual stabbing itself, but at what happened the first hour after it occurred. It was pure luck. One of my photographers had a police radio and phone in his car. He heard a squad car being ordered to an address in Beverly Hills. It was the code for murder. So many famous people live in Beverly Hills that such a call immediately alerts reporters and city desks. As soon as I heard the address, I knew it was a major headline. It was the house where Lana and Johnny were shacked up.

Both the photographer and I took off with engines burning. The squad car had beat us there. A cop on the door barred the photographer, who had all his paraphernalia strung about him. He asked who I was. "Coroner's office," I said. He stepped aside.

I followed the sound of voices upstairs to Lana's bedroom. The first thing I noticed was Stompanato's body on the floor with a hole in him big enough to see daylight. Lana was crying hysterically. So was Cheryl. Another cop was holding the butcher knife, big enough to slice up a cow, with a handkerchief so as not to smudge fingerprints. In the midst of all this was Jerry Giesler, the famed criminal lawyer. Jerry was a companion of movieland trouble and tragedy, from the Monroe–Di Maggio divorce to something like this. Lana, who had never met Giesler, called him before the police—not an unusual thing to do in Hollywood.

Lana was sobbing as the house soon filled up with homicide detectives. Clinton Anderson, chief of the Beverly Hills police, took charge of the questioning.

"Cheryl has killed Johnny," said Lana. "He threatened to kill me, and poor Cherie got frightened. My poor baby. Please say that I did it. I don't want her involved. Poor baby. Please say that I did it."

Lana must have repeated that last sentence a dozen times to Chief Anderson. Then she got hysterical again. Giesler calmed her: "Your daughter has done a courageous thing. It's too bad that a man's life is gone, but under the circumstances the child did the only thing she could do to protect her mother from harm. I understand your concern for the child's welfare. But you won't get anyplace by hiding the truth. Will she, Chief?" Anderson nodded assent.

Giesler's advice calmed Lana, and she started telling a straightforward story. Although her voice shook slightly, she appeared, all of a sudden, to be a remarkably composed woman. Stompanato, she said, had threatened to beat her up, even disfigure her.

"He said he would cut my face with a razor. He told me, 'If a man makes a living with his hands, I would destroy his hands. You make your living with your face, so I will destroy your face. I'll get you where it hurts the most—your daughter and your mother.'"

Lana also told Anderson that Stompanato had choked her into unconsciousness during an argument in a London hotel room, when she was making a movie over there.

"I didn't see any knife," Lana continued. "I truthfully thought she had just poked him in the stomach. He didn't say a word, just gasped. He grabbed his stomach, walked a little way, half turned and fell, dropping on his back. He didn't talk, just kept gasping."

Over the years many have doubted this story because Stompanato was a former U.S. Marine with hand-to-hand combat experience. How could a sixteen-year-old girl stab him to death? As Cheryl told her story, it all made sense.

Cheryl, it developed, had been cowering in fear behind a door listening to Stompanato making those horrible threats to her mother. At one point Cheryl came into the bedroom, took her mother into the bathroom, and said: "Mother, why don't you just tell John to leave?" She said that her mother replied: "You don't understand. I am deathly afraid of him."

As the fight tempo increased between Lana and Stompanato, Cheryl went into the kitchen and got the biggest knife she could find. "I just walked between them and did it," Cheryl told Anderson.

Stompanato, in a rage by this time, suddenly broke away from Lana and walked right into the knife held poised by Cheryl. Like Lana, he, too, had not seen a knife. In his fury, you might say, he impaled himself on the knife. It was such a surprise that there were no words spoken, as Lana said. That explains how a scared sixteen-year-old girl can kill a former combat Marine.

After all the statements, Anderson said that Cheryl would have to go to the police station and be booked. And once again, Lana pleaded with the chief. "Can't you arrest me instead? It was my fault. Poor baby's not to blame for all this mess."

The chief and his men conducted a thorough investigation and concluded that it all happened the way Lana and Cheryl said it did. Anderson told me at the time: "We had been expecting this ever since they moved into that house. Stompanato always has been a shady character and he had a reputation of beating up on other wealthy women in town."

When I first knew Stompanato, he was a strong arm man in Mickey Cohen's mob. His family back in the midwest always was quite sensitive about calling him a hood, but that's what he was when I knew him. He was always in Cohen's entourage until he started the Beverly Hills wealthy women routine. Johnny was one of a breed of studs who prey on lonely women in Beverly Hills and Bel-Air. Often the women are divorced, more often they are married to producers and other executives who work fourteen hours a day and bang starlets for a pastime. All these women have one thing in common—great wealth.

The cops are wise to them but, as Anderson said, "Lana was too scared to file a complaint on Stompanato and most of the other women don't want their husbands to find out. The police can't act without a complaint."

Stompanato's final rage was triggered when Lana refused to have him as her escort of the Academy Awards. She was nominated for best actress for *Peyton Place* but lost out to Joanne Woodward in *The Three Faces of Eve*. Stompanato in the bedroom was OK. At the movie industry's fanciest party of the year, covered by television, he was the guy you kept in the closet.

Lana went to the awards—it was her first nomination in twenty years of the business—with Glenn Rose, her publicity man and close friend. The ceremony came more than a week before the stabbing, but Lana's refusal to be seen with him in public put Stompanato into a sullen mood, climaxing in his final rage.

The year 1958 was a big one for Lana. The Oscar nomination was a thrill because Jerry Wald, the producer of *Peyton Place*, had cast her in that picture over the objections of the 20th Century-Fox front office.

"The front office thought I was nuts," said Wald. "Lana had had seventeen straight flops, a record that would have killed off a lesser star."

Peyton Place was such a big box office success that it launched a new career for Lana. She did *Imitation of Life* and *Portrait in Black* soon after. All of a sudden, she was making as much money as her old MGM colleague—Elizabeth Taylor—and she pushing forty at the time.

But she never could pick men. Probably one of the sexiest stars ever to be in the movies, she was always being chased by them. "And I usually wound up with delinquent adults," she once confided.

One night at a party, Lana and I kidded each other because, as I told her, "I'm stupid about women and you're stupid about men."

"You can say that again," said Lana. "I really am stupid about men."

21

Big Duke and the Big C

THE PRESS RELEASES all said the same thing: John Wayne was in Good Samaritan Hospital for treatment of an old leg injury suffered when he had fallen on his yacht.

Everybody believed it, including me. Guys like Big Duke never get sick. They only get injured brawling or falling.

So one afternoon I was driving by Good Sam and decided to drop in on Duke just for a friendly visit. A registered nurse stopped me at his door.

"Mr. Wayne is seeing no visitors," she said.

"OK," I said, "just tell him that Jim Bacon stopped by to wish him well." And then I started to walk away.

A booming voice came from within the suite: "You can let that son-of-a-bitch in," said the voice that had scared movie Indians for forty years.

I had barely sat down when Duke bellowed: "Well, I licked the big C."

"What?" I practically screamed.

Then he went into gory detail of how they had found a malignancy on his lung, removed the lung, and then he had had a relapse because a severe coughing spell opened up all the stitches.

"What's all this shit about the ankle injury?" I said.

"Those bastards who got me in pictures only think of money. They figured Duke Wayne with cancer was not a good box office image. Hell, I was doped up. I didn't know what they were saying. I don't lie. You know that."

I said, "There's a hell of a good image to Duke Wayne licking cancer, too. It would give a lot of hope to a lot of people."

Duke agreed: "Let me get on my feet and I'll talk them out of it. Don't print anything yet. I'll give you the go-ahead when the right time comes." Little did I know that I was to sit on that story three months before breaking it exclusively.

In Hollywood, rumors spread fast. Everybody knew that Duke smoked five packs of Camels a day, six when drinking late. Bogart, who had died of cancer, was a five-pack-a-day Chesterfield smoker. The whole world knew of the relationship between cigarette smoking and lung cancer.

Duke left the hospital in a few weeks. Reporters asked him if he had heart trouble. No. Did he have cancer? No.

"Duke wouldn't lie," said his wife. "Fortunately, the doctors told us that they had gotten all the cancer and none of the reporters asked if he had *had* cancer."

The ankle injury story was amended to say that Duke also had an abscess taken from his lung. But no cancer. Movie moguls are funny people. So are actors. They abhor publicity on sickness. The main reason is insurance, a must for movie-making. Duke returned to his office.

The rumors persisted. My friend Earl Wilson came out from New York and heard them. Duke said that Earl confronted him with the rumors, saying he was going to print them—the next afternoon, in fact. A typical reply came from Duke: "Print any goddamn thing you like."

The next move shows you the integrity of the man. He started running me down and finally found me at the Tropicana hotel in Las Vegas.

"Earl Wilson says he is going to print the rumors that I had cancer in tomorrow afternoon's *New York Post*. Go ahead with your story."

Well, the beauty of working for the Associated Press was its instantaneous transmission of news. My story started rolling around the world within two minutes after Duke had reached me. It was a page-one banner from Los Angeles to Tokyo to Cairo. Even the *New York Post*. I hated to do that to a close friend like Earl, but I knew he would understand. When he told his editors that he was going to have a Duke Wayne cancer story, they told him that Jim Bacon already had it. Earl called me the next day and I explained how long I had been sitting on the story and also about Duke's phone call to me in Las Vegas.

"Well," said Earl, "I have to admire his honesty and loyalty to you. You can't win them all."

The doctors, of course, ordered Duke to quit smoking. He did, for a few years. But a lifetime of inhaling cigarettes was not an easy habit to shake. The next thing you knew, he was chewing tobacco. I was up in Durango, Colorado where he made *The Cowboys*. He had a violent coughing spell one day and I thought he was going to cough up a lung. I suggested that chewing tobacco may not be the best thing in the world for a guy with one lung.

"It wasn't the chewing that caused the coughing," he replied. "It's that goddamn dust around here."

Next time I saw him, he was smoking a cigar. Now I had covered the famous press conference of the president of the American Cancer Society in which they revealed that they had found no evidence of cigar- or pipe-smoking contributing to lung cancer or heart disease. The reason for that, of course, is that few people inhale such strong tobaccos. Duke had given up chewing tobacco because he was losing his voice, an actor's most valuable asset. It was getting particularly raspy.

I watched Duke smoke a couple of cigars. I was amazed to find that he was inhaling them just as deeply as he used to do with his Camels.

"Christ, Duke," I said one day. "I'm a cigar smoker, but I would turn green if I inhaled them like you."

Duke said, "I can't smoke if I can't inhale."

Not long after that, Duke and his wife Pilar split up after nineteen years of marriage. No one has ever come up with an official reason for that split, but the word I got was that Pilar was not about to sit around and watch her husband kill himself. It led to violent arguments and finally the end of the marriage, but who knows?

The cigar smoking sent Duke back to the hospital again. There was no word that cancer had reappeared, but serious respiratory problems had, including pneumonia.

Let's hope by the time this book comes out, Duke is a good boy again. Last time I saw him, he was going easy on the cigars but he was still heavy on his favorite tequila

—Sauza Conmemorativo. Duke and I and his secretary companion, Pat Stacy, were drinking the potent brew in his dressing room, where he was doing a Bob Hope TV show.

"I like tequila," said Duke, "because it doesn't give you a hangover. You may get some broken ribs and broken legs from falling down, but no hangover."

Duke is one of Hollywood's legendary drinkers. He has spent forty-five years on rugged locations drinking with stunt men, wranglers—and John Ford. He's not a guy who needs a drink. In fact, he goes weeks without one but when he goes, no one can keep up with him.

I remember once in Camargo, Mexico, when he was making *Hondo*. A big poker game was organized, and the bottles were on the table. There was a dog featured in the movie, so that meant that the famous dog trainer, Rudd Weatherswax, was there, too. Rudd owns and trains "Lassie," which is like owning the Bank of America.

Rudd, figuring that Duke was drinking pretty heavily, felt the game was safe enough to join. What Rudd didn't know is that the more Duke drinks, the better he plays poker. When that game broke up in the small hours of the morning, Duke owned Rudd's car, his money, and Lassie. The next day Duke said, "Hell, I can't keep Rudd's car and his dog. That's how he makes his living." So he gave them back. I once figured that Duke gave up about $25 million when he gave back Lassie because the TV series had not even started in those days.

When Duke is drinking, he will drink with anybody. The whole world knows his views on communism, but once in New York he ran into the Soviet delegate to the United Nations. To a visiting Russian, Duke, Gary Cooper, and Johnny Weissmuller, who played Tarzan in those days, were the only recognizable stars. I found that out when Nikita Khrushchev visited Hollywood for a famous industry luncheon.

The Soviet delegate kept saying to Duke: "John Wayne, you come to my country."

"I wouldn't go to that goddamn commie country," said Duke.

But before the night was over, Duke and the Russian

were at the delegate's house, eating caviar and drinking vodka until 7 A.M. By that time, Duke was ready to visit Russia by the next plane.

Duke and I have been good friends for more than twenty-five years. Since he moved out of the San Fernando Valley and down the coast to Newport Beach, I don't see as much of him as I used to. It may be one of the reasons I am still alive.

People continually ask me: What is Duke Wayne really like? Well, the simplest answer is that what you see on the screen is what you see in person.

He is absolutely fearless. Once I visited him in Madrid where he was making a movie with Rita Hayworth and Claudia Cardinale called *Circus World*.

I took a jet. Duke and his crew sailed his converted mine-sweeper *The Wild Goose* to Spain. The ship, which floats like a matchstick in heavy seas, as any ex-sailor can tell you, hit one of the worst Atlantic storms in years. His crew, all navy and maritime veterans, were ashen white when they arrived in Barcelona. "I didn't think we would make it," one crew member told me, his hands shaking.

"How about Duke?" I asked.

"That crazy bastard. We would all be below during the heavy seas, while he lashed himself on deck and loved every minute of the trip. He said it was the greatest trip he ever had on his yacht." Duke wasn't kidding.

Once, during the old Republic days, I visited him on the back lot, the scene of so many westerns that it was called the Republic Range. Duke and I were talking when Herb Yates, the boss of Republic, came on the set. As soon as Duke spied him, he ran and vaulted on a horse from the rear, like a kid playing leapfrog, and took off like a shot. Duke was much younger in those days and doing his own stunts. With the horse spurred into lightning speed, Duke was doing all the fancy riding tricks, rolling under the horse's belly and all that.

Coming up to Yates's party, he took a fall under the horse's hoofs, rolled over, and got up. Brushing himself off, he went up to Yates and drawled: "Let's see your goddamn Roy Rogers do that."

Duke is very loyal to old friends. That's why you saw

Bruce Cabot in every Wayne movie until lung cancer took that old-timer.

He's a very trusting guy. In fact, he will trust anybody —no matter how miserable a bastard he is—until he catches him in a lie. He believes everybody until they lie to him, and then he's through with them for good. He's usually more hurt than angry when he's been taken. And if Duke likes you, no one can backbite you when he's around. Only you can lose favor yourself.

It's happened with business deals. That's why Duke is still riding the range at an age when he should be fishing all the time. In the fifties, he had been so victimized by people he trusted that he found that, after twenty-five years of major stardom, he didn't have a penny.

"I was luckier than most. I found out by selling everything I owned that I, at least, didn't owe anybody."

Things were so tough that in the winter of 1965 he was working down in Durango, Mexico, in one of the most rugged of all his westerns, *The Sons of Katie Elder*. This was only a few months after his cancer operation. For the first time in his career, he had to be helped up on a horse. And riding it was sheer pain because several of his ribs had been removed to get at the diseased lung.

One morning I watched him shoot take after rugged take in a mountain stream where the water was 40 degrees. He never once complained, although you knew he was in agony. And that 7,000-foot altitude could have used more than one lung. Yet there he was throwing punches at the bad guys in the icy Rio Chico River. The wardrobe department wanted him to wear a frogman's rubber suit under his western garb, but Duke would have none of it.

Dean Martin, his co-star, commented: "I couldn't get my breath in that water, and I got both my lungs."

The first time I ever did a story about Duke, I made a personal observation about his acting style. I said, "Duke doesn't act. He re-acts." He liked that. So much so, that he has been using it in interviews ever since. Now he thinks he originated it. "Let those actors who pick their noses get all the dialogue," says Duke. "Just give me the closeup reaction."

Joel McCrea, an old-timer like Duke, says Duke is the

foremost exponent of "the shit kicking school of acting." Joel includes himself in the same school. "It was originated by Charlie Ray in the silent movies. He became a hit playing a farm boy who kicked the shit in the barnyard during a romantic scene and said something like 'Shucks, Miss Nancy.' Gary Cooper, Duke, Jimmy Stewart, and I did the same thing in talkies. Instead of being on a farm, we were on a ranch. But we were still kicking shit."

McCrea exposes another facet of Duke's longevity: "None of us learned to act in acting schools. We learned in front of a camera, by osmosis. And one of the first things you find out is whether a picture is going to be good or lousy. If lousy, you keep yourself away from center camera, preferably out-of-focus. The picture comes out and it stinks, but the critics and the public haven't noticed you. If it's going to be good, then stand right up front. And first thing you know, people only remember you from the good pictures." Lee Strasberg doesn't teach that in class.

That osmosis theory works because Duke owns one best actor Oscar and could well get another before he hangs up his spurs. Kate Hepburn, who co-starred with him in *Rooster Cogburn*, acted him mano a mano and said: "He's the most underrated actor in the business."

Duke and Kate worked off each other like Kate and Tracy used to do.

"I soon let her know she wasn't fooling around with some amateur," says Duke. "I had great respect for her talent and she had the same for mine."

You want to have fun with Duke, get him in a Spanish session and have the mariachi band play "Granada." Duke has had three Spanish wives and, wherever he goes, he is always serenaded with "Granada." He hates the tune.

When John Ethan, who has to be fourteen now, was baptized in Encino, Duke threw a christening party that began at 1 P.M. Sunday and wound up at 6 A.M. Monday morning. It would have gone on much longer had I not told the mariachi band leader that Duke's favorite tune was "Granada." They must have played it twenty times between 4 and 6 A.M. That ended the party.

22

Hollywood's Greatest Romance

AT THE TIME OF Spencer Tracy's death, newspapers dutifully reported that among the visitors at the little house in which Tracy had lived was "his longtime friend, actress Katharine Hepburn."

What a kiss-off for one of Hollywood's greatest romances—one of its all-time great love stories. In another part of this book I tell about incurring Kate's wrath once when I took Spence home drunk to the beach house the two shared. I wasn't supposed to know about the romance —although everyone in town did. But when Tracy died in 1967, the rest of the country was horrified to find that Spencer Tracy and Kate Hepburn had lived as common-law husband and wife since 1941.

I once asked Tracy how come he had escaped the headlines while so many of his contemporaries could bring out the bold, black type for an illegal left turn. Tracy knew he could give me an honest answer because he knew that the Associated Press would never carry news of a clandestine romance on its wires.

"Kate and I never go anyplace where you bastards (meaning the press) will see us. It's as simple as that," he replied with that famous Irish grin. Then he added: "People who get headlines are the ones who ask for them."

I had to agree that he had a point. As a longtime Hollywood reporter, I had written stories on both Tracy and Kate, often when they were in the same movie, but on everything other than their love affair. Maybe the Hollywood press corps had too much respect, as I did, for their perfection in the craft of acting, but I doubt it. My relations with Spence were always cordial, but it was not so with most of the press. In his later years, he was an irascible old Irishman who couldn't care less about catering to the public's appetite for news about its favorite stars. And Kate's views about publicity were even more outspoken. So it was not a love affair between the press and the principals that kept the story off the entertainment pages all those years. What was it, if not respect?

Perhaps Spence summed it up best himself when I came on the set of *The Devil at 4 O'Clock,* which he made with Frank Sinatra.

"You don't want to talk to me," said Tracy. "You want to talk with the other fellow. My life's too dull for you. He's news." All during the making of that film, Tracy always called Sinatra "the other fellow." He never once referred to him by name.

Kate set her cap—she always wears one—professionally for Tracy in 1941 when she demanded and got him for her leading man in *Woman of the Year.* It was the first of nine pictures, all successful, the two were to make, including his last *Guess Who's Coming to Dinner?*

"Spence and Laurette Taylor are the two greatest actors I have ever seen," said Kate. And she stuck with that appraisal all through the years.

Humphrey Bogart always said Spence was the greatest. He put him on the same level with "Larry Oliver," which is what Bogey always called Laurence Olivier. He thought Olivier sounded phony. I told this to Tracy once, and he said: "What the hell does 'Humphrey Bogart' sound like?"

When Tracy and Hepburn made *Woman of the Year,* a set romance developed. It often does because there is so much time between camera setups. Great romances between leading men and women most often take place on big-money movie sets, seldom on TV sets or low-budget movies. The leisure time between TV camera setups is too short. Remember that the next time you read about a movieland divorce.

Most of these set romances last only through the picture, especially if one or both of the stars are married. Gary Cooper made *Saratoga Trunk* with Ingrid Bergman, who is such a dedicated actress that she usually falls in love with her leading man.

"On that picture," Cooper once told me, "Ingrid loved me more than any woman in my life loved me. The day after the picture ended, I couldn't get her on the phone."

Not so with Tracy and Hepburn. Their romance lasted twenty-six years and was ended only by Tracy's death. Kate was not a home wrecker when she fell in love with Tracy. The hard-drinking, charming Irishman had long been estranged from his wife.

Before Kate, there was a particularly torrid one with the beautiful Loretta Young. This too was little known because of Tracy's low-key profile. But Loretta, in her pre-religious days, would talk about it at length.

"I was madly in love with that man," she once told me.

Some of Tracy's friends in the Irish Mafia of Hollywood say that Tracy and his wife, a former actress, drifted apart because of her total devotion to their son John, born deaf. With true maternal love, she dedicated her life to the arduous, almost impossible task of teaching her son, now past fifty, to talk and read. "Louise had the patience. I didn't," Spence once told me. "I was willing to put up the money." And that he did.

Out of the mother's devotion grew the John Tracy Clinic for the Deaf, one of the world's finest. Tracy, despite the Irishman's traditional love of the bottle, stayed with his wife until the birth of their daughter, Suzy. But it was a losing marriage almost from John's early childhood. Through the years Spence and his wife remained friendly. He was very devoted to his children and a good father. If he lacked the patience of his wife, he made up for it in other ways. He concentrated on his career to become the great actor he was—probably the best the movies ever produced. And with fame came lots of money—money that was largely channeled into his wife's project for helping the congenitally deaf.

A lot of people in town thought Tracy might divorce his wife to marry Loretta. It was a different era then in Hollywood. It was the time of the Breen office, the Catholic Legion of Decency, and a puritanical spirit in the United States. Tracy and Loretta were both Irish Catholics. So their romance, doomed by the church, ended.

Enter Miss Hepburn. Here was a Women's Libber when no one knew what the term meant. Tracy, the Wisconsin Irishman, and Hepburn, the Connecticut intellectual. She could talk knowingly on any subject—and Tracy was no dummy himself. Bogey once said that Kate was an expert on St. Thomas Aquinas's *Summa Theologica* and also on the spreading of manure on diochronda.

Tracy basically was a simple man. He could be a mean bastard if he got too drunk, but he possessed all the Irish charm and the storytelling that goes with it. Above all, he was a man.

Once, in my salad days with Kate, she asked me what size shirt I wore. I told her size 17.

"Spence has a bull neck too," she said. "Size 17 is a man's neck."

Tracy's charm used to melt the iceberg loneliness that was Kate at times. What at first was deep professional respect for each other turned into enduring love. Both loved the sea. And together they would walk every foot of the beaches at Malibu and Trancas. Each loved to paint, and they painted together. Kate was a free spirit. She didn't care much for marriage and she never bugged Spence about it. It really was an ideal relationship. They traveled around the world. They drank at sidewalk cafes in Paris and visited museums in Rome, unrecognized by tourist or native. And they played hard, too, especially Spencer.

One morning I was playing golf with Ernie Borgnine, not long after he had won his Oscar, out at Riviera Country Club. The course marshal dashed up in his golf cart and yelled: "Jump in, Mr. Borgnine. There's an emergency call for you at the clubhouse." Ernie, fearing disaster at home, hurried away. In a few minutes, he rejoined our foursome and said: "That was my agent. I may have to go to Cuba tonight. Tracy, Hepburn, and Ernest Hemingway got drunk in a saloon last night and smashed the place. Jack Warner said the owner wanted $100,000 for the damage. Warner says if he has to pay it, Tracy's through and they want me to take over for him."

Borgnine never did. Tracy finished *The Old Man and the Sea;* the Havana innkeeper must have come down on his price. The picture, with a cast of only an old man, a little boy, and a big fish, cost $5 million to make and never made its money back. But it was a tour de force for Tracy the actor.

Little is known, and you'll never find out, if Kate and Mrs. Tracy met or talked through the years, but they were together on an early, hazy morn at Spence's house in West Hollywood where, an hour or so before, his housekeeper had found the noted actor dead in bed. There in that monk's cell of a room with one oak chest and one chair, the wife and other woman mourned together for the man they both loved.

"The spirits of the two women were sad but friendly," recalls another person in the room. "On the old bed covered with a plain white sheet was the man both had loved. And now he was gone and neither could do anything about it."

Two days later, Miss Hepburn decided to stay away from Spence's funeral. Her New England upbringing told her that his family, and his family alone, deserved the privacy and sanctity they sought.

Kate had had the best years of Spence's life—and those memories were too private to spoil now in public glare.

23

Mae West, Still the Queen of Sex

MAE WEST ADMITS to eighty-three years of age (her sister Beverly says she is two years older) but she still has an active sex life.

I've known Mae for twenty-five years and I was first custodian of her famous secret of youth. Mae in her eighties has perfect teeth and wrinkle-free skin. She never has had a face-lift. One day in her bedroom, where she always entertains men, she had me feel behind her ears for the telltale scars of a plastic surgery job. There were none. I'm not saying Mae looks nineteen. She doesn't. But she doesn't look a hell of a lot older than the days when she titillated a nation out of its Depression woes.

A visit to Mae's apartment on North Rossmore in Hollywood—the same one she rented when she first came out here from New York in 1933—is a delight.

She always receives me in her bedroom, in a nightgown, with her famous bosom prominently displayed. It is all there—the mirrors on the ceiling, everything conducive to making love. Mae is living proof that you are never too old for sex. She always has an ardent stud on call, usually a boxer or wrestler. At one time she had a big thing, at age seventy-five, with the University of Southern California's National Championship football team. The All-Americans were having such a good time in Mae's apartment that Coach John McKay made it off limits during the season. Look it up. It's a matter of record.

How can this happen when other women at her age are barely able to play shuffleboard at Sun City? I once put the question to her directly. Her answer:

"I don't drink. I don't smoke. I sleep until two o'clock in the afternoon, unless I'm working, and I take low colonics. My mother was just like me and did the same thing. The poisons that seep through the lower colon are what cause wrinkling and loss of vitality. I've taken them daily for forty years." (This was 1968.)

I then asked her what her doctor thought about such a debilitating procedure.

"He's appalled, naturally, but it's what's up front that counts."

I was writing a column for a Hollywood trade paper that year. At most it had 10,000 circulation. I teased those readers, all in show business, with the fact that I knew Mae's beauty secret but it was too indelicate to print.

What a furor that caused! People in town saw Mae at parties. I was deluged with phone calls and mail. Even some stars like Ethel Merman, who had no use for me personally, used devious means to pry the secret from me. I told the secret to all who called me. Most of them would ask, "What is a low colonic?" When I told them it was similar to an enema, most lost interest. It was too high a price to pay for no wrinkles. I got calls from Europe, Latin America, even Australia.

One caller from Mexico City offered to trade me Dolores Del Rio's secret, which, if true, is quite sexy. When I told him what Mae did, he felt sort of let down. But I never printed Mae's secret because, as she herself once put it, "Who wants an image of sitting on a pot?" The tease even penetrated the Iron Curtain. I got off a plane in Belgrade, Yugoslavia, one day and was met by a local reporter accompanied by an interpreter. The first question, of course, was what was Mae's secret? I answered and got this response—first and only time it ever happened. "Does she use hot or cold water?"

Other old-time stars like Gloria Swanson, who also doesn't look her age, were asked by friends to get in touch with me for the secret. The Australian calls stemmed from an interview given to the Australian press by Stella

Stevens. In response to a question, she said she owed her good looks to Mae's secret, which she was sworn not to reveal. It was a lot of fun while it lasted. I don't think Mae, at her age, gives a damn now whether it's printed or not.

One prominent book publisher called me from New York City and asked if I could write a book on it. I told him I could give him the whole thing in thirty seconds over the phone. How could you stretch that into a book?

Mae paid me the greatest compliment I have ever received. In her autobiography, *Goodness Had Nothing to Do With It,* she tells of a lover named Ted with whom she made continuous love for fifteen hours. He has got to be the all-time champion, because Mae told me privately that the guy came thirty-three times in that period.

"How did you keep score?" I asked.

"Well, I used to buy condoms by the dozen. I had three boxes, and there were only three left in the last box."

A few days later, she sent me an autographed copy of her book, inscribed: "Jim Bacon. Best wishes. Sincerely, Mae West. 1959." And then, as a postscript, she added: "Reminds me of Ted." I told Mae that I will always treasure that. It's like comparing my golf swing to Jack Nicklaus's.

Mae is more comfortable around men than women, but occasionally she will open her beach home at Santa Monica to a charity tea or something for the Beverly Hills matrons. I happened to be there one day when she was entertaining some prim and proper ladies. In the course of the affair, the front doorbell rang and Mae answered it out of sight of the matrons. It was a photographer assigned to take a picture for my story. Since it was a hot summer day, he didn't have much on but Bermuda shorts and his paraphernalia. The ladies almost went into shock when they heard Mae tell him: "Take out your equipment and wait for me in the bedroom."

Mae even injects sex into such academic functions as honorary degree ceremonies. Delta Kappa Alpha, the cinema fraternity at USC, awarded Mae, Jimmy Stewart, and Director Mervyn LeRoy honorary degrees for their movie achievements. Mervyn and Jimmy received theirs in traditional academic style. Not so Mae. No folding chairs or microphones for her.

As vignettes from three of her pictures were shown on the screen, stagehands hurriedly set up a satiny double bed, a full length mirror, and all the other accoutrements that befit the Queen of Sex.

The movies over, a spotlight was on a side stage. Dr. Norman Topping, who had been dozing all through the ceremony up till then, suddenly came alive. As president of USC, he had been through hundreds of these ceremonies, but he couldn't believe what he saw onstage. There was Mae in the spotlight, wearing $250,000 worth of her own diamonds and swiveling her hips as only Mae can swivel. Even Presley can't beat her at that movement.

"I want to thank you for your generous applause— and your heavy breathing," said Mae to a thunderous standing ovation, including Dr. Topping. Her dress revealed more curves than Nolan Ryan ever threw. She stretched on the bed, surrounded by three USC All Americans, the great O.J. Simpson among them.

Into this setting came Director Robert Wise and George Cukor, who—conscious of the academic occasion—prepared to question her about her early life and career. Mae put up with this for awhile and then she nodded to her piano player—and wouldn't you know, his name was Sam? —to hit a few bars. Enough of this university horseshit, Mae seemed to be saying; the audience had come to see the one and only Diamond Lil. Sam soon was giving up with a few introductory bars of pure whorehouse piano. Dr. Topping was sitting on the edge of his chair, wide awake and smiling broadly. And then Mae, a terrific singer, started telling the musical story of Diamond Lil and her involvement with Spider Kelly and that most famous of Chinamen—Hung Lo Lee. With that story finished, she swang right into "Frankie and Johnny." No one sings this song like Mae, and no one else should be allowed to sing this folk classic. *Oh roll me over easy! Roll me over slow!* We all fell in love again with Mae that night. The USC campus has never been the same.

Mae is extremely talented. She has never uttered a word on stage or screen, since becoming a star, that she hasn't written herself. Her dialogue is so sharp that her entrance line in her first movie, which she wrote, made her a star overnight.

In *Night After Night,* starring George Raft and Constance Cummings, Mae walks into Raft's speakeasy and checks her mink coat. The hatcheck girl looks at her jewelry.

"Goodness, what beautiful diamonds," says the hatcheck girl.

"Goodness had nothing to do with it, Dearie," says Mae as only she can deliver such a line. And a living legend of the movies is spawned.

Now, nearly forty-five years later, Mae West is a cult figure among teenagers. Her apartment building in Hollywood reports that a dozen or more teenagers a day try to see Mae. The old movies on television are responsible, but so is a rock 'n' roll album she made with a teenage rock group a few years ago. It's called "Way Out West," and Mae, pushing eighty then, sounds better than any of the girl rock singers around. "The kids write me letters all the time, and I see some of them. Some of the guys are downright cute." She has defied every rule in the book about aging. When, at eighty-two you can be an inspiration at both the corner malt shop and Sun City, you've got something.

It all goes back to that personal Fountain of Youth. It's amazing. I still am asked questions about it by some of our biggest stars—Lana Turner is typical. After the story of my being privy to the secret, even the great Greta Garbo, in one of her rare visits to Hollywood, said that she wanted only to meet one star—Mae. Naturally, they discussed that Fountain of Youth.

Mae is still working on a script for a TV special or maybe another movie. Her latest, *Myra Breckenridge,* was a disaster—not for Mae personally, but as a picture. It was directed in chaotic fashion and the result was chaos. Mae will be more careful her next time out.

The money means nothing to Mae. Like Bob Hope, she is very rich: "I always like to invest my money in something I can watch—like diamonds and real estate." What Bob Hope doesn't own in the San Fernando Valley,

Mae does. Both of them bought this land in the thirties, when the huge valley was nothing but bean fields and was selling at $30 an acre. Today those bean fields support a million and a half people, with all the shopping centers that go with such a population.

One day back in the thirties, Mae and her business manager took a Sunday drive through the valley. In those days it was a scenic drive, much like going through the farmlands of extreme Northern California.

"We came upon a grove of huge deodara trees—they look like Ponderosa pines. I looked out the window at them and told my manager: 'Look into that. It looks like a nice place to build a house someday.' We never stopped. The next day the manager told me that it was owned by a Mexican family and was about to be sold for $600 back taxes. I said, 'Give them $6,000 for it.' That was the happiest Mexican family you ever saw. They were about to kiss my feet."

The punch line, of course, is the land that she bought is now three blocks in the heart of the Van Nuys business district and worth millions. In those days, it was the Depression for everyone but the movie industry. People had little, but what little they had went for food and then the movies. It was their only escape from misery. Movie stars like Mae were earning $5,000 a week and keeping most of it. Land was cheap and Mae could buy it.

Then came World War II and postwar booms. Every GI who had ever been stationed in Southern California, and there seemed like millions, wanted to get away from the frozen East and settle here. The San Fernando Valley became Los Angeles's favorite bedroom community—or communities—although nearly all of it is within the Los Angeles city limits.

No, there will be no benefits for Mae West.

24

Sinatra:
Las Vegas's Swinging Image

OTHER THAN THE TIME he almost ran me down with his car, I have always found Frank Sinatra to be the essence of charm.

That famous car incident at Los Angeles International Airport has become somewhat akin to the passenger list of the Mayflower. The Queen Mary couldn't have carried all the Mayflower ancestors that are claimed by descendants of New England families. The same with all the Los Angeles reporters who claimed to have been at the airport that night, twenty-five or so years ago, when Frank and Ava Gardner tried to sneak into town on a private plane. The reason the two had to sneak was that Frank, although separated, was not divorced from Nancy, Sr. at the time.

The tipoff on the clandestine arrival came on a message from the Mexico City bureau of the Associated Press, giving the plane's schedule. The message was seen on the wire by the Los Angeles AP, of course, the *Los Angeles Times*, the *Los Angeles Examiner*, the *Los Angeles Herald-Express* and the *Los Angeles Mirror*. In those days the Times-Mirror Corporation also owned TV station KTTV, which was alerted by the *Times*.

At most there were six people there, including me. KTTV sent a cameraman who was crippled and kept shining a bright light right into Sinatra's face.

Frank was angry. Who wouldn't be getting that reception when you expected solitude?

The plane landed in the relatively quiet, noncommercial area of the airport, and Frank's car was waiting for him on the field. Frank and Ava ran to the car in flight from the pursuing reporters. Frank took the wheel, stepped on the gas, and the car came right at us, pinning us all against the fence and just missing us by a hair's width. No one was injured, but one photographer later sued Frank. At the time I didn't write about Frank running over reporters because I am of the school of journalism that believes the public isn't interested in how a reporter gets a story; it's just interested in the story. End of lesson.

A year passes, and I'm at a party in Romanoff's, sitting with Prince Mike and Bogey. Frank joins our table and turns to me:

"I want to apologize for that thing at the airport. I was madder than hell, naturally, because I thought you guys had planted that cripple there, with the light shining in my face, so I would take a poke at him. I got in the car and stepped on the gas and the wheels were turned. I would have gone right through that fence and over all of you if I hadn't gotten them straightened out. I'm sorry."

Well, I figure if the guy is big enough to apologize, I'm big enough to forget. That was a quarter century ago, and I would have to put Frank on a par with Cary Grant as Charlie Charm.

I have printed things that have horrified some of his entourage, such as: "The Pope is going to make Frank a cardinal. That way, we will only have to kiss his ring."

And after Carl Cohen, the casino boss of the Sands Hotel in Las Vegas, belted him in the mouth, right after the Six Days War in the Middle East, I sent him this wire: "Frank, if I've told you once, I've told you a thousand times. Don't fight Jews in the desert." Frank loved it. At this writing I am still one of the few press names on Frank's carte blanche list, with open access at all times to the Chairman of the Board.

One night I was discussing this with Nancy, Sr., mother of Frank's children. He is very friendly and devoted to her.

"I can't believe it," she said. "I know it's true, but I can't believe it. You'll get yours someday."

The secret of dealing with Frank is to treat him fairly. I have never seen Frank be anything but professional with reporters who were professional with him. But there are those who bug him, especially photographers. There are some gentlemen among photographers, but, as a class, they are not God's most lovable people. There's a professional reason for that. A reporter can come a half hour late and get the story, but the photographer has to be there the instant it happens to get the picture. That's why they are so aggressive.

When Frank testified before the Los Angeles County Grand Jury about his part in the famous Joe Di Maggio "Wrong-Door Raid" on Marilyn Monroe's apartment, I came up in the elevator with him. A small army of photographers met him, all of them shouting things like "Hey, are you really Perry Como?" and "How about posing for a picture, Mr. Damone?" And so on. What they wanted, of course—and what their city editors probably insisted on getting—was a shot of the famous Sicilian temper exploding. But Frank kept his cool. There was a time when he wouldn't have.

You often wonder how rich Sinatra is. I once judged his worth, solely on his life-style, at about $75 million. A multimillionaire ex-partner of his pooh-poohed that: "At the most, he's got only six or seven million." I commented, "That means he will have to sign up for Social Security at age sixty-five, at the rate he is spending it." No one lives like Sinatra; he gives away more than most multimillionaires spend.

It's very hard to be a close friend of Frank's because every night is New Year's Eve. I've heard him ask his guests if they wanted Mexican food for dinner. When they answered in the affirmative, Frank would pile them in a limousine and fly them in his private jet to Acapulco for a Mexican dinner. (Incidentally, it's very hard to get Mexican food in Acapulco at any of the posh places. I once asked for a taco one night at Las Brisas Hotel, and the French chef threatened to walk out.)

No use going into Frank's charitable deeds; that story has been done to death. But some of them are unique.

One day at breakfast in the Sands Hotel, he read a news story about a sailor, discharged and on his way home after duty in Vietnam, got rolled in an alley. All his money had been taken. Frank turned to one of his associates: "Take a plane up there, find the guy. The Navy will know where he is. Give him back what he lost, plus a few C's more." It was done. And no one ever heard about it. The sailor— on Frank's orders—never knew from where the money came.

I've been with Frank drunk and sober and still find him charming. I have never asked him for a favor, and he has never asked me for one. Maybe that's why we get along. "I can't stand people tugging on my sleeve," he once confided.

He sometimes gets playful when he drinks. Once he and Ava, who likes a drink, too, shot out all the street lights in a desert town near Palm Springs. Nothing was ever printed about it because Frank paid off enough money to get the town new street lights that were better than the old ones.

But one story was well-publicized: how he tried to demolish the Sands Hotel after his gambling credit was shut off. That was enough to make anyone mad, and Sinatra had made the Sands the number one hotel in Las Vegas.

Of course, the Sands had done a lot for Sinatra back in the days when no one else would. Jack Entratter and Jakie Friedman had sold Frank a few points in the hotel for the giveaway price of $50,000. This was before *From Here to Eternity,* when Frank couldn't get himself arrested in show business. But that was a smart move on the Sands's part; Frank brought in his pals—Dean Martin, Sammy Davis, Jr., Joey Bishop, and others—so that the Sands was the place to go on the Las Vegas Strip. Frank shot movies there, threw parties there, and saw that it did the best business in town. The Sands, when it lost Frank, never regained that stature, even with Howard Hughes money.

Now Frank, followed by his high-rolling friends, has switched to Caesars Palace—although he has had some problems there, too.

Still, he remains a popular fellow. Hank Greenspun, the fiery publisher of the *Las Vegas Sun,* once editorialized in print that Frank Sinatra in town was the equivalent of three conventions for the town's economy.

A few weeks after that, one of the bosses pulled a gun

on Frank at the baccarat table. Somehow Frank emerged the heavy. The district attorney, running for reelection, said: "Frank Sinatra was being his usual, miserable, rotten self." It is not unusual for a Las Vegas politician to side with the casino bosses, but it's politically damaging to go against Sinatra. Those waitresses and captains to whom Frank gives $100 tips vote too. The DA was not reelected.

A close friend of mine was an eyewitness to the whole fracas. He doesn't want his name used because he is a Las Vegas performer himself and the bosses, not Sinatra, are the ones who sign the lucrative contracts. Here is his account, as impartial as can be; he is not a Sinatra buddy:

"It was early in the morning, almost dawn, and Frank had won a bundle at baccarat the night before. He plays at $8,000 a hand, so he asked to double his limit to $16,000 because he was losing this time. The house refused. Frank didn't sing any love sonnets, but he didn't throw money around either. He merely threw his cards down on the table and said: 'You guys better get another boy singer up on that marquee for tonight, because I ain't going to be here.' At that, Sanford Waterman, one of the casino bosses, pulled a gun. That was the end of any argument on Frank's part."

Some have said that Waterman was afraid that Frank would win again with the double limit. No casino executive wants that on his conscience the next morning, when the big boys come on duty. Others have said that Frank didn't always pay his markers. This I find hard to believe, because Frank is the kind of guy who always pays his debts.

It's no secret there always has been bad blood between Frank and Waterman, ever since the two were partners in the Cal-Neva Lodge at Lake Tahoe. The Cal-Neva Lodge is on the north shore of the lake, and the state line runs right through the lodge. The casino and part of the hotel are on the Nevada side, and most of the hotel is in California, which doesn't permit gambling. Nevada, of course, allows gambling, but it has an unwanted list of notorious mobsters whom the state prefers not to have around.

Both Waterman and Frank lost a mint when the Nevada gaming commission took away their gaming license, after Salvator (Sam) Giancana visited the Nevada side of the lodge to see his girl friend, Phyllis McGuire of the McGuire Sisters, who were headlining there.

"I didn't even know he was at my place," Frank told me. Frank later gave Giancana such a bawling out—which took more courage than I've got.

In those days, Sam was Godfather in Chicago. He was tough, but he had a thing for Phyllis, who learned to sing in a small-town, Ohio Sunday school. Sam was slain last year in his suburban Chicago home, in Chicago style. After his death, stories came out telling how he had once had the CIA bug Dan Rowan, the comedian, because Dan and Phyllis were having an affair.

Frank once told me: "I knew Giancana had this thing for Phyllis, and I knew he was staying over on the California side in a motel. He knew he was on Nevada's list of unwanted visitors, but Phyllis called him up and invited him over. When I heard about it, I raised Holy Hell with him. His visit cost me my license."

Whatever the reason for Frank's later troubles with Waterman and the gun, it has all been smoothed over and Frank is once more selling out Caesars Palace.

Las Vegas is a funny town. Back in the old days it was run by the Mafia and run quite efficiently. You could see the greatest entertainment in the world at low cost. Now that the town is run by businessmen, the prices are outrageous. The town is run by computer. Every department must show a profit. In the old days, the Mafia let the casino carry the whole operation. Then, the town was filled with gangsters. I used to see Meyer Lansky at the Flamingo, and I met Giancana many times.

I had known him from Chicago and Henrici's Restaurant, where Charlie Dunkley, the "mayor of the Loop," and I used to dine every night. Dunkley was the AP midwest sports editor and one of the most colorful figures I've ever known. He's the guy who hung the sobriquet "The Galloping Ghost" on Red Grange and wrote the famous "Say it ain't so, Joe" story about Shoeless Joe Jackson and the Black Sox World Series scandal of 1919.

For some reason the Chicago mob loved him, and I met them all through him—Charlie (Golf Bag) Hunt, the Fischetti brothers, Louis (Little New York) Campagna, and the rest.

Somehow the word gets around. When I first started going to Las Vegas in the postwar years, I was treated like a king. In those days Las Vegas had no crime because a common crook was scared to death to pull off gunplay or a heist in a town the Mafia had declared an open city. They wouldn't even kill off their own enemies in Las Vegas.

Gus Greenbaum, one of the early owners of the Flamingo and later of the Riviera, double-crossed somebody. The whole town knew he was living under a death sentence, but he kept on working as usual for five years, secure in Las Vegas. Then he got careless and took his first trip out of town to Phoenix. Both Gus and his wife, an innocent bystander, were found slain there in a hotel room. Their throats had been slit—the Mafia code for double-cross.

Now businessmen and their computers run Vegas, and it has one of the biggest crime rates in the country. Figure that one out.

A lot of people have wondered why Howard Hughes invested so heavily in the town. Someone high in the Hughes organization once told me that when Bobby Kennedy was Attorney General, he asked Hughes to move in, appealing to his patriotism. Howard always loved Vegas as a town, even in the old days. It's nocturnal in its habits, as he is, and it's a great place to get lost—which Howard also likes. It's the world capital of anonymity; that's because gamblers don't see anything but the numbers on dice. Hughes is probably the only man big enough to take on the Mafia and win. He could make them offers they couldn't refuse.

Hughes changed the whole character of the town. Banks and insurance companies started investing in hotels. It used to be that most of the hotels were built on loans from the Teamsters Pension Fund. But many of the big casinos have huge markers outstanding. So far the businessmen haven't found the Mafia's secret of collection, which is probably a good thing for anyone who owes a casino. In the old days, the Mafia collected all overdue bills. You either paid or had your kneecaps broken.

The big salaries to entertainers are mostly paid on the basis of how well they attract the high rollers. That's why Sinatra, at an estimated $250,000 a week, is numero uno. Dean Martin is another big high roller draw, as is Shecky Greene, a Las Vegas favorite.

The biggest draw in Vegas, rivaling Sinatra, is Elvis Presley, who doesn't mean a thing to the casino. But he is a gold mine for the Hilton Hotel operation. At every Elvis engagement, the 2,200-seat room is filled to capacity, the biggest in Las Vegas. And he's the only one who fills it for every show. When Elvis appears, secretaries and shopgirls from all over the world save up their money and spend every night at his show for a week. They come from Australia, Ireland, England, even from behind the Iron Curtain. It's really one of the great phenomena of show business.

But other than a few moments at the nickel slot machine, Elvis's fans walk right through the casino. Frank, on the other hand, has followers who live in the casino. Danny Schwartz, one of Frank's buddies and partners, lost $260,000 one night playing baccarat at $8,000 a hand. He paid for Frank's salary in a couple of hours. I watched the whole thing. I call Danny the baccarat king. "One more night like that one and I'll abdicate," says Danny.

A lot of people would like to see Sinatra do more acting. Bogey used to say that Frank would be the new Spencer Tracy if he paid as much attention to acting as he does to singing. It's true in a sense. Frank is a perfectionist about his music or saloon appearances. In his movies, he prints the rehearsals.

But Frank has given some marvelous performances with his one-take style. In *Man With the Golden Arm,* Director Otto Preminger allotted one week to do the drug withdrawal scene. Frank came on the set and said: "Ludwig, start the cameras rolling. I don't need no rehearsal." The whole scene, a classic one, was shot just that way—one take, no rehearsal. A half day's work in a week allotted.

Frank can do it, but the other actors working with him can't. Once Edward G. Robinson, a dear friend of Frank's, said he could not work with him in a movie. Eddie was a perfectionist and he thought Frank was not. Director Frank Capra, a fellow Sicilian, solved it beautifully:

"I just had another actor rehearse Frank's lines with Eddie. When Eddie felt he was ready, I brought in Frank to do the scene in one take. I noticed that the first take with Frank was always the best, that he lost spontaneity when the scene dragged."

Frank had a lot of trouble with Marlon Brando when they made *Guys and Dolls,* a horribly miscast movie. Knowing that Brando is a twenty-five take man, Frank wouldn't come out of his dressing room after a while.

"When Mumbles is through rehearsing, I'll come out," Frank told Joe Mankiewicz.

That musical, which is my all-time favorite, should have had Sinatra as Sky Masterson, singing all those great Frank Loesser songs, instead of Marlon Brando. Marlon, who insisted on singing the songs himself, has a voice like —as the late Joe E. Lewis used to say—the all-clear signal in a floating crap game.

But somehow Frank was miscast as Nathan Detroit. Jilly Rizzo should have played the role.

25

Elvis: He Made an
Aircraft Carrier Rock

It was 1955, and Milton Berle and I were flying down to San Diego, where Mr. Television was going to do his show on the U.S.S. *Enterprise,* an aircraft carrier. This was the famous "Texaco Star Theater," which built television and sold more sets than RCA. I asked him who were the guest stars.

"Well, there's Harry James, Esther Williams, and some guitar player the William Morris office sent over. I need him to fill a spot for my wardrobe change," said Milton. Milton, who, with Ed Sullivan, was TV's top buyer of talent, couldn't remember the guitar player's name. "I never heard of him before, but the Morris office says he's good."

Came show time and the carrier filled with naval personnel and their families, including the usual number of teenage daughters. They were all there—from the admiral's family to the seaman's. I was sitting in the front row. Came time for Milton to announce the guitar player, whose name he now knew—Elvis Presley.

Elvis was an incongruous sight in those days. No one wore long sideburns, but he did. He looked exactly like what he had been—a truckdriver from the Deep South. A twang on the guitar, a sexy thrust of the pelvis and rock! The song was "Heartbreak Hotel." I was not prepared for what happened behind me. Such screams!

I turned around and saw that the kids, especially the young girls, were going wild, just exactly the way I had seen them do for Sinatra a decade or so earlier. Parents were trying to quiet the girls but it was no use. Navy discipline was helpless here. Elvis was getting to the glands of girls too young to know they had glands. It was pandemonium.

When Elvis's bit was over, Milton came out dressed like a woman. I dashed down in the carrier's wardroom to find out more about this phenomenon. I introduced myself to Elvis and Col. Tom Parker, whom I had heard about from an old friend, Gene Austin. I learned that Elvis had done some things in the South and caused a stir. Then he had made a television appearance or two with the Jimmy Dorsey Orchestra, which was a summer replacement for the Jackie Gleason show, but that was about it. This was Elvis's first big-time break. After all this chatting, Elvis took me aside.

"You're from Hollywood, huh?"

"Yes."

"Have you ever heard of a producer up there called Hal Wallis?"

"Yes."

"Is he reputable?"

"None more reputable," I answered. Then I asked Elvis why he wanted to know. He told me an amazing thing:

"Well, I'm going up to Paramount Pictures tomorrow and test for a contract with him."

I knew how Wallis had discovered many a talent long before they had become famous. I had just done a story on how he had gone backstage between the first and second acts of *Pajama Game* and hired Carol Haney's understudy. That was Shirley MacLaine, who had yet to appear in her first picture and, other than understudying Miss Haney, had done nothing out of the chorus. And now she was in Hitchcock's *The Trouble with Harry*. So it really wasn't surprising that Wallis had spotted this guy that Berle and I had never before heard about.

Next day, back in Hollywood, I started writing a story about Elvis rocking the aircraft carrier. I called Wallis, who confirmed the screen test and said: "I saw this guy on the Jimmy Dorsey Show one night, and I decided he had the same animal magnetism as Brando. I couldn't care less about his singing." Hal was very impressed when I told him what happened on the aircraft carrier.

My next call was to Teet Carle, publicity director of Paramount. I asked him for a picture of Elvis Presley. "Who?" asked Teet. "No one could have a name like Elvis Presley. What is an Elvis Presley?" Then I told him that he was being tested at that very minute on the Paramount lot by Wallis. Soon Teet called back: "If I hadn't seen it, I wouldn't have believed it. He's got a crazy manager too; he's out there trying to sell autographed pictures of Elvis to the crew."

Well, you and I should have the millions Hal Wallis made off of Elvis Presley in the movies. Elvis had the animal magnetism of Brando all right, but not the acting talent. He did sell tickets, though.

Elvis and I still reminisce about that first meeting. He still calls me, "Mr. Bacon"—the only person in show business who does, but that's because of Elvis's perfect manners. Elvis's late mother, to whom he was very close, certainly taught her boy well. He is, without doubt, the most gentlemanly of all superstars. He is also among its greatest lovers.

Years ago, Mamie Van Doren, who knows a thing or two about men, had a close friendship with Tuesday Weld, who also knew men well in those days. Mamie once came up to me in Palm Springs and we discussed lovers. She had known a few, including Jack Dempsey, this virile ex-heavyweight champion of the world, then in his late fifties.

"I want to meet Elvis," sighed Mamie. "Tuesday tells me he really rocks around the clock."

26

King Richard
and
Queen Elizabeth

IN AUGUST 1974, writing in a national magazine about the Burtons who were then getting a divorce, I said: "As one who has been through concubinage, marriage, and divorce with the Burtons, I predict these two will eventually get back together again. They cannot live without each other. They make love by fighting." It was one of my better predictions. I also wrote: "But how many reconciliations are there on the fire?"

By the time this book comes out, who knows what will happen? Let's hope they're still together because the Burtons together mean about twenty-five columns a year to me. Apart, maybe ten at most.

The public really wasn't interested in Elizabeth when she was with Henri Wynberg, her used-car consort, during the fourteen months the Burtons were separated. It was too sad an ending for one of the public's favorite idols. It was like reading about Lana Turner and her Johnny Stompanato or Ava Gardner and her beach boys.

Elizabeth and I were the closest of friends over the years until I wrote a story about Wynberg. She didn't like it, although deep in her heart she knew it was true. I suppose it hurt her ego more than I realized, but it was my love for Elizabeth that prompted me to print it. I didn't want to see an old friend—the screen's greatest beauty—go the gigolo route. In retrospect, it was none of my business, and I'm sorry now I wrote it.

It all happened when a member of Elizabeth's entourage called me from Rome one day and described a hilarious scene in which Elizabeth hid Henri in a closet when Richard made an unexpected visit to Elizabeth's hotel suite. It all sounded like a French bedroom farce, with Richard coming in one door while Elizabeth pushed Henri out another. Richard and Elizabeth were separated at the time and I wrote it as funny as it sounded. It was not a malicious story in any way.

The story had an amazing reaction from a group of Henri's colleagues in the used-car business. They called me and told me that Henri, already into them for some money, had proposed a way to be paid off with interest. The way was to marry Elizabeth Taylor, a wealthy woman. One highly reputable dealer, told me that a group of car dealers had at Henri's request, formed a syndicate to finance his wooing of Elizabeth in Rome. They even showed me the cancelled check—drawn on a Paramount, California, bank, if I recall, to the tune of $14,525. The reason they called me was that they were starting to worry about their investment. Last I heard, they haven't recouped.

For fourteen months, Henri was live-in stud with Elizabeth, from Beverly Hills to Leningrad. One of his used car backers described the loan quite bluntly. "We know the size of Henri's cock. That was our only collateral." I wrote about the syndicate without using the blunt language describing the collateral. Elizabeth, for obvious reasons, didn't like that either.

It's doubtful that Henri got anything out of Elizabeth except expenses. When he went with her to Leningrad while she did *The Blue Bird*, each member of the Soviet-American Company was allotted $20 a day for expenses. Elizabeth demanded and got an extra $20 for Henri. That tells it all.

I find it hard to believe that Elizabeth could exist on $20 a day—not the way the Burtons lived. I once spent a week in Paris while they were staying at the Hotel Lancaster, a plush hotel on the Rue de Berri. Dick Hanley, who was Elizabeth's secretary at the time, told me that the Burton entourage occupied twenty-one rooms, and the usual weekly tab was $15,000. Everybody in the Burton entourage always lived high on the hog. And Richard paid all bills. In fact, Elizabeth never lived like the movie queen she really was until she married Burton. She got a brief taste of it with Mike Todd, but until *Around the World in 80 Days* hit big, Todd was pretty much living a hand-to-mouth existence. He spent it but he didn't have it. Burton's got it.

Early in Burton's career, long before he became an international star, he became a Swiss resident. All the big money he has made since has escaped heavy taxation. He's got most of what he has made. Last time I talked with Aaron Frosch, the Burtons' longtime lawyer, he estimated Richard's fortune at $70 million. Even when Elizabeth was a major star and married to Michael Wilding, the two couldn't afford to buy a movie star house. MGM advanced them $85,000 on her future salaries to buy the home they lived in on Beverly Estates Drive, off Benedict Canyon in Beverly Hills. The house was recently offered on the market for $250,000. During all the years of marriage to Burton, she never had to touch her own money. She told me herself that Richard picked up the tab for everything.

Elizabeth, with Wynberg, was picking up all the tabs. That's why she worked so long and so boringly in Leningrad—to make money. Even her closest friends were appalled. Dr. Rex Kennamer, her private physician and dearest friend, told me recently: "The only thing Henri did was to keep Elizabeth working. He couldn't sell enough used cars, even if he were in the business, to keep her in the life-style she is used to. Why in the hell else would she spend such a miserable winter in Leningrad?"

Elizabeth, at age forty-four, hasn't got that many working years left. It's a sad thing about the movie business. A woman star, even at age thirty-five, has trouble finding good roles, while a man is just beginning. Elizabeth has endured longer than most because she is so breathtakingly beautiful and is, in my opinion, the screen's greatest instinctive actress. Her only avenue from now on is character parts.

I recently ran into Elizabeth in the lobby of the Beverly Hills Hotel. Her violet eyes flashed as she said: "He was my dearest friend. Now he writes with a sweet pen," she said in an aside to Henri, who said nothing. She offered her cheek for a conciliatory kiss. I held both her arms at her side as I kissed her. That gesture made her laugh. Elizabeth doesn't hold grudges long. It made me all the more sorry that I had written the stories about Wynberg. After all, it was her life. And none of my goddamn business, even if I am a gossip columnist.

It never pays to be a Good Samaritan. It backfired on me first with Katharine Hepburn, the time I took the drunken Spencer Tracy to the beach house they shared. And now Elizabeth. I didn't give a damn about Kate. I never really liked her anyhow, but Elizabeth I loved. You couldn't help but love Elizabeth, one of the great basic broads of all time.

We had shared so much together. How could I forget that Saturday morning, March 22, 1958? It was about 7 A.M. and my home phone rang. The voice on the other end of the line said: "Thank God, you answered." It was the AP bureau in Albuquerque. "Do you know there's a plane crashed near Grants and that your name is on the passenger manifest?" It was Mike Todd's plane. I knew that immediately.

"Do you have the serial numbers?" I asked. The voice on the other end of the line gave them to me. "It's Mike Todd's plane. Is everybody dead?"

"Burned beyond recognition," was the answer. Later Mike's body was identified only by a pair of cuff links that Eddie Fisher had made especially for him by Tiffany's. They were solid gold and made in the shape of shirt buttons.

A half hour before departure the night before, I had called Mike at Burbank Airport and told him I was cancelling out of the flight. There were a lot of reasons. It was one of the worst nights in Southern California history, with rain, sleet, lightning, thunder—the works. The reason for the trip was we were all going back to a special roast the Friars were giving Mike in New York. Mike's plane, luxurious as it was, was a prop plane that would take ten hours to make a flight that the new jets could make in four and a half. Frankly, I asked myself, is this trip necessary?

"You son-of-a-bitch," he said. "You're not going because your girl friend Liz is not going." It was the first I knew she wasn't going. Mike explained that she had a virus and a fever and he didn't want her to make the trip. "I want her to stay home with the baby—not get sick. She wanted to go, but I laid down the law. So she's not going."

Mike's plane was called *Lucky Liz*. And Mike called her "Liz Schwartz." She hates the name Liz. Whenever you hear someone purport to being a friend of the Burtons and then call them Liz and Dick, beware. Richard says Dick is an appendage, not a name.

But with the confirmation of the crash that Saturday morning, there was only one thing to do. I called Dick Hanley, then Mike's secretary.

"I knew something was wrong," Dick said. "Elizabeth has been calling me all morning. Mike was supposed to call her from Tulsa, where they were to refuel. We'd better get Dr. Kennamer and go over there. Jesus, I hate this."

Rex and Dick were already at the home on Schuyler Road in Beverly Hills when I arrived. Both lived in the Beverly Hills area. I had to drive over the mountain from the San Fernando Valley. I got there in time to see Elizabeth, in a short, see-through nightie, run screaming from room to room in the big house. Kennamer grabbed her and stuck a hypodermic needle into her. It quieted her quickly. Then, with the help of servants, they took her upstairs to bed, where she was knocked out for hours. Hanley and I talked.

"The minute we walked in the door, she was waiting for us," said Dick. "She knew. She screamed: 'He's dead, isn't he? I've been up since two o'clock. He promised to call me when they stopped in Tulsa. He never did. I know something's wrong.'

"We didn't even have to say a word. Then she started screaming like a wild woman. Perhaps it was good she was an actress and could burst out with extrovert emotions. She just ran screaming from room to room. If we hadn't blocked her, she would have run into the street."

Kennamer stayed up in the bedroom with her. Soon the street outside was filled with reporters and television people. All of them were grumbling because I was inside and they were out. They didn't know of my tragic involvement.

But MGM police—Elizabeth was working there at the time —were keeping out everybody but authorized visitors. Bill Lyon, an MGM press agent, reasoned with the reporters that I was inside because I was a close personal friend, one who was supposed to be on the plane.

Debbie Reynolds and her husband, Eddie Fisher, came; so did Shirley MacLaine; Helen Rose, the MGM designer; Michael Wilding, her ex-husband; and Kurt Frings, her agent. Kurt, too, had been booked on Mike's private plane, but he had cancelled for basically the same reasons I had.

It was the major story of the day around the world and the press was getting angrier because I was inside; it didn't matter that my stuff on AP would be available to all of them. Louella Parsons called Howard Strickling, head of publicity at MGM, and put all kinds of pressure on him to get inside, too. He refused, but he relayed Louella's— also Hedda's—complaints to Bill Lyon. I told Bill that, to avoid any unpleasantness in such a tragedy, I would go outside. There I acted as a spokesman for what had happened inside. I told them that Elizabeth was under heavy sedation and that Debbie had taken the Wilding boys and baby Liza over to her house. This seemed to quiet everybody somewhat.

The houseman then came out and spoke to me: "Mrs. Todd is awake, and she wants you back in the house." So I went back in as unobtrusively as possible. It was past deadline time for most on this Saturday morning and there was little or no grumbling. Even Louella had given up— although she was a little cool toward me for a few weeks.

All of Elizabeth's friends visited her in the bedroom. She talked constantly—while sipping a stiff drink. Who could blame her? Rex thought it good therapy for her to be surrounded by friends. It really was.

"I begged him not to go—to wait one more day. I don't think he wanted to go. He came upstairs to kiss me good-bye six times before he left the house." As she rambled on, spurred by drugs and whiskey, a phone rang downstairs.

"I can't bear to hear that phone ring. I feel everytime that it's Mike calling. I loved him so much. And he loved me. No one can ever know how much. If only I had been on that plane with him. I feel like a half pair of scissors.

That's what he always used to tell me when he was away from me."

I remember that scene so vividly. Here was this girl, heavily sedated and drinking and without sleep most of the night, and how beautiful she looked! Maybe it was because of that memory that I wrote the Wynberg piece years later, hoping to bring Elizabeth back to her senses.

Then Kennamer suggested that Elizabeth get some more sleep, and we all went downstairs. I got in a long conversation with Debbie. She and Eddie had traveled all over the world with the Todds.

"She and Eddie are so close. You know Mike is like a father to Eddie but when we go anyplace, it's always Eddie and Elizabeth who seem to talk with each other for hours, leaving Mike and me alone. I don't know what they find to talk about for so long."

I thought nothing of that conversation until many months later when all hell broke loose. Eddie, the all-American boy singer, left Debbie, the all-American girl, to take off with Elizabeth, the all-American femme fatale. Everybody was typecast for their roles in the scandal of the century except Eddie. He has never recovered from it.

When it broke, Debbie's business manager called a press agent by name of Irwyn Franklyn over to help her handle the media. The yard of the Fisher home in Beverly Hills was filled with press, all clamoring for a picture. Debbie didn't want to pose, but Franklyn told me that he urged her to make a brief appearance—if only to get some diapers drying on the line. He took the credit for sticking the diaper pins in her blouse. Whoever did it ruined Eddie's career with that little touch. It was the Wirephoto seen around the world, and Eddie's been trying to make a comeback ever since. You can get into any kind of a scrape in Hollywood if you're typecast for it. Eddie wasn't.

After that picture there was nothing for Eddie and Elizabeth to do but get married. No matter all that stuff you have read about Elizabeth saying she was in hibernation after Mike's death until she met Richard—she was in love with Eddie Fisher. Who knows what might have happened if Fox had gone through with its original casting of Steve

Boyd as Marc Antony and shot it in London instead of Rome, a year later with Burton? Eddie recalls that it all happened on Elizabeth's thirtieth birthday:

"I came into her dressing room and found her gazing into the mirror, searching for wrinkles. I couldn't believe that look. Here was the world's most beautiful woman scared to death of turning thirty. It was sad."

It's understandable, for the movie business likes its whiskey aged and its women young. Any leading lady dreads that thirtieth birthday. That's why the year of birth is seldom listed in studio biographies—although Elizabeth's is—1932. Could that fear of aging have spurred her to conquer Burton who, by his own admission, was the greatest womanizer in the business?

When the romance on the *Cleopatra* set first started, Eddie recalls Sybil Burton telling him, "Don't worry, Eddie. It will pass. Richard always must have these flings with leading ladies." Eddie said that Sybil just waited in the wings, hoping it would pass like all the others.

Richard once, over a few drinks, bragged that he had batted a thousand with his leading ladies. From observation, I would say that was a little high, but maybe .900. On *Ice Palace,* he jumped everything that moved, including one fifty-year-old production assistant who is still eternally grateful. His most serious affair on that picture was beautiful Diane McBain, who played his granddaughter. She was an eighteen-year-old virgin out of Glendale, a town where they have a lot of virgins. When Richard turned his charm on her, she fell and fell hard. She didn't know he was married, and when she found out, it was too late; she was hopelessly in love with him. And she was gorgeous.

Once, in an apartment she shared with actress Sherry Jackson, she described to me how Richard had taken her virginity. Sherry, who once played Danny Thomas's daughter on TV, listened rapturously and sighed: "What a way to go!"

One night Richard and Sybil dined at Chasen's with Jim and Henny Backus. Jim, who was also in the picture, had become a pal of Richard's.

In the course of an evening's drinking, Richard excused himself to go to the men's room. By coincidence, Diane, who had been dining in another part of the restaurant, came to the ladies' room. Neither one ever went back to their respective parties.

"It worried hell out of Henny and me," Backus recalls, "but it didn't seem to bother Sybil. She took it all in stride."

As it was, Richard and Diane didn't come back for three days. I had been sitting at another booth in the restaurant and was aware of the Backus's concern for the missing Richard. A week or so later, I ran into Richard out at Warners and asked him: "Christ, Richard, what the hell do you tell your wife when you take off like that with a young girl?"

Richard, using that great cathedral he carries around with him, resonantly replied: "My good Jim, I tell her nothing."

"Doesn't she ask questions?"

"She wouldn't dare."

Really, I'm surprised that Richard ever left a wife like that—even for Elizabeth Taylor. It reminded me of what Sessue Hayakawa, the great Japanese star, once told me. Sessue, so great in *Bridge on the River Kwai*, was shacked up with a young French girl in Paris in 1941 when Pearl Harbor hit. Nothing else for Sessue to do but stay with the French girl for the duration. In 1946, he returned to Tokyo to his wife, also a famous actress.

"She Japanese wife," said Sessue. "She never asked where I had been. She wouldn't dare."

So it was with Burton and Sybil, but Richard had never encountered a man-eater like Elizabeth before. She was no one-night stand, like the hundreds of others before her. Only once in all the years had I seen Sybil be anything but the passive wife. That was on New Year's Eve, 1952. At the stroke of midnight, Richard was dancing with the gorgeous Jean Simmons, his co-star in *The Robe*. Richard gave Jean a long and soulful kiss in the time-honored tradition of the New Year. He had overlooked Sybil at the moment. She walked out on the dance floor, hauled off and belted Richard, and then left the party. The Burtons had been houseguests of Jean and her husband, Stewart

Granger. They moved out shortly and became the guests of the James Masons.

It was inevitable that Elizabeth and Richard would have to get together sometime, but there is no use going into all that gory detail again.

After *Cleopatra*, Richard went down to Puerto Vallarta to do *The Night of the Iguana*. Elizabeth and I were down there with him. I spent six happy weeks in that seaside Mexican paradise, and how I got there is quite funny.

One afternoon I bumped into Sarah Taylor, Elizabeth's mother, in the Polo Lounge of the Beverly Hills Hotel. She told me that she had just gotten an urgent cable from Elizabeth to hurry down to Puerto Vallarta. I asked what that meant. Maybe marriage?

"Could be," said Mrs. Taylor. "I've been to all of Elizabeth's weddings."

I told my bosses of the conversation. A marriage between these two, of course, would be a banner around the world. I was sent to Puerto Vallarta, then a sleepy village. Burton was smart. He bought up a lot of property at sleepy village prices. Today, when Puerto Vallarta is on the verge of becoming another Acapulco, those same holdings are worth millions.

It was true. Elizabeth wanted a wedding, but Eddie Fisher was the stumbling block. He wouldn't give his consent to a Mexican divorce. At one point, I heard Elizabeth tell her lawyers to offer Eddie $1 million as a settlement. He turned it down, much to his later regret. Meanwhile, there was nothing to do but have fun.

Came Thanksgiving Day, 1963, and Elizabeth invited me to go out to Mismaloya, the movie location that was reached by launch. I noticed that she had big picnic hampers and buckets filled with cooling champagne. With us were the children and Mike Wilding, her ex-husband, who had now become Elizabeth and Richard's agent. It was about time for the cast and crew to break for lunch.

Richard joined us on a huge rock jutting into the ocean, and Elizabeth spread out a tablecloth. From out of the hampers came roast turkey, cranberry sauce, mashed potatoes, and pumpkin pie—everything the folks back home were eating for Thanksgiving. I'll never forget the sight on the movie location. Sue Lyon, who was working that day, and the rest were eating tacos. It really was one of the most memorable Thanksgivings of my life. How in the hell Elizabeth ever got all that stuff together down there, I did not know.

But I know now, because years later I returned to Puerto Vallarta when the Burtons were there, and one of their underlings intercepted me at the airport with a suitcase full of bacon, hams, breads, and all the other American things you couldn't get in Mexico. I almost got a double hernia carrying the suitcase full of goodies. I dropped it off over at Gringo Gulch where the Burtons were. A drunken nanny took it as if I were a delivery boy. That was the last time I ever carried groceries for the Burtons.

Life in Puerto Vallarta, with the Burtons, was fun. I was there for six weeks straight except for taking the weekend off for Christmas, 1963. It was tough on the liver and even tougher on Burton's.

One night when Richard was on the wagon, we all went to the Oceana Bar. In all fairness, Richard knows he drinks too much and tries every now and then to cut down. But Elizabeth never lets up. And she can be a barracuda at times. She can outdrink any man I have ever known, including Burton. That may have been the ego buster that broke up the marriage for fourteen months.

This one night at the Oceana, everybody was drinking but Richard. He was charming as always. Then suddenly Elizabeth turned to him and said: "Richard, take a drink. You are so goddamn dull when you're not drinking."

I was sitting next to Richard and he turned to me and said: "Keep count."

I did. That was the night I saw him drink 23 straight shots of tequila, with a few bottles of Carta Blanca beer as chasers. It's a wonder it didn't kill him. I know it was twenty-three because Richard was the only one at the table drinking tequila, and I got stuck with the bill. He couldn't even see the waiter who brought it, but I must say that he got up under his own power and made it to the Jeep, where his driver was waiting for him to take him and Elizabeth up the hill.

The amazing thing about Richard is the more tequila he

drank, the more eloquent he became. About the twelfth or thirteenth shot, he decided he wanted to do some *Hamlet*. He asked Elizabeth to do Ophelia but she refused.

"Lady Macbeth's more my meat," she said.

I volunteered to read Ophelia's part. Did quite well, too, especially in the mad scene. I am probably the first Ophelia in Shakespearean history ever to do it with musical accompaniment. During my whole six weeks in Puerto Vallarta, I never went anyplace without Julio Corona, my personal guitar player and minstrel. Julio was an old friend from Palm Springs. He had played there many years with the Guadalajara Trio. My first night in Puerto Vallarta, I found him singing for cerveza in the Oceana. I was on an unlimited expense account, so I kept him in beer for six weeks. This particular night, during my mad scene, he played and softly sang that great Mexican song "Cu Cu Ru Cu Cu." You would be amazed at how well this adapted to Shakespeare. In fact, after the Burtons left, Julio and I strolled along the waterfront singing it. Finally, after what seemed like miles, we were under Elizabeth and Richard's balcony still singing it. Elizabeth loved it. Richard dropped a flowerpot on us, which, due to his tequila content, missed. Oh, those were the days.

There was something about Puerto Vallarta then that caused everyone to drop inhibitions. A sedate schoolteacher sent down to tutor the sixteen-year-old Sue Lyon suddenly kicked off her prim background, smoked opium, and shacked up with one of the natives. Last I heard, she was still down there on the beach.

Ava Gardner took up with a twenty-one-year-old beach boy who continually beat her up in public, much to the amazement of the tourists from Des Moines. John Huston took up drinking an illegal native brew called raicilla that was 180 proof and went down like Drano. Burton and I tried it, too. It's a wonder any of us have any stomach left.

Press people came from all over the world to the site because the presence of all these crazy people in a little Mexican fishing village was just too much to ignore. And the town affected the press even more than it did the actors who, after all, had a movie to make and less time to play.

One particularly conservative journalist who is a long-time friend of mine and not much of a drinker decided to challenge Richard to a drinking bout. Richard, like a gun-fighter of the old West, is confronted with this sort of thing every day. He complied. After five or six rounds, the journalist, a well-known Hollywood writer, suddenly dis-appeared. No one thought anything about it until hours later when he showed up in his jockey shorts covered from head to toe in grease, like somebody about to swim the English Channel.

Earlier he had scared the hell out of Ava Gardner when he jumped over a brick wall at a bar where she was drink-ing. She didn't know what the hell to think until she recognized him through the grease. Before she could help, he fled again and appeared at the Oceana, once more ready to challenge Burton in a drinking contest.

Greg Morrison and Ernie Anderson, the press agents on the movie, figured the best thing to do was to get him back to his hotel room and let him sleep it off. He was staying at a place called the Del Rio, which had a peculiar way of treating guests. It used to move them from room to room without telling them beforehand. The reason was that if someone who had stayed there the year before made a reservation, they always gave them the same room. I know it sounds crazy but that's the way it was in Puerto Vallarta in those days before civilization moved in with the Burtons.

Well, Ernie and Greg took our journalist—who might even be called ultraconservative—and hauled him off to his room. A middle-aged tourist couple now occupied the room. They were in bed. Ernie took the journalist's key and opened the door, awakening the couple. Imagine what they saw? Two guys holding up the Creature from the Black Lagoon.

When our journalist saw this, he said drunkenly: "First the bastards tar and feather me and now they steal my goddamn room."

The story is now a fixed part of Burton's repertoire. He tells it every time he drinks with newspapermen. The story is much funnier if the identity of the journalist is known, but the organization he works for, a huge wire service, is really ultraconservative and they might cut off his pension.

That story is mild compared with what happened to a beautiful young Swedish journalist who came down on the plane with me. It was her first trip to Mexico and I was introducing her to the joys of tequila—which I described as a quaint native drink. She said that it reminded her of aquavit from her native land. By the time she got off the plane she was flying. Ernie Anderson met us, and the girl, beautiful as most Swedish girls are, said she had made reservations for a hotel recommended by SAS.

"Fine," said Ernie, "except for one problem. The hotel isn't built yet."

The tequila was working on the girl and we had to drive miles out of our way to show her the concrete frame of a hotel called Posada Vallarta. That's all there was—just a mass of concrete and steel. "But SAS confirmed my reservations," she insisted.

Ernie took her to the Tropicana, right on the beach, and that seemed to soothe her. We all went out for dinner, driven by Ernie's crazy Indian driver, who obviously led a double life. He would come to work in the morning with fresh machete scars—he was part barbarian, no doubt about it.

Our beautiful Swede continued with the tequila. She drank it like Burton. About this time, Ernie suggested that we all go up to his house and try some raicilla. Ernie, a bachelor, obviously had some designs on this good-looking chick. He poured us healthy glasses of the potent brew. All of us—including the Indian driver—sat in chairs and drank it. Kerplunk, Ernie went out like a blown fuse with his. The Swedish girl gulped hers and asked for another. Mine went down deep into the intestines and burned each one individually.

I suggested that we go back to our hotels. The Indian driver dropped me off first and then proceeded with the Swedish girl since she lived further away. I thought nothing of it until the next morning, when the Swedish reporter pounded on my door and told me a horrifying tale.

The Indian driver had taken her up into the mountains and raped her, tearing off most of her clothing. The driver then dropped her off at the Tropicana, where she explained to the night manager that she was afraid to stay alone in her room because of what had happened. Since she explained that I was her only friend, the night manager gallantly offered to drive her to the Oceana Hotel, where I was staying. On the way, she found herself again being driven to the mountains, where the night manager raped her. The rapings didn't seem to bother her when she appeared at my door for help.

"I lost my passport," she screamed. "How will I ever get out of this awful place?"

Then, from Australia, came another beautiful journalist —a twenty-one-year-old girl who bore a striking resemblance to Jackie Kennedy. One of the really big people on the picture, very big in Bel-Air and Beverly Hills, took after her. At the end-of-the-picture party on Mismaloya, he got her into a bedroom and started taking off his own clothes furiously.

The girl said: "But I'm a virgin."

The Hollywood big shot had never coped with this situation before. The girl told me that he turned so white that she feared for a heart attack. "He grabbed his clothes and ran," she said. You can see that the Burtons, although they are blamed for everything, were by no means the only hell-raisers in Puerto Vallarta.

Elizabeth vowed that she would not leave the Mexican resort unless she could go out as Mrs. Burton. In those days she was Victorian about such things. That live-in situation with Wynberg was quite surprising to people who know her well. She's had a lot of men in her life, but mostly one at a time and mostly as husbands. Maybe the reason Wynberg didn't make it as a husband was because although he may have known what to do, how could he have made it interesting?

Elizabeth worked feverishly for a divorce in Mexico although the law in the state of Jalisco required that both parties consent, and Eddie steadfastly refused. Even years later, he told me, "I am still legally married to Elizabeth Taylor."

I told him, "Let me be the first to tell you that Richard Burton is having a hell of a lot of fun with your wife."

Eddie's lawyers and Elizabeth's lawyers were in constant

meetings in the tropical paradise. One Sunday afternoon, Mickey Rudin, now Frank Sinatra's lawyer, told me that the divorce meetings were suddenly shifting to New York, where the divorce probably would be worked out and announced. All the lawyers were going there in a private jet. No room for me. There was nothing to do but go commercial to follow the action.

Every plane—and I stress the singular—was booked. Not a chance. Then I remembered the words of General Obregon, who once had been president of Mexico. He said, "None of my generals can withstand the blast of a $100,000 peso note." A few thousand pesos distributed in the right places, and I was on the last plane out of Puerto Vallarta. I checked my bag all the way through to Mexico City, where I had to change airlines for New York. The Mexican plane made a stop in Guadalajara, and before long we were in Mexico City.

I was wearing cotton pants, a tropical shirt and sandals, nothing else. I had enough time to change clothes in Mexico City—except that when all the bags came off the plane, mine was not among them. Telex messages and phone calls. My bag was finally located in Guadalajara. It would be delivered by first flight next morning. My plane was due to leave any minute for New York. I got on it without even a toothbrush, looking like a beachcomber. It was January.

My plane landed at JFK—I think it was still called Idlewild then—at 6 A.M. in the midst of the worst blizzard New York had had since the winter of 1897. I walked outside the terminal in my tropical getup—I even had a coconut hat—and hailed a cab that was driven by a fellow who told me he was New York's oldest cabdriver. He was eighty if he was a day.

"I almost didn't pick you up," he said. "I thought you were another one of those damn Puerto Ricans coming up to live on welfare."

I got to my hotel, which, fortunately, had a Rogers Peet store in the lobby. I charged about $500 worth of winter clothes to the AP and was in business.

I checked in with Rudin, who was at the Algonquin. The big meetings were on for that day, but no word. Next day he advised that I fly back to Puerto Vallarta—that the New York meetings with Eddie's lawyers were a bust. So back to Puerto Vallarta. I landed there in 90 degree heat and humidity, carrying a topcoat. No one seemed to mind.

In a few days the local judge, whom I had gotten to know very well, told me that he was going to grant Elizabeth a divorce by default since Eddie had been properly served. He did. Surprisingly, she and Richard did not marry in Puerto Vallarta. Instead, it was about time for Richard to go on the road with his fabulous *Hamlet*— which I had helped him rehearse many nights in the Oceana Bar—and they got married in Montreal, disconcerting everyone, even me. I protested to Elizabeth that it was the first of her five marriages that I had missed.

"You are so diabolical and such an evil companion to Richard," she cooed, "I just didn't want you there—or anybody else.. This marriage will last forever, and I didn't want it spoiled at the outset."

How many times over the years was I to hear this evil companion routine from Elizabeth?

She had a point.

Richard, although a champion of the grain and grape, has never been able to drink me under the table, although young girls and old women have. Just as the arch-conservative journalist had challenged him in Puerto Vallarta, I represented a challenge too. In London, Budapest, Paris, and Rome I have encountered Burton on the wagon and he invariably has gone off it because of me.

He claimed to have bested me in Budapest—where he was making *Bluebeard*—one afternoon in his dressing room. And I would have gone on thinking so if I had not met Jeannie Bell, the gorgeous black doll who was living with Richard in Switzerland until the Burtons reconciled.

"Richard has a great story about you in his repertoire," she said when we first met.

"Oh, yes," I said. "He can't prove a thing."

"He tells about the time he drank you under the table in Budapest," Jeannie continued. "And Bob Wilson, his valet, was fixing the drinks. Bob served you double scotches and Richard iced tea." I will sample Richard's drinks the next time we meet.

Elizabeth has remained a superstar longer than most women in the movies—almost a decade longer—because she is the secret envy of every housewife in the world. I have never met a woman who didn't envy Elizabeth. She is to women what Sinatra is to men. There's a kind of a public-be-damned attitude in them that appeals to something basic in all of us. The housewife ironing the shirts in a hot, midwestern kitchen would like to kick her husband in the ass and take off with some young stud. To hell with everybody. I have deduced this from many years of giving lectures to convention crowds, women's groups, and college audiences. No other star elicits the questions Elizabeth does from other women. Even now, at age 44, she's still my number one lecture topic.

What is Elizabeth really like?

You hear all sorts of pronouncements from her, downgrading her beauty. I once heard her tell a press conference that Ava Gardner is more beautiful than she. Ava, in her prime, was a beautiful woman, but she couldn't carry Elizabeth's makeup case. Elizabeth's eyes are really violet. Her eyelashes are really double. Everything about her face is perfection. She is a little dumpy in build, but her magnificent breasts overshadow that slight defect.

On top of all this she can outdress any other star. I have been in rooms filled with all the top feminine stars dressed to the teeth. In would walk Elizabeth and overwhelm the room both in beauty and style.

She's basically a nice person, a good mother and kind, but she can be insulting. At times she has three sets of balls, and that's when she is at her worst. That is undoubtedly why she and Burton had that split. Richard is too much of a man to live with that. Bette Davis once said that a great actress can be married only to a weak man. Well, Elizabeth is a great actress. If you notice all pictures ever taken of Elizabeth with Fisher or Wynberg, you will see that these two are always trailing her, sometimes carrying her purse. Pictures of Elizabeth with Mike Todd and Burton show Elizabeth trailing. She fought more with these two than any other husbands she ever had.

Once, in Todd's Rolls Royce, I sat between the two of them during one of the most violent arguments on record.

Elizabeth, absolutely gorgeous, was furious at Mike for putting Marlene Dietrich in *Around the World in 80 Days*. It was obvious that this young dream was jealous of an old dame like Marlene. Once, Mike had had a little fling with Marlene.

I'll never forget the shock I felt when Elizabeth's beautiful mouth kept yelling, "Fuck you" at Mike. It shattered a dream. Mike spoke in four-letter words, but he was one of those rare people who could use them without offending those who heard him.

I remember one night at a party he threw after *Raintree County*, which I still think is Elizabeth's greatest performance. Mr. and Mrs. Norman Chandler came in. Now the Chandlers, who own the *Los Angeles Times* and half of Southern California, were the crème de la crème of Los Angeles society. Mike offered Buffy Chandler his seat next to Elizabeth. She demurred.

"Come on, honey, set your little ass down here," said Mike.

Buffy, for whom the Dorothy Chandler Pavilion is named, sat down smiling. All through the meal, Mike would drop a fuck here and a fuck there. Buffy didn't seem to mind. Had any other host in town talked liked that, she would have walked out in disgust. But that was Mike. I was sitting next to Norman Chandler at the meal. He thought it was hilarious. "At home, if I say hell, I catch it from Buffy."

Elizabeth changed over the years; she got tougher. You have to, to survive as a superstar. Pan Berman, the producer, told me a story about Elizabeth that about sums it all up.

Pan was the producer of *National Velvet,* the movie that made Elizabeth world famous, while still a little girl. It was the story of a beautiful black horse Elizabeth fell in love with. When the picture ended, she begged Pan to give her the horse. Pan went to Louis B. Mayer and made the same plea. L.B. was not about to give away such a beautiful horse, not when he had his own stables, but Pan was so convincing that L.B. gave in. Elizabeth got the horse.

Many years and many husbands later, Elizabeth is cast in *Butterfield 8,* the movie that won her her first Oscar.

Pan is the producer. The first day on set, Elizabeth sees Pan and says, "Aren't you the producer who gave me the horse from *National Velvet?*" Pan nodded affirmatively. "Well," said Elizabeth, "I'm still feeding that son-of-a-bitch."

I found my own close relationship with Elizabeth slipping little by little after she married Burton, although Richard and I had been friends since 1949. We still are good friends. But Elizabeth knew me as a drinking buddy of Richard's from the old days when he was knocking over leading ladies right and left. I was an evil companion from an evil past. Elizabeth and I remained friendly and cordial at all times, but I sensed something was wrong. She was running scared of Richard. In fact, she was running scared of a man for the first time in her life. It really changed her personality. She started surrounding herself with sycophants. Sometimes good friends couldn't get through to her. It was like a little court, with everybody vying for the queen's favor.

In Budapest, the marriage almost fell apart. When she wasn't on the set of *Bluebeard* herself, her entourage was. The hairdresser and her paparazzi husband, who was the only one allowed to take pictures of Elizabeth, were there, plus the new secretary.

Soon tales were coming back to the Intercontinental Hotel suite that Richard was having affairs with Raquel Welch, Joey Heatherton, Virna Lisi, and some of his other leading ladies in the film. Elizabeth came back on the set like a policeman, even though no one actually confirmed that any dalliances had taken place. It soon led to a major battle—and I was there.

If you are Elizabeth Taylor and your husband is rumored to be fooling around, where do you go? Or rather, whom do you fool around with? Elizabeth took off for Rome and had a big night on the town with Aristotle Onassis, Jackie Kennedy's husband. Where else can you go when you are Elizabeth Taylor? I, by coincidence, had left Budapest and gone to Rome. Both Elizabeth and I were in suites on opposite ends of the same floor in the Grand Hotel when all this was going on. I wrote at the time that the Onassis headlines were but forerunners of bigger headlines to come in the Burton marriage. Elizabeth vowed that I would have to eat those words, but this, too, was one of my better predictions. It was only a matter of months until the Burtons got a divorce.

I hope they're still together when this book comes off the presses. . . . Too many good memories—like the time Clark Gable and I were having lunch in the MGM commissary in late 1948 or early 1949. Suddenly, the King dropped his fork and said, "Jesus, just look what came in the door."

What had come in the door was the sixteen-year-old Elizabeth, developed enough to play Robert Taylor's wife in a movie called *Conspiracy*. She was the most breathtakingly beautiful woman I had ever seen. And Gable, who had been around a few beauties in his time, was as excited as I. All of a sudden the pretty child of the lot, the one who had starred in *Lassie, Come Home* and *National Velvet*, had become a full-blown woman. And what a woman!

And then there was the time Elizabeth and I got drunk together one night and we kissed. I don't think either one of us remembers much about that night. And I'm afraid to ask. At least I don't remember getting my face slapped.

And then the most poignant memory of all. While she and Eddie Fisher were having a clandestine live-in at the old Ty Power house on Copa del Oro road in Bel-Air, she grabbed my hand and said: "I have something for you that I know Mike would want you to have."

She went into a bedroom and came back with the button-like, gold cuff links that he had worn on that fatal flight. I didn't have the heart to tell her they were the cuff links used to identify Mike's charred body. I think she knew.

They were the first of a kind in those days. It was a touching gift. And I still wear them.

27

Steve McQueen:
Hollywood's Most Miserable
Movie Star

STEVE MCQUEEN is Hollywood's most miserable movie star—and he loves it.

Once I got a telegram from him inviting me to a screening of his picture *Junior Bonner* at the home of his agent, Freddie Fields. I showed up—the only member of the press in the small group which included McQueen, Richard Thomas of "The Waltons," a few producers, and a few agents. It was obvious that the screening was just for me and that McQueen and everybody else there, except Thomas, was selling the picture.

Everybody greeted me but McQueen, who purposely avoided me the whole evening. At times, he went out of his way to be rude. It was a hell of a way to sell a picture, and maybe that's the reason it was one of his biggest flops. Columnists, armed with a typewriter, always get revenge. The next day I wrote that McQueen was felled by a virus during the making of *Getaway*. The crew voted 80 to 79 for him to get well. But despite Steve's rude behavior, I liked *Junior Bonner* and reported so in print.

Warren Cowan heads one of the biggest publicity firms in show business. He has never met a client he didn't like —until McQueen. McQueen is the only client, and there have been thousands, that Warren has ever fired.

"No amount of money is worth that grief," says Warren. And McQueen loves it. He boasts proudly of being fired by Cowan.

McQueen's faults are numerous. He is rude, ill-mannered, and thoroughly disagreeable. I once, in a sense of fairness, mentioned to Bobby Darin—who had just finished a picture with McQueen—that Steve perhaps is his own worst enemy.

"Not while I'm alive," said Bobby.

McQueen realizes he is filled with anger and hostility.

"Thinking back," he says, "I feel that I must have spent a third of my life being angry and not knowing why."

The first time I ever met him he was doing a TV series called "Wanted—Dead or Alive," in which he played a bounty hunter. He was married to Neile Adams, the dancer, at the time. I asked him casually how long he and Neile had been married.

"Do you mean counting all the years we shacked up before we got married?"

It means nothing nowadays, but in the fifties it was an arrogant thing to say. And the way he said it made me dislike him immediately. My sense of decency was not offended because, God knows, this book proves I am no prude. It was just his prickish way of saying it that rankled me.

"Maybe my hostility comes from my street upbringing. It made me feel like a second-class citizen and brought out rebellion," says McQueen.

In a word, Steve is saying that he has that trait common to all actors—insecurity. But does that excuse some of McQueen's behavior among co-workers and employees? There are actors and crew members in town who will not work on a McQueen picture, no matter what the money. But this sense of controlled hostility on screen and off is what makes him one of the biggest superstars. So why should he change? He's the new Jimmy Cagney—without the Cagney warmth and humor.

Steve believes that there are lots of nice actors in the Hollywood unemployment line. The bastards live in the wooded estates of Beverly Hills and Bel-Air. And, for the most part, he's right.

I have my own personal theory on McQueen's hostile attitude. He's a guy who had been stepped on all during his early life. Now that he's made it, he's going to step on people before they step on him. It's that simple.

Much has been written about his upbringing in the Boys Republic of Chino, an institution for wayward youth. He has never hidden the fact—just the opposite—he could be described as professional reform school graduate. But he is bothered by his lack of a good education. Unlike Marilyn Monroe, who read voraciously to overcome the same problem, McQueen gets rid of his hostility when he is given words of more than one or two syllables in his dialogue. One of his early directors found this out quickly. "Steve has always been bothered by a lack of education, and he is a pussycat when he is given dialogue in words of one or two syllables in short takes. But give him long words in long speeches, and you have a bastard on your hands." The director doesn't want his name used because he likes to work steadily, even with McQueen.

Maybe Ali MacGraw, who left studio tycoon Bob Evans to shack up with McQueen when they made *Getaway* down in Texas, can help. Now his wife, she can give McQueen some refinement if he isn't too hostile. Ali is a Wellesley graduate. However, she admits freely to friends that since marrying McQueen she is visiting a psychiatrist.

Of course, for an actress in Beverly Hills to see a psychiatrist is like belonging to the Book-of-the-Month-Club.

The Day David Niven
Lost His Sponsor

DAVID NIVEN, along with Dick Powell, Ida Lupino, and Charles Boyer, formed a very successful TV company in the days when movie stars wouldn't touch television. It was called Four Star Television. Dick, an able businessman, was president. David was vice-president. He was much too playful to be anything else.

One day I had an appointment with him in his big office at Four Star. This was just before David was to leave for Italy to make the original *The Pink Panther*. At one point in the movie he was to be dressed as a gorilla.

Before my appointment, the United Artists wardrobe people came over and fitted David in his gorilla suit. He begged them to leave it with him. He fixed up a double martini for me and one for himself. Then he dressed up in his gorilla suit and waited for me.

Came a knock on the door and Niven, thinking it was I, roared as he opened the door and handed my drink instead to a man who had come there with his wife and three children. It turned out to be the sponsor of one of Four Star's most profitable series. The guy had no sense of humor and cancelled his sponsorship a few days later. Niven had been full of apologies as he took off his ape mask, but sponsors take a dim view of vice-presidents who go around dressed as gorillas and drinking martinis.

I arrived a few minutes later. So we had a few more martinis.

Sophia's Language Teacher

SOPHIA LOREN today speaks English like a British duchess, but there was a time when she had Frank Sinatra as teacher and she spoke English that would have made George Burns blush.

I met Sophia when she first arrived in this country on a polar prop flight that took twenty-seven hours to make it from Europe. As an opening remark, I asked her how the flight was.

"It was a fucking gas," said Sophia.

Then one day after she had been here awhile, I heard her say to Carlo Ponti, later to become her husband: "Hey, Carlo, how's your cock?"

She would deliver these four-letter words with such innocence that you could see immediately that she didn't have the slightest idea what they meant. I finally found out why. When she had done *The Pride and the Passion* in Spain, Sinatra had taken charge of her English lessons. He told her that "fuck" was a form of endearment in the English idiom; that she should use it as much as possible. And "How's your cock" was the same.

I gave Sophia a little English lesson myself and told her she should have taken lessons from Cary Grant instead of the incorrigible Frank.

Sophia and I run into each other all over the world.

Once she was making a movie in Paris with Paul Newman. She took me aside on the set one day and asked: "Do you know a cowboy in Hollywood by the name of Clint Eastwood?" I told her he was an old friend. "Well," said Sophia, "he is the biggest box office star in Italy, bigger than Mastroianni. He made a picture called *A Fistful of Dollars* and at every theater where it's playing the lines are four blocks long and four abreast. I have never seen anything like it."

I knew that Clint, during a hiatus in his "Rawhide" TV series, had gone to Spain to make the first of the spaghetti westerns. He had done it for $15,000—peanuts. I also knew he was about to make another one for the same money. As soon as I got home, I saw Clint and relayed Sophia's message. He hadn't heard a damn thing about the picture. In fact, didn't even know it had been released in Italy. I caught him in time to renegotiate the contract so he could get a piece of the action. A series of these spaghetti westerns starring Clint made him a fortune and also made him into the number one box office star in America and a top draw around the world. Clint is now the world's richest cowboy. Last time I saw Sophia was in an Etruscan field near Rome, and we talked about the conversation in Paris some years previously.

Sophia and Clint have never met, but Clint is eternally grateful to her. He had figured that *A Fistful of Dollars* was a European western and nothing more. He was convinced that he had been paid $15,000 for a disaster:

"You can't imagine the problems I had making that picture. The director and producer wanted me to wear tennis shoes instead of cowboy boots. It took me a week to talk them out of it. Then the character killed everybody in sight. He was supposed to be the hero, but he was one of the rottenest villains alive. I never dreamed it would catch on." The Europeans love violence and Clint gave it to them. "I come into town to save the place, then proceed to kill everybody in it and finally burn down the town—and be heroic about it."

Amazingly, the pictures became as big a hit in the United States as they were in Europe. Some theaters showed all of them at one time—a Clint Eastwood festival—and the lines were just as long as they were those first days in Italy.

Sophia knew what she was talking about: "I was in Rome and I saw this line trying to get in to see an American cowboy I had never even heard of. I got out of my car and introduced myself to the theater manager, who let me right in. I had to see him for myself."

Clint had director Sergio Leone over a barrel when he negotiated for that second picture. All told, Clint made millions off his spaghetti westerns—the three made with Leone, followed by three of his own American-made films of the same genre. The money is still coming in. The least Clint could do, it seems, would be to do a picture with Sophia. Those two would be dynamite together.

Sophia's two years in Hollywood from 1957 to 1959 were disastrous, except as a language course. She forgot everything that Sinatra had taught her about English and, indeed, did learn from Cary when they made *Houseboat* together. It was the only good picture she made at Paramount, which miscast her in such films as Eugene O'Neill's *Desire Under the Elms*. In those days, Sophia had not yet married her mentor, Carlo Ponti. And although both will deny it to this day, Cary and Sophia fell madly in love during *Houseboat*.

Cary says only: "I adored her—still do." But he says it with the same urbanity with which he has made the same statement about Grace Kelly, Ingrid Bergman, and all of his ex-wives. Sophia told me the same thing once in Paris, almost the same words and in the same way. But she knew —and still knows—that I know better.

I have always said that Sophia is the world's greatest advertisement for spaghetti and Dago Red. At age seventeen, nourished by noodles and chianti, Sophia sighed in a low-cut peasant blouse and a star was born. Hollywood tried to reshape this greatest masterpiece of Italian architecture since the Renaissance. Paramount told her to forget the pasta and live on broiled lettuce. She got sickly thin. Remember, this was the time when Audrey Hepburn was the biggest and thinnest thing on the Paramount lot.

"I don't belong here," Sophia said one night as we stole pizza together. "Hollywood bosses don't like their women to look womanly. They want them to look like boys." It was a shrewd appraisal. Then, as she took a bite on her pizza, she added: "I'm going back to Italy. Americans have even ruined the pizza that is a Neapolitan invention." When I printed that, it created a furor among Italian-Americans in the pizza business—a front-page controversy.

But look what happened. Sophia returned to Italy, ate fettuccine, drank plenty of red wine—and won an Oscar when she made *Two Women* for her favorite director, Vittorio de Sica. When Sophia first returned to Italy, she was so undernourished that de Sica wanted to cast her in the movie as Anna Magnani's daughter. Then hitches developed. Anna had other commitments. Meanwhile, Sophia ate the spaghetti and drank the wine. Soon she was the Sophia of old, with more curves than the Appian Way.

After the nominations were announced, I talked with Sophia on the phone in Rome. I urged her to come to Hollywood for the Oscars. I was sure she would win.

"What if I should lose?" she said. "I could not stand another embarrassment in America like the last one."

She made airline reservations, but the fear of losing caused her to cancel at the last moment and thus miss a great moment in her life. She won going away, of course.

Writing about Sinatra's English lesson and de Sica reminds me of the great director's first visit to Hollywood in the early fifties.

A huge reception complete with receiving line was staged for him at Romanoff's. In those days, there was an Australian journalist in town, a likeable although pompous fellow by the name of Jonah Ruddy. He and I stood together in the receiving line waiting to be introduced to de Sica.

"Jim, old man," Ruddy said, "you are a man of the world who has traveled in every country. What would you say is the intimate greeting in Italian that would befit this occasion?"

My weird sense of humor prevailed.

"I grew up in Pennsylvania with many Neapolitans. They always greeted their close friends with the word 'fungu.'" Well, fungu is an Italian slang term which means what you think it means—fuck you.

Ruddy was introduced to de Sica ahead of me. Sure enough, he greeted him with "fungu." De Sica was furious, and Ruddy kept apologizing, saying that I had told him it was the warmest greeting you could give to a Neapolitan.

Maybe that's why Sinatra and I get along so well. We both have perverted senses of humor.

PART IV

The Drinkers

*Bogey, Big Duke (again), and
Sinatra (again)—unique,
because there is not one Dean
Martin drinking story here.
That's because Sinatra spills
more than Dean drinks.*

30

Actors I Have Known
above and under the Table

THE QUESTION most often asked about my column in the
Los Angeles Herald-Examiner and syndicated around the
world goes something like this: "Don't those stars, such as
Richard Burton and John Wayne, ever get teed off at you
for writing so informally about their drinking habits?"

Believe it or not, I have gotten but one complaint about
my drinking man's guide to Hollywood. And that came
from Wayne. He didn't complain about what was written
about him, but he jumped me for including Gene Autry
among the great drinkers of Hollywood.

"Why, when Ward Bond and I were over at Republic
with Autry, he couldn't carry our ice," stormed Big Duke.

That may well be true, because it would take a combination of W.C. Fields, Burton, and Jackie Gleason to stay
with Duke when he settles down for some serious drinking. But Autry in his prime did all right. Like every other
country and western singer, he's in the major leagues when
it comes to booze.

In the history of show business, no star, male or female,
ever made the spectacular entrance Autry once made at
Madison Square Garden—helped by a fifth or two of
scotch and a new horse. Back in the days before Autry
became the multimillionaire tycoon he is now, he used to
travel between pictures with his own rodeo. It was a
blockbuster in more ways than one. Gene, resplendent in
white cowboy suit, would make his rodeo entrance by
riding his famed horse, Champion, through a huge paper
hoop some fifty feet in diameter. It was a thrilling sight,

as man and beast came crashing through the hoop into
the arena. It never failed to thrill the audience—but only
once the way it did this particular opening day in New
York.

Gene had started his cocktail hour a little early this day,
around 9 A.M. The show was due to open at 8:30 P.M.,
some twelve hours away.

As sometimes happens with movie horses, the star lasts
longer than the horse. So it was that on this particularly
scotch-misty day, a new Champion was to make his debut.
To the public, he looked the same as the original, which
had been retired to stud. But there was one major difference. The new Champion was young, balky, and completely
lacking in the show business docility of its predecessor.
With all that in mind, a wrangler approached Gene and
suggested that this horse needed a little work before making that entrance through the hoop.

"Mr. Autry," said the wrangler, "you're asking for
disaster without rehearsing this horse. That entrance is an
unnatural thing for a horse to do. They like to see where
they're going."

Gene, scotch in hand, brushed aside the wrangler with
these words: "I was born on a horse. I can ride any son-
of-a-bitch horse that ever stood on four feet. And I can
ride him through fire, hell, or high water."

The wrangler could do nothing but walk away shaking
his head.

Came show time and Gene got on the horse for the entrance. He wasn't quite sure whether he was getting on a
horse or an elephant.

"I knew it had to be a horse because I never rode an
elephant," Gene later said.

On cue, the band struck up Gene's theme, "Back in the
Saddle Again," and Gene took off his big white Stetson
and whipped it across the untried horse's rump. The two
took off like Eddie Arcaro and Whirlaway in the 1941
Kentucky Derby. The hoop smashed, and the next thing
the 20,000 spectators saw was Gene Autry sailing head-
first—minus horse—into the arena. It was like that guy
shot out of a cannon in the circus. The horse galloped like
the wind until it reached the hoop. Then it stopped on a

dime. And that's when Gene left it. To Autry's credit, he brushed himself off and took a deep bow, as if he always made his entrance that way.

One thing about Autry, he never was hypocritical about his drinking.

"No one ever saw me drinking martinis out of a teacup like Roy Rogers."

Gene, who since has mellowed, had a few 502's for drunk driving. I once suggested that anyone as rich as he was should have a chauffeur. He allowed that that was a good idea. Next week Gene was booked again on a 502. He was pinched when a cop saw him driving astraddle an open excavation, with the workers ducking into the ditch, as in a Mack Sennett comedy. Gene's new chauffeur was passed out on the seat next to driver Gene.

Gene was back in the saddle again.

Humphrey Bogart once had a theory that the whole world was three drinks behind, so he launched a one-man crusade to rectify that awesome situation. Bogey formed his own drinking club, complete with meetings and by-laws. It was called the Holmby Hills Rat Pack. Mrs. Bogart (Lauren Bacall) was appointed den mother for the unlikeliest group of adult delinquents ever assembled.

Some of the regulars were Frank Sinatra, David Niven, Prince Michael Romanoff, Judy Garland, Agent Irving (Swifty) Lazar, and others who were transient members. The latter included such regular drop-ins as Adlai Stevenson, author John O'Hara, director John Huston, Peter Lorre, and horror cartoonist Charles Addams, along with the beautiful long-tressed wife of those days who was the model for Addams's witch drawings. I was the only member of the press considered a member, although Bogey christened me an honorary mouse.

"Any writer with as much circulation as you've got, I don't want to call a rat," explained the publicity-oriented Bogart.

Members all had a few things in common—a love of social drinking and an intense loyalty to the Democratic party. Prince Mike, a rugged individualist if there ever was one, was the only vocal Republican. "The Democratic party is for commoners," said Mike. At the time, Mike was grateful to the Eisenhower administration. He had posed for so many years as a phony prince that he could produce no proof of citizenship. So J. Edgar Hoover and other high-placed friends in the administration approached President Eisenhower. An act of Congress made Mike a U.S. citizen, even though he had never officially renounced his claim to the throne of the Czars.

Meetings of the Rat Pack always were hilarious affairs and sometimes unruly, especially when the athletes played a game called killer croquet, a sort of dirty version of the ancient lawn game. One day, after about the sixth round —drinks, not croquet—Bogey pushed little Swifty Lazar, fully clothed, into the pool.

"Why?" I asked Bogey.

"The little son-of-a-bitch is cheating. He's walking through the wickets."

One Saturday night we held a meeting of the pack in the Bogart den. Judy brought along her then husband, Sid Luft, who has been known to take a drink.

Sinatra, as secretary, was in the act of reading the minutes of the last meeting when Luft quietly crawled into a bookcase alongside the Bogart fireplace. He mumbled something unintelligible as he brushed aside the books and curled up into a space too tiny for a midget. All of us sat in awe because Luft, who is a giant, had done something impossible. After what seemed like minutes of silence, Bogart spoke: "I'll lay anybody ten to one he can't get in there sober tomorrow."

Sinatra continued with the reading of the minutes. And then, for entertainment, Bogey sang a few obscene sea chanteys. Came time for the party to break up, and Luft was still asleep in the bookcase. Bogey was about to waken him, but Judy said that Sid often slept in their own bookcase. I escorted Judy home, a few doors down Mapleton Drive from Bogey's house.

The next morning, around 11 A.M., my phone rang. It was Bogey.

"Hey, that bastard Luft is still asleep in the bookcase. What the hell shall I do with him?"

I advised, "Let him sleep until he wakes up. The guy's a frustrated bookend."

So Bogey went sailing and left Sid asleep among the bound copies of *High Sierra, Casablanca, The Maltese Falcon,* and other Bogart masterpieces.

A week later, I bumped into Sid at Romanoff's.

"You bastards," he stormed at Bogey and me. "Do you realize this is the first day in a week that I have been able to stand upright?"

Bogey was a rarity among actors in that he was completely honest. He didn't turn his charm on and off to make points. You took Bogey as he was—no other way. That's why, years after his death, the modern antiestablishment youth has made a cult of him.

He loved to needle the big studios. He wasn't tight with a buck, but he lived by the principle if he could get the studio to pick up the tab, that was real living. He secretly admired the press, which in Hollywood never has to buy a drink. The town is so dependent on publicity as its lifeblood that an alert press agent is always nearby to pick up the tab. It's not bribery, as such, just a way of life. It's always charged to the budget of a particular movie. Accordingly, Bogey dubbed me King of the Freeloaders. For years, I could never walk in Romanoff's—Bogey's home away from home—without hearing the chant from his booth: "Hey, Bacon, when is the press ever going to buy a drink?"

Much as I liked and admired Bogey, this got irksome after awhile. One day I had lunch with Marilyn Monroe at Romanoff's. I asked maitre d' Kurt Niklas to seat us on the other side of the room, far away from Bogey. I even sneaked in without his seeing me. But who could miss Marilyn in any size room?

Soon the chant started: "Hey, Bacon, when is the press ever going to buy a drink?"

Half of Beverly Hills was lunching there that day, and the whole restaurant kept gawking at me and Marilyn. I was getting as much attention as Marilyn because of Bogey's endless chant. He had just celebrated his eighth scotch of the lunch.

I excused myself from the puzzled Marilyn and walked over to Bogart's booth. He was sitting with Romanoff, director Joe Mankiewicz, and wife Betty Bacall. I said to Mike: "Give me this prick's tab."

It soon came. I took the tab over to a table where Milton Weiss, press agent for John Wayne's production company, was sitting with a couple other Batjac executives. Miss Bacall had just finished co-starring with Wayne in *Blood Alley* for Batjac.

I handed Bogey's tab to Milton, who promptly signed for it, charging it to *Blood Alley*. I returned to the Bogart booth and handed it to him and Mike.

"Don't ever say again, Bogey, that the press never bought you a drink," I said, walking back to rejoin Marilyn.

I never heard that chant again. And I miss it to this day.

In 1958, I was in Monaco with Sinatra, Peter Lawford, and Pat Kennedy Lawford. Frank was doing a gala for Princess Grace and Prince Rainier.

In those days bourbon was hard to find in European bars. The only whiskey in Europe was scotch. So Frank got on the plane in Los Angeles with about twelve cases of Jack Daniels, the official beverage of the Holmby Hills Rat Pack. I think he was charged more for excess baggage than he was for first-class fare.

We all settled in the Hotel de Paris in Monte Carlo. The first day, Grace invited us up to the palace, which has something like 900 rooms. Bill Miller, Frank's longtime accompanist, was in the group. Bill, like many musicians, has a nighttime pallor that is somewhat lighter than a bass's belly. Naturally, Frank always calls him "Sun Tan Charlie."

After the tour, during which Sun Tan Charlie never opened his mouth, we all descended on the elevator. Then he spoke: "No one told Grace how much we liked her house." This broke up Sinatra—a 900-room house.

The Hotel de Paris has been rather a sedate hotel since the Russian Grand dukes became impoverished by the Communist Revolution. Dowagers, elderly American millionaires, British industrialists, and an occasional title frequent the hotel.

Sinatra and his group, it was not yet ready for.

To Frank, as I said, every night is New Year's Eve—no matter where he is. Our nightly procedure was to leave the Casino at 2 A.M. and then meet in Frank's suite for a party. Invitations for Frank's parties always read, "black tie and sunglasses."

Frank somehow had a grand piano installed in the suite. Noel Coward was installed as house piano player. There was lots of singing but, unfortunately, none by Frank. I am probably the world's worst baritone but at 6 A.M. at these parties I had one devoted fan—Sinatra. He would invariably put his famous brown straw hat on my head and request numbers. No matter what he requested, I always sang "Come Fly With Me."

Actually I couldn't sing a medley with the drinks I had consumed, but with Coward at the keyboard, I was a smash—at least to Frank. No one else would listen to me —not even Coward, who often was playing some of his own songs. But Frank did. And when I would finish, he would applaud and yell: "One more time!"

I still have the brown straw hat Frank gave me in appreciation. My fans may be small in quantity, but you can't top the quality.

No chapter on movieland drinkers would be complete without mention of the one and only Errol Flynn, as charming a rogue as ever lived.

Errol was a fifth-a-day man at takeoff, two fifths at cruising speed. I was present with Errol on many drinking escapades, but the most hilarious one was the time he got arrested before even getting to the bar.

Movie press agents used to toss an annual Ballyhoo Ball. One year Errol, always a favorite of the publicity department and vice versa, was invited as guest of honor. This particular ball was held at the Riviera Country Club in Pacific Palisades and was well in swinging tempo by the time Errol showed. The club, with some necessary precaution, had hired an off-duty Los Angeles cop as a security guard, in case the guests started wrecking the joint. This was a real possibility.

When Errol arrived, one MGM press agent was tearing off the front of a busty starlet's see-through dress. Some of the guests had passed out on the dance floor, but no one seemed to mind as they danced over and around them. It was that kind of party.

I happened to be the first friendly face Errol saw as he came in the door, and his first greeting naturally, was, "Which way to the bar?" I started to escort him in the right direction when the cop interrupted with typical fanlike adulation.

"My wife," said the cop, "is the hatcheck girl. She's your greatest fan. Come on over and say hello."

Errol, charming as always, explained that he was on his way to the bar and then he would gladly visit the checkroom. It was, said Errol, an old tradition with him never to mingle until he first had glass in hand. But the policeman was so insistent—almost to clamping an arm lock on Errol—that there was nothing else the wild Irishman could do but go along to the checkroom. It so happened that the cop's wife was as good looking as any starlet in the house, a fact readily noticed by the dashing Flynn. Such a fan rated more than an autograph, so he kissed her full on the lips. And the Flynn charm oozed as only this charming man could ooze it.

It was obvious that the cop thought that Errol was overdoing his charm, especially with the effect it was having on the ecstatic wife. Apparently to get back into the ball game, the cop displayed his LAPD badge to Errol. Errol, always playful, snatched the badge and started a friendly game of basketball with it among all of us—perfectly harmless horseplay that wasn't appreciated by the badge's owner. He arrested Errol on the spot and said he was charging him for being drunk and disorderly.

This infuriated Errol, who screamed that his constitutional rights were being violated. No citizen can be cited on such a charge without first having a chance to visit the bar. The cop was not impressed. He had the handcuffs on Errol in a second and soon he was in the officer's car headed for the West Los Angeles Police Station.

The desk sergeant heard us out patiently and was all for forgetting the whole thing. He looked disgustedly at the off-duty cop. We could have all gone back peacefully to the party, but Errol was carried away with the injustice of it all. So he made a speech.

"I demand the rights given me by the Constitution of the United States," Errol said, with perfect elocution. I honestly don't know if Errol ever had become a U.S. citizen, but he kept quoting the Constitution as if he had. "The inalienable rights of any citizen arrested for drunken behavior decree that he first must be able to visit the bar. I demand a trial by jury of my peers. I will not leave this edifice until this matter is legally adjudicated."

The more Errol spoke, the more evident it became that he had visited a bar someplace before he showed at Riviera. Somehow it weakened his argument, although his constitutional points were valid.

"After all," he continued, "I sued *Confidential* magazine and won. My future is in litigation."

I tried to shut him up, but he was just reaching the climax of his oratory. He was Robin Hood berating the Sheriff of Nottingham. He raved on and on, and the desk sergeant was getting more disgusted by the minute. In conclusion, Errol declaimed: "I will not be satisfied until I am behind bars. This is another Dreyfus case." At that, the desk sergeant stood up and in about five seconds Errol was in the drunk tank looking out.

It was a Saturday night, and the tank was filled with Mexican farm workers who had been rounded up at a wedding with heavy tequila content. The wetbacks—because that is what they were—had been deposited in the drunk tank until U.S. Immigration could deal with them in a more sober way. They were singing all the gay ranchero songs of their homeland. At first they didn't notice Errol, but when they did the music stopped as if on cue.

There was stunned silence as the Mexicans looked at the new guy in the cell. Then one shouted: "Viva El Capitan Blood!" And the singing resumed, with Errol a new voice.

Meanwhile, I was on the phone to Jack L. Warner explaining Errol's latest escapade—the type of story J. L. had heard a hundred times before. He listened in silence and then said: "You have reached a disconnected studio boss."

The next call was to Jerry Giesler, the famed criminal lawyer, who keeps popping up, who promptly got Errol sprung, as he had done so often before.

Errol walked out of the jail with head high, his principles

of democracy intact. Thomas Jefferson would have been proud of him that night.

Whiskey almost got me a look at one of the most famous surgical operations of all time.

About six months after Christine Jorgensen had that famous change of sex in Denmark, I interviewed her in the Chateau Marmont, a famous Sunset Strip hotel for actors.

We were drinking together and she was telling me the story of her operation and how it had affected her life. I must say she made a lot of sense.

After about the fifth scotch—and all this surgical talk—I was overwhelmed by a tremendous curiosity. I wanted to see where it had been cut off and what had replaced it.

Finally, I no longer could contain myself. I practically shouted: "Christine, let me see it!"

To my surprise—also glee—Christine stood up as if to pull up her dress. You won't believe what happened next.

A rabbit came through the window—believe me, a beautiful brown and white rabbit. It started running wildly through the suite, chased by Christine's poodle, me, and Christine in high heels. The Keystone Kops in their heyday never came up with a chase like this, in and out of rooms and closets and bathrooms. Finally, Christine caught her dog and locked it in the bathroom. I caught the frightened rabbit. It was a beauty, obviously some child's treasured pet.

Immediately, Christine's operation was forgotten. I was concerned with returning this beautiful animal to its master or mistress. Bright idea. Why not call my good friend Johnny Grant, a disc jockey at Gene Autry's KMPC, a 50,000-watt radio station that covered Southern California like the smog? Johnny was the afternoon disc jockey and I got him on the phone immediately.

"Johnny, I'm over here in Christine Jorgensen's apartment at the Chateau Marmont and she was just about to show me her operation when a rabbit came through the window."

Johnny stopped me with these words: "Ladies and Gentlemen, this is my friend Jim Bacon, who writes about all the stars for the Associated Press. He often has strange things happen to him. And now a word from our freeway cruisers on traffic problems."

I had blurted my story to millions of listeners. Now I was telling it privately to Johnny while the freeway traffic bulletins were broadcast. I explained that I had called him because the rabbit obviously belonged to some child who probably was crying his eyes out for him.

Traffic and commercials over, Johnny went back on the air as I listened by phone.

"Believe it or not, ladies and gentlemen, a rabbit really did come through Christine Jorgensen's window and Jim thinks it may belong to some child. If any of you has lost a rabbit, just call Christine Jorgensen's room at the Chateau Marmont and ask for Jim. Thank you."

Within two minutes, the phone rang. It was Patrice Wymore, wife of Errol Flynn. The rabbit belonged to one of the Flynn children. It seems that Pat and her kids were also staying at the Chateau Marmont. She retrieved her rabbit. Everybody was happy. To this day, I have never seen Christine's operation.

But I did a good deed.

In the whole history of show business, there never was such an appetite for food and drink as that of Mario Lanza.

Mario was one hell of a tenor, too. I only heard Enrico Caruso on records, but Mario had one thing more than Caruso: Mario had balls.

I've had some wild drinking escapades with Mario. Once in the Polo Lounge of the Beverly Hills Hotel, he left Jack Keller, his press agent, and me and wandered down a corridor of the hotel. A door was open, and standing inside, packing a suitcase, was the ugliest girl anyone has ever seen. Mario, feeling no pain, went in and gave her one of the nicest bangs any girl would want. He later expained: "I felt sorry for such a homely girl." The girl never filed any charges of molestation, rape or breaking and entering. No doubt, she packed her suitcase happily, knowing that she had just been jumped by the greatest tenor alive.

Later in his career, Mario signed to make his Las Vegas

debut at the Last Frontier hotel. Never has such a debut been preceded by so much fanfare. Photographers shot Mario as he boarded the Union Pacific's City of Los Angeles for the train ride to Vegas. More photographers shot him as he arrived. The press was brought in from all over the country for the show the next night. Mario rehearsed beautifully the day of the show, knocking off by 5 P.M. Showtime was 8 P.M. that night. Now what I am going to tell has never been told before, but it will solve a great mystery. Anyone who ever knew Lanza will readily believe it.

Mario, with a little time off, wandered over to the Sands Hotel and was walking through the casino when he spotted me having a drink with Ben Hecht.

I introduced Mario to Ben and then invited him to have a drink with us. That invitation, innocently made, cost the Last Frontier hotel hundreds of thousands of dollars. Mario started out by ordering one double martini. An hour later, he was ordering them by the tray. He never did show up for his performance. In fact, he never made it for the rest of the engagement. Mario died without ever playing Las Vegas.

Few people except close friends knew it, but Mario Lanza was a better mimic, when drinking, than Rich Little or Frank Gorshin could ever hope to be.

One day I was in his dressing room at Warner's when he was making a movie called *Serenade*. For some strange reason, I have a record of being an evil companion to movie star delinquents. It was 10 A.M., and he immediately broke out a bottle and refused to work the rest of the day.

Mario was particularly incensed about some item that columnist Sheilah Graham had written about him. The more he drank, the more he cursed Sheilah. "That cunt," he said over and over again.

Finally, he picked up the phone and said he was going to tell her that to her face. I didn't try to stop him. I knew from past experience that you risked mayhem if you tried to stop Mario from doing anything. He was a bull, even used to work out in the ring with Rocky Marciano, the world's heavyweight champ. So I just sat back and sipped my drink as Mario got Sheilah on the phone.

Well, you can't believe what Mario told Sheilah. He called her a cunt, a whore, and some other things that weren't so friendly. But he did it all with a perfect imitation of George Sanders's voice, never once revealing that it was Mario Lanza talking. It was one of the more memorable mornings of my life because it was the pure genius of mimicry at work.

A few days later, I saw Sheilah and said, "Someone told me that you and George Sanders are having a feud."

"Are we?" Sheilah stormed. "He called me the other morning and called me terrible names, and I haven't printed anything but nice things about him for years. I think his marriage to Zsa Zsa Gabor has driven him insane." I said nothing. If Sheilah buys this book, she'll learn something.

As I said, Mario didn't work any more that day. We wandered over to another soundstage, where Liberace was making a movie called *Sincerely Yours*, one of the all-time disasters. But that's another story.

Now, the sweetest man in the world is Liberace. It was his first movie and the crew loved him and he loved the crew. And he was especially sweet and loving to Henry Blanke, the veteran producer. All of us were talking at one point. Blanke told Mario and me that in all his years of producing movies, he had never met a more cooperative actor than Liberace. Liberace gave us all that famous smile. I looked at Mario and the devil was working on him, you could see it.

From Warner's, Mario and I went to an Italian restaurant in Hollywood, where we ordered wine and pasta. Now you have never seen anyone eat unless you saw Mario eat spaghetti. He didn't order it by the plate, he ordered it by the tureens. Filled with spaghetti and wine, Mario turned to me and said, "Let's go to my house. I've got a great gag I want to pull."

We went home and were met by his wife, Betty, who loved this man so much that she literally died of a broken heart six months after his great heart gave out in Rome. Betty brought out more wine chilled. I still remember it. Soave Bertani.

Mario dialed the phone. I heard him begin: "Henry, you miserable asshole. What a prick you are. I won't be on that set tomorrow unless my dressing room is redecorated. And I don't want to see your horse's ass of a face around there." Mario, for fifteen minutes, used the most vile language I have ever heard, making impossible demands for script revisions, firing of actors, and every other picayune thing you can think of. And with a perfect— I say perfect—imitation of Liberace's voice.

The next day on the set, Blanke walked with trepidation. But Liberace was all smiles. Sweet as ever.

It really threw Henry, but Mario liked Henry too much. He went up to him and started repeating all those nasty things in his Liberace voice.

Blanke, in his German accent, could only say, "You bastard." And then laugh like hell.

They called him Doc over at the Formosa Bar across the street from Goldwyn Studios. Doc for years and years was in charge of the first-aid station on the Goldwyn lot.

When I knew him, he was spending all his time at the Formosa drinking and dancing. It was not unusual to drink at the Formosa, but it was unusual to dance. No one danced in the Formosa but Doc. Occasionally one of the girls who came in would dance with him out of pity, but most of the time Doc filled the jukebox and danced by himself. He would dance happily for hours. Everybody from stars to grips knew him. No one bothered him because his was a sad story.

For twenty-five years, twice a week, Doc was Sam Goldwyn's most intimate employee. He was a big man among the little people at the studio because no one got closer to Sam the tycoon than Doc. Doc's main job with the boss was to have Sam drop his pants twice a week and then Doc would give him a Vitamin B_1 shot in the ass. Everybody on the lot knew this. It made Doc a big man, a man of distinction among the little people.

Then one day, after twenty-five years, during one lunchtime when the lot was filled with workers, stars, directors, and producers, Goldwyn yelled out of his window at Doc who was passing by. The whole studio stopped for a moment and looked up.

"You want me, Mr. Goldwyn?" said Doc, gleefully.

"Yes, you son-of-a-bitch," said Sam, running his hand around the trim of his bald head. "Look at this lousy haircut you gave me."

After twenty-five years, Goldwyn had confused Doc with the studio barber. There was nothing for Doc to do but go to the Formosa and get drunk—and dance by himself.

Strange things happened at the Formosa. Walter Brennan used to drink martinis straight up and then, under the influence, do a perfect imitation of his boss, Sam Goldwyn.

One day Walter was drinking with a wardrobe man. The wardrobe man went back to work on the lot. Walter stayed for a few more martinis. I was there at the time. Walter was no longer the three-time Academy Award winner, he was Sam Goldwyn. I didn't stop him because I thought it was a funny gag at the time. Walter, in his best Goldwyn voice, called up the departed wardrobe man and fired him.

A half hour later, the wardrobe man came back to the table in the Formosa practically in tears. "After thirty years in this studio, Goldwyn just fired me for no reason at all." We all laughed. It was funny at the time, but then it wasn't funny. Walter confessed to the crestfallen man that it was he, imitating Goldwyn, who had fired him. But no amount of talking could convince that guy he had not been fired by the boss himself. Brennan excused himself and said he was going to speak to Goldwyn personally on behalf of the man.

Within minutes, the bartender called the wardrobe man to the bar phone. You could see him smile and hear him say, "Thank you, Mr. Goldwyn."

He gave us a parting shot: "Walter got Sam to rehire me."

The wardrobe man left, and soon Brennan returned. We all knew what had happened, but Walter told us anyway: "I fired him in Goldwyn's voice so the only thing I could do was rehire with Goldwyn's voice." At that, Walter ordered another double martini straight up.

People don't think of Walter as a martini guzzler, but

he was a charter member of Lakeside Golf Club and never played one round of golf. And you used to see him every day over at Lakeside when he wasn't working.

"They make the best martini in town here."

That explains why W.C. Fields, Oliver Hardy, Forrest Tucker, George Gobel, and a few others have long belonged to Lakeside.

For months George Kennedy, after he won his Oscar, begged me to take him up to meet his idol and my old friend, Jack Oakie.

I arranged the meeting for a Sunday night at Oakie's estate in Northridge. Kennedy's wife, Revel, came along. I warned Kennedy not to try to match Oakie drink for drink because Jack downs a quart of J & B in ninety minutes, sometimes faster. Kennedy, a giant, is a giant in his appetite. My warning went unheeded. Before long, George was smashed while Oakie was still giving him lessons in how to make an exit through a door so you can't be cut out of the picture. It was the funniest acting lesson I have ever witnessed, but its hilarity couldn't be transferred to print even by Ring Lardner or Robert Benchley.

Suffice it to say that Oakie and I steered, pushed, and shoved Kennedy out the front door to his car. George insisted on driving, although his wife had not had a drink all night. We couldn't talk him out of it, and he was too big to fight.

George took his keys out of his pocket and inserted them in the trunk lock. For five minutes, he kept turning the key. Finally, he said: "The goddamn battery's dead."

You can't speak of Hollywood's legendary drinkers without mentioning George Gobel. George and I often played golf over at Lakeside, the only club I know that keeps a fully staffed bar on the ninth hole.

One day as we drove up to the bar, George ordered eight martinis put on the cart.

"You can't get another drink until you get in the clubhouse," explained George. It made sense at the time.

On the 18th tee, I told George I couldn't hit because there were four balls on the tee.

"Swing," said George, "you got four clubs in your hand."

Another time, George was playing in a foursome behind then President Nixon, Bob Hope, Jimmy Stewart, and about twenty Secret Service men. Once again he put the eight martinis on the cart and wound up feeling no pain in the locker room with President Nixon.

Now George Gobel drunk is the same George Gobel you see on the stage. That's because he won't go onstage without a drink or two or three. Those pauses, masterpieces of timing, are alcohol induced. George was hilarious in the Lakeside locker room that day, so hilarious that the President of the United States lingered longer than he had expected because George was so funny. Finally, the inevitable call from George's wife, Alice, came, demanding that he come home.

"I can't leave the President of the United States," he pleaded. Alice was furious: "What a lousy excuse." You could hear her screaming at George.

The president, sensing the domestic crisis, took the phone and explained that he indeed was having a drink with George. No one knows what Alice said to the president, but when the phone was handed back, Alice stormed again: "George, I know you. You're drinking with Rich Little again."

When Bela Lugosi died, I met Peter Lorre for a few drinks before going to the funeral. At the funeral we met Boris Karloff. At the conclusion of the services, the mourners were invited to view the body of Count Dracula.

Boris, Peter, and I were together in the line. As I watched Boris and Peter looking down on Bela's remains—and what a picture that would have made—I heard Peter say: "Come now, Bela, quit putting us on."

Capt. Horace Brown, who had married Marion Davies, was a playful drunk. I got a tip one night that he had tried to shoot Mary Pickford while drunk at a party at Marion's home. Calls to the Beverly Hills Police Department were fruitless because, if you are a resident of Beverly Hills, you would have to kill the chief of police to get your name on the Beverly Hills police blotter. It's a closed corporate state. So I called Mary. She gave me the whole story.

"Yes, Horace did shoot at me, but he didn't mean to, and besides, he missed. The bullet just grazed my head. He was a terribly naughty boy that night, and he should never have been showing off his guns. Before he did that, he slashed all the tires in the driveway and all the guests had to take taxis home.

"And then he pushed Marion's sister Rose into the pool, which wouldn't have been so bad but she was confined to a wheelchair at the time."

Spencer Tracy was one of the legendary drinkers of Hollywood. When he went on a binge, he went all out. He was the typical Irishman in that respect.

One day at the Bistro Bar, I ran into Spence and his brother Carroll. He invited me to have a few drinks with him. Then he told a funny story about the time he, Clark Gable, and Eddie Mannix, an MGM boss, all went down to Tucson for some reason or other.

After a few bottles of booze had been downed in their suite at a Tucson hotel, someone suggested they play games. Toni Mannix, Eddie's wife, got a brilliant idea—jacks. She somehow rustled up a set of jacks and a rubber ball, and a wild game was on. Can you imagine Tracy and Gable in a game of jacks?

As the game got wilder and wilder, the phone rang. Tracy answered it. It was L.B. Mayer calling from MGM in Culver City, urgently wanting to speak to Mannix, one of his top executives. Tracy told L.B. that Mannix couldn't come to the phone. Mayer demanded to know why.

"Because he's on his threesies," said Spence and hung up.

More stories and more drinks, Spencer's head fell on the bar; he was in no condition to drive home. Since I was in the best condition, I offered to drive. Brother Carroll and I put Spence in my car and I did. Turned out it was the right home—but I wasn't supposed to know about it.

I had taken him to the Trancas Beach house he shared with Katharine Hepburn.

I, as a Good Samaritan, knocked on the door with

Tracy's body hanging limply by my side. I was doing my best to hold him up. Now, Spencer Tracy and Kate Hepburn carried on one of Hollywood's great illicit romances for thirty years, but no one was supposed to know about it. I took Tracy to the house because it was owned by a friend of mine, Frank McFadden, and his wife had told me they had leased it to Tracy and Hepburn. To be honest with you, I didn't know where in the hell else to take him because his brother was in no shape to give directions.

Well, if you have ever been bawled out by Kate Hepburn, you know what it is to get dressed down. She called me every name under the sun. The one that hurt most of all was when she said: "You have always been a bad influence on Spence. He gets drunk everytime he's with you."

I didn't think Kate knew me that well but all I could say was: "Katharine, don't you think it's a little late in life for anyone to be a bad influence on Spencer Tracy?"

I left because she had picked up something and I knew I was going to be hit over the head with it. It looked like an umbrella.

I avoided Kate after that. I would occasionally see Spence, but I never mentioned the incident to him. I liked him and it wasn't his fault. I'm sure he didn't remember my taking him home.

Years pass, and so did Spence. I am in the south of France at the Negreso Hotel in Nice. Kate is there making *The Madwoman of Chaillot* with Danny Kaye, an old friend, and I go out to the studio in Nice and are walking across the lot to the soundstage.

All of a sudden, Kate comes riding by on a bicycle. She waves at Danny and gives me a cold stare. I couldn't care less except that she almost hits me with the bike. I notice she gathers up speed, comes up again, and almost knocks me on my ass.

Danny comments: "Doesn't Kate like you?"

I said, "I hardly know her."

We go inside an office on the soundstage—Danny, I, and director Bryan Forbes. Soon Kate comes in, sees me, and beats a hasty retreat to the corridor. She has important business with Forbes but refuses to discuss it with me in the office. She stands out of sight in the doorway and does her business and then leaves.

Sometimes it doesn't pay to be a Good Samaritan.

I was working in Chicago in 1946 when an old newspaper friend, Mark Hellinger, called and said he wanted me to meet a circus acrobat who was going to be the next great movie star. Mark had given up the life of a Broadway columnist to become a successful Hollywood producer.

So I went over to the Hotel Sherman for lunch with Mark, who was on his tenth brandy of the day by that time. He introduced the acrobat—a fellow by the name of Burton Lancaster. As the drinks progressed, I expressed my expert show business opinion that Burton Lancaster as a name was too long for a marquee. What this guy needed, I told Mark, was a name like Tom Mix or Bob Hope.

You could see that Lancaster wasn't taking too kindly to this, although Mark was. Burt was in *The Killers,* the Hemingway work.

A few years passed and I went to Hollywood. Burt Lancaster was a major star, and he told me the trouble I had caused him with Hellinger. Mark wanted to change Lancaster's name to Stuart Chase but Burt resisted. The only concession he made was to shorten it from Burton to Burt.

The night Burt won his Oscar for *Elmer Gantry,* he spotted me backstage and said: "I accept this in the name of Stuart Chase."

Private joke.

Burl Ives is another prodigious drinker, and especially when he is with his press agent, Ernie Anderson.

One night in Galway, Ireland, Ernie and Burl hit all the pubs. The pubs close in Ireland at 11 P.M. as a matter of civic self-defense.

But it's hell on guys like Burl and Ernie, who are just getting started at that time of night. It was too early to go back to their hotel and besides, as Burl explained, they had probably been locked out anyway. So they got themselves a jug of poteen, the illegal Irish moonshine that's about 180 proof.

Burl, one of the greatest of the folk singers, always gets cultural on poteen. In County Galway is buried one of the legendary Irish minstrels. After a few more swigs, Burl decided that he and Ernie should make a pilgrimage to the grave of the minstrel, Blind Lafferty.

So they got into the car and started driving down the narrow Irish country roads in search of the minstrel's grave. They drove and they drank. "We pushed ever onward," Ernie recalls. "Burl was driving." Finally they came to a fork in the road. Now poteen is fighting whiskey, and the two friends all but came to blows over which fork of the road to take.

"To hell with it," said Burl. He took neither fork and drove instead between them across a field. They drove for miles and finally got stalled in the turf. Dawn broke, and the Irish farmers came out in the chill air to work. Burl and Ernie shared their jug of poteen with the farmers to take the early morning chill off. Finally Burl asked the farmers if they knew where Lafferty's grave was.

One farmer put down the jug and said: "Ye be standin' on it."

And, sure enough, they were, headstone and all.

Col. Tom Parker is not a drinking man himself, but he once got half the teetotaling Baptists in the Bible Belt drunk and discovered Elvis Presley in the process.

The colonel has been everything—from a barker in the carnival, where Gene Austin discovered him and made him his road manager to a con man who once painted sparrows yellow and sold them as canaries who had laryngitis. But his greatest trip was when he was the medicine man for Hadacol. Now Hadacol was sold as tonic and it made $18 million for its inventor, a Louisiana state senator. A bottle of Hadacol had about as much alcohol in it as a triple martini, maybe more.

The colonel was hired to get up a medical caravan just like the old time medicine shows and sell Hadacol through the South. He took his show and tonic deep into the Bible Belt, where the Southern Baptists abhor alcohol by church edict. Some stars, such as Mickey Rooney, were in the show, as well as the unknown guitar player out of Tupelo, Mississippi, and Memphis, Tennessee. The colonel sold the Hadacol. The Baptists came in droves to see the show, all of them complaining of aches and pains. A bottle or two of Hadacol, and they all vowed they never felt better in their life. No wonder. They were stoned.

The colonel left the medicine show in Memphis and took along one bottle of Hadacol, for medicinal purposes, and also the guitar player. The Hadacol is long gone, but the colonel still has Elvis, which is like owning the Bank of America.

My most frightening experience with drunks came in an unlikely place—the headwaters of the Amazon, where the men hunt with blowguns and the women are topless all the time.

I went there on my honeymoon. And how many newly-wed couples have you known who have spent their honeymoons in the headwaters of the Amazon?

There's a little show business angle to all this, because I remember going into a grass hut in an Indian village with these primitive people and seeing a picture of Vic Mature as Samson smashing the pillars in *Samson and Delilah*. The picture somehow had floated down the river, and the Indians, thinking that it represented some kind of god, had hung it in a place of honor in their hut. I later told Vic about it, and he was not the least bit surprised.

"I always told Zanuck that I had fans everywhere," said Vic.

We got friendly with the Ticuna Indians up the river from the nearest civilized post—Leticia, Colombia, where Peru, Brazil, and Colombia come together on the great river—so friendly that we were permitted to join in a rare —for outsiders—puberty rite. When a Ticuna girl first starts to menstruate, usually around eleven or twelve, she is isolated from the rest of the tribe and put in a bamboo cage. The drums then start, not to stop for three or four days. Women of the tribe mix a potent brew, about 180 proof, from the local yucca tree, and the serious drinking begins. The young girl is also fed the brew, else she never could stand the ordeal, which when you read it, will set breakfast back twenty years.

These Indians really go native and dance around a big communal hut until they fall. Each time they pass this poor child in a cage, one of the elders pulls out a strand of her hair. This is done one hair at a time and ends only when the girl is completely bald.

We visited the village several times during the three days of drunken revelry. The final night my new wife, Doris, who is a natural blonde, was spotted by the chief, who made an overt pass at her.

Now here I am surrounded by 300 drunken Indians, and their chief wants my wife. What the hell do you do in a situation like that? Not even Marlon Brando or John Wayne could have handled it.

But then help came from an unexpected—maybe not too unexpected—source. The old chief's wife came over and grabbed him by the ear and pulled him away from my wife.

Who says squaws aren't liberated?

My second most frightening experience with drunks started innocently enough one night in Madrid. A group of Apostles, Roman centurions, even Christ himself, from the movie *King of Kings,* had dinner and then decided, for a nightcap, to go to a flamenco nightclub for the traditional singing and dancing.

One by one, the various actors all left—including Jeff Hunter, who played Christ—because of early calls the next day.

Finally, at 2 A.M., only Ron Randell, the Australian actor, his wife, Laya Raki, a sort of German version of Charo, and I were left. Ron, who was playing the Roman centurion at the foot of the cross, also had an early call. But that never bothers Australians when they are drinking. I should have known better from past experiences with such as Rod Taylor, Peter Finch, and Chips Rafferty.

Ron and I decided that the flamenco music we had just heard was strictly for tourists. We wanted the real stuff, so asked a cabdriver who, as I recall, looked like a gypsy. He knew just the place. Well, we took a sixty-mile cab ride, which didn't seem unusual at the time, and wound up in some caves in the mountains. All of a sudden we were up to our ass in gypsies—real ones. Ron and I were feeling no pain, so even that didn't seem unusual at the time.

The gypsies were serving us a wine called Tinto. The

dancing was wild, and the guitar playing was the greatest I ever heard. If I knew where the hell we had been, I'd give it the highest recommendation. Someone later told us it was Granada, but I don't think we went that far into the south of Spain. Of course, it was one of those nights and anything is possible. This was back in the days when a cab ride from the center of Madrid to the Castellana Hilton—a good three miles—cost only fifteen cents. Our fare this night was well over $100, including tip.

Laya must have gypsy blood in her because, once she got in those caves, she had the gypsies applauding her flamenco. She danced so sexily and wildly that a handsome gypsy buck started dancing with her. It was obvious that he was about to take her into his wagon for no good purpose. At this, Ron parted the two and then drunkenly threw a punch. It missed the gypsy and hit Laya, knocking her down.

I can't adequately describe the feeling I had at this time, as an innocent bystander, watching all this. The best I can come up with is that I figured, right then and there, that both Ron and I would have our balls cut off.

The gypsies around the cave were stunned for a moment—and then they cheered. Ron, all of a sudden, had become a hero. What he had done was pure macho. He had socked his wife for enticing the gypsy. It was a typical gypsy reaction, and they loved it.

We got home safely to Madrid just in time for Ron to get into his armor and ride a horse all day—with a hangover. Me? I spent all day bleaching my face. Tinto is just what the name implies. Besides a hangover and a night to remember, I had a purple face.

I often wonder: How could anyone get in trouble after an evening with Christ and the twelve Apostles? But then, years later I was to get drunk with Annette Funicello, who had to drive me home. Maybe it's me.

31

What the Stars Do
for That Hangover

SINCE THIS BOOK deals so much with the drinking habits of movie stars, it is only fitting that there be an educational chapter on hangover cures.

Richard Burton, who gets monumental hangovers from monumental drinking, is a great believer in chili and beer for breakfast. It's a breakfast that he has had so often that even Elizabeth got in the habit of going that route, instead of having bacon and eggs.

Errol Flynn, one of the most charming men I ever knew, used to charm doctors into giving him narcotic shots, mostly cocaine. I don't recommend this because the cure is worse than the disease. When Errol died, he was fifty, but he had the organs of an eighty-year-old man. By the time he had his shots, Errol was already at work on his next fifth.

Humphrey Bogart believed that the only way to cure a hangover was to get drunk again. A lot of stars use that formula.

Bob Mitchum is a Bloody Mary man. And Frank Sinatra advocates Ramos gin fizzes. Ramos was an old-time New Orleans bartender who had to contend with those rugged Creole drinkers. He concocted a drink with cream, which gives a great stomach lining plus a little of the dog that bit you. It's a very specialized drink, if you can find one bartender out of a hundred who can make it properly.

Once, years ago, Frank and I dressed like maharajas when the Sands Hotel took over the Dunes in Las Vegas. Frank even rode around the town on a camel. Needless to say, there was considerable drinking. The next morning, we were both holding our heads; I think it was those bouncy camels that did it. But Frank began ordering Ramos gin fizzes by the tray. Soon the world was round and spinning on its axis again.

Dean Martin is a great believer in vanilla ice cream or a heavy malted milk. And wouldn't that make a great picture? A malted is a great stomach liner, and the glass is easy to hold with two hands.

Jackie Gleason has the most scientific approach to hangovers. "Alcohol dehydrates the brain," expounds Jackie. "It's very simple, when you drink, if you take a few salt tablets to prevent dehydration. There is one hazard, however. After about the sixth or seventh drink, who the fuck cares about salt tablets?"

Some people, like the late Bud Abbott of Abbott and Costello, never had a hangover. "I wish I could get one so I would have an excuse to give up drinking." Few people knew it, but a half century ago, Abbott entered Johns Hopkins hospital, where he was diagnosed as an epileptic. "The doctors told me that if I took another drink, I'd be dead in six months. It so scared me that I was drunk every night for the next fifty years."

A postscript on that Errol Flynn cure by shots: When Errol was making *Roots of Heaven,* deep in darkest Africa, he conned a Belgian doctor to do double duty—cure his hangover and facilitate his sex life.

It seems that the particular Ubangi tribe on the location was about 96 percent syphilitic, which scared even Errol. But over a bottle one night with the doctor, Errol found out that shooting the natives with a huge dose of penicillin rendered them noninfectious for about six hours. All night long, Errol's tent had a steady parade of Ubangi maidens. Errol had a quaint way of putting things: "One has never had one's cock sucked until sucked by those Ubangi lips."

PART V

The Presidents
(of the U.S.A.)

They're a little bit of
Hollywood, too—even the
one who is merely a
secretary of state.

32

How in the Hell
Do You Say "No Comment"
in French?

IN 1958 I was invited by Princess Grace and Prince Rainier, along with Frank Sinatra, Pat Kennedy Lawford, and Peter Lawford, to a gala in Monte Carlo.

About this time, former President Harry S. Truman and his wife, Bess, were motoring through the South of France just like ordinary tourists. Prince Rainier put the whole government of Monaco into the search for the Trumans so they could be invited to the gala. Grace, daughter of one of Pennsylvania's top Democratic leaders, was a friend of the Trumans.

Came the day of the gala—no Truman. Prince Rainier told me it was impossible to find anyone, even a former president of the United States, on a motoring trip.

"He could be anywhere in the South of France," said the Prince.

At the same time, the Associated Press, my employer, was frantically looking for Truman for a different reason. This was during the time when the Eisenhower administration was rocked by the Sherman Adams scandal. You remember the $800 vicuna coat? Well, it seems that a number of U.S. newspapers thought that Harry Truman's comments would be pertinent, since he and Ike had parted enemies from the White House.

ABOUT 3 A.M. one morning, I got a frantic call from the AP bureau in Paris. All the resources of the AP and French newspapers couldn't find Truman. Would I help?

I volunteered to try. Truman's early morning rising habits were well known, so at 6 A.M. I went down to the lobby of my hotel and asked the concierge a simple question. "Where, monsieur, would you stay in the South of France if you were a former president of the United States on a motoring trip?"

Before answering, the concierge started dialing the phone and then started speaking in rapid French to someone at the other end of the line. Then he spoke to me: "There is only one place: St. Paul de Vence." Then he handed me the phone. On the other end of the line was Harry Truman.

I told him that it was urgent that I speak with him since the AP wanted his comment on an important story.

"Get the hell over here, and we'll go for a walk."

It took a half hour or so, and Harry was waiting for me in the center of the quaint walled village, one of the great remnants of the Middle Ages. He was not Give-Em-Hell Harry as we walked through the village, quite briskly.

"I know how tough Ike's job is," said Truman. "I'm not about to add to his burdens. Just tell your bosses that you talked with Truman, and he said, 'How in the hell do you say "No comment" in French?' "

And that's what I phoned back to the Paris bureau of AP.

After our walk, Harry and I stopped in the famous Colombe d' Or restaurant. No one was in the place but a chef or two. They served us some hot croissants and a jug of white wine, the house wine. And it was delicious.

"This beats that horrible French coffee," said Truman. And it did.

What a wonderful early morning! It goes down as one of the most memorable happenings of my life. Truman enjoyed it too. I once casually mentioned in a column that I had walked through the streets of St. Paul de Vence with Harry Truman, omitting all the details. This was a good decade later and Milton Lewis, a movie executive and correspondent of Truman's, sent a clipping back to HST in Independence, Missouri.

Truman wrote back, thanking Milt for reminding him of a very pleasant experience.

President Eisenhower was our golfing president. When he came west to Palm Springs, it usually meant a two week, all-expenses paid, luxury vacation. There was little work connected with Ike's visits to the desert. We would watch him tee off the first tee and then go back to our hotel to enjoy ourselves.

As I recall, the biggest Ike story I ever wrote during those trips was a description of the menu when Ike cooked steaks for his golfing and bridge pals, including Freeman Gosden, the Amos of the original "Amos 'n' Andy." For the White House press corps, it was always two weeks of idyllic life as a millionaire.

The only time the routine was broken for me came after a press briefing by Jim Hagerty, the White House press secretary who was more like an assistant president. I had known Hagerty from the days in Albany, New York, when I was covering Thomas E. Dewey as governor of New York. He had the same job with Dewey.

Hagerty called me aside this one day and said, "The president wants to see you out at La Quinta as soon as possible." I drove the half hour or so out to La Quinta, where Ike was staying. He had not started his morning golf game yet, and the Secret Service, whom I knew, waved me into the house. All the way I kept asking myself: "What the hell does the president of the United States want with me?" I couldn't imagine. Ike knew me as one of the reporters who always joined the regular White House press whenever he came west, but that was it.

Now here I was face to face with the president of the United States and he was greeting me as an old friend. He put his arm around me and said, "Jim, I'd like you to do a favor for me."

"Anything, Mr. President."

"Well," he said, "Mamie and I would just love an autographed picture of the Lennon Sisters." Then he went into rhapsodic praise of the Lennons and Lawrence Welk. "We love that little one. She's as cute as a bug's ear."

"You mean Janet?"

"Yeah, that's the one."

I went back to the White House press room, called a

press agent friend of mine at ABC-TV, and told him Ike's request. It's the sort of news press agents love to hear.

Never heard anymore from Ike, but Merriman Smith, the famous UPI reporter who was dean of the White House press corps, later told me I had made Ike very happy with his autographed picture of the Lennons.

Janet, a wife and mother now, is a sexy performer on-stage. In those days, she was about twelve and a president's favorite.

Ike lived the quiet life in Palm Springs. JFK, also a regular visitor to the desert, went the swinging route. It was New Year's Eve every night when he was in town.

Frank Sinatra spent hundreds of thousands in overtime pay to fix up his place for JFK's visits, but the president, although very fond of Frank, never stayed there. Sinatra always blamed it on Bobby Kennedy, but Bobby had nothing to do with deciding where the president stayed. It was strictly a Secret Service decision enforced by Kenny O'Donnell. He and Dave Powers were the two people closest to JFK, outside of his family.

Kenny said Sinatra's house on the seventeenth fairway at Tamarisk Country Club was too hard to protect, too much open space surrounded it. So they chose Bing Crosby's home, which was backed up against a mountain and could be entered only by a solitary road from the front. Bing's friends—writer Bill Morrow and composer Jimmy Van Heusen—had homes in the same remote conclave, and these were used for Secret Service and staff housing. It was an ideal setup—and the president always used it.

This naturally irked Frank, not because they had chosen a rival singer's home, a Republican at that, but because Frank had gone to great expense to build a winter White House. He even had lumber flown in by helicopter and had carpenters working around the clock (they used spotlights by night) to get the house ready. When Kenny told Frank's pal, Peter Lawford, that they weren't going to use the Sinatra house, Peter said: "Frank's not going to like this."

Which is true. He and Lawford, once the best of pals, haven't spoken to each other to this day. And Frank blamed Bobby Kennedy who thought Sinatra too controversial a figure for JFK's image.

"Bobby never had a damn thing to do with it," Kenny told me.

No one had worked harder than Sinatra to get JFK elected, and his staging of the Inauguration Gala was a classic. I almost got involved in that. Frank called me up and said: "I'd like to get you sprung from the AP for a couple weeks to handle the press for me back in Washington. I don't want any Hollywood press agents involved." I told Frank to call Wes Gallagher, general manager of the AP and ask him, since I couldn't spring myself. Sinatra's request to Gallagher was turned down, so I missed the JFK gala.

During JFK's time, I broke a number of stories that made front page. Two of them got surprisingly big play. The first happened during the Democratic convention that nominated him.

JFK had rented a small hideaway penthouse apartment on North Rossmore Avenue in Hollywood. It was owned by actor Jack Haley, and the apartment beneath it was rented by actor William Gargan. Bill had been sworn to secrecy about his famous neighbor, but he didn't keep his vow. The apartment wasn't a secret hideaway long. Soon the press was staked out in front, complete with television cameras.

Gargan, in the backyard one afternoon, saw an amazing sight, which he promptly relayed to me. Coming down a fire escape, carrying a pair of swimming trunks, was JFK. Gargan then told of how the future president climbed over a back fence and disappeared.

I wrote the story, quoting Gargan, and it got banner play. Columnists like Walter Winchell picked up on it and speculated that our most romantic of presidents was having a little dalliance the very day of his nomination. The rumor at the time—and it's still alive—was that JFK had gone to see a certain diplomat's wife with whom he was having an affair. Not so, as Kenny and Dave Powers later told me, along with Marion Davies.

JFK and Powers, who also came down the fire escape, just jumped into a waiting car and sped off to Marion Davies's home in Beverly Hills. Joe Kennedy, the president's father, was an old friend of Marion's from his days in Hollywood, when he owned RKO studios. Joe was

Marion's guest in her home, and with the TV and press outside his place, JFK just wanted to sneak away for a swim and get a quiet look at the convention on TV.

He later went back to the apartment, climbing over the fence and up the fire escape to the hideaway penthouse—from where he later emerged to go to the Los Angeles Sports Arena to acknowledge the nomination.

A funny sidelight to all this came from Marion. When Wyoming's votes gave the nomination to JFK, she said: "I looked over at Joe Kennedy in his easy chair, and he was asleep. He had missed the whole damn thing. Then Jack called, and I had to wake up Joe and tell him his son was nominated so he wouldn't be surprised."

The other story that broke very big was one I wrote about JFK putting a $100 note in the collection basket at the Church of the Good Shepherd, where Kennedy often attended mass when he stayed in Beverly Hills.

If Kennedy had lived, I could be a candidate for Heaven. It was always my job to accompany him to mass whenever he visited the West Coast. This particular morning I sat directly behind him on the aisle. The Secret Service was so used to me by this time that the proximity didn't bother them.

I took a good look when composer Jimmy McHugh, another Boston Irishman, passed the basket in front of JFK. The figure 100 was clearly visible on the bill. Now, a C note in the collection box is big news, even for Beverly Hills. So I wrote a story about it, making the $100 bill the lead item. This story got bigger play than any of the speeches the president delivered that day.

Years later, Dave Powers saw me at the Bel-Air Hotel and told me the aftermath: "The next day in Washington, Jack called me into the office and said, 'Look at Jim Bacon's story here in the morning papers. Did you give me a C note?' The president was horrified. He never carried any money on him, and I always handed him a $10 bill for collection. I told him that's what I had given him in Beverly Hills, but I had folded the edges so that it looked like $100. I knew you were back there watching the collection plate. The President loved it. He said, 'Wait until I rib Bacon about that.' " He never did.

Another story about JFK that got attention was when

he took that famous swim in the Pacific Ocean outside Peter Lawford's Santa Monica beach house.

Lawford had a great party going that afternoon. Marilyn Monroe was there, Angie Dickinson, Milton Berle, Greg Peck, and scores of other Hollywood stars. I was standing by the gate that led out to the public beach when the president took off for his swim. I walked beside him and Lawford, and as the president stepped into the water he took off his sweat shirt and handed it to me to hold. Soon he was swimming through the surf, and literally thousands of bathers surrounded him in the water. A photographer with his clothes on waded into the surf and took a historic photo.

Meanwhile, still clutching the president's blue sweat shirt, I dashed down the beach to a public telephone and dictated a story about his plunge.

I vividly recall the presidential perspiration smell in the hot phone booth. I thought to myself: Give this thing a good washing, and you have a nice souvenir of the president. Just about that time, there was a knock on the phone booth. It was one of the Secret Service guys. I opened the door and the agent said: "The president wants his sweat shirt back."

I handed it to him with these swords, "Tell him to wash it. I almost asphyxiated myself with it in here."

The agent laughed. "I know what you mean."

I first met JFK when he was a young congressman, not yet married to Jackie. It was a long ago Hollywood party, and he told a group of us a hilarious story about a well-known Broadway actress and himself.

He had met her at a cocktail party in New York City just a few weeks before. At that time she was just getting started in the theater and was not a well-known name. I remembered her name because it was such an unusual one.

As JFK told it, it seems that this girl was so dedicated to the theater that she would not sleep with anyone outside of show business. Actors were her favorite. She was a particularly delicious looking girl in those days and JFK struck up a conversation with her. One thing led to another and soon the two were in a bedroom off the party area, making love. That over, the two rejoined the party and took off in different groups.

JFK remembered that he was talking with a group of friends when the actress burst upon him and yelled, "You son-of-a-bitch, you're not Arthur Kennedy!"

The last time I spoke to JFK was in September 1963, his last visit to Palm Springs. When Air Force One landed at the airport, the presidential party got off wearing very Washingtonian business suits. And there I stood in yellow Bermuda shorts with shirt and socks to match.

JFK spotted me and came up to me and said, "No one but a Hollywood writer would greet the president of the United States dressed like that." He laughed. There had been a couple of parties at the Crosby estate and I had made it to the airport just before the president arrived.

One of the Secret Service guys took me aboard the plane to look around. I had never been inside it before. We got to the president's bunk, with the covers neatly turned down. There on a little stand was a package of Winston cigarettes stamped with the Presidential Seal and Air Force One.

I picked them up and told the Secret Service agent to tell the president: "Just say that Bacon took them for a souvenir to make up for the sweatshirt. He'll understand." I still have the cigarettes to this day.

The president soon got on the plane and took off. A few months later, he went to Dallas.

I finally made an Inauguration Gala—President Nixon's in 1973—but only because I went with Bob Hope, as a token Democrat.

When you travel with Hope, you mix in the high echelon group. After one of these affairs in Washington, a bunch of us were sitting around in our tuxes at a private dinner. As is often the case, you rest your arms on the table and the cuff links flash. Imagine my embarrassment: I was the only one at the table not wearing the presidential cuff links. Henry Kissinger, the president, of course, and Hope —and here I was with my Swifty Morgan cuff links.

Now Swifty Morgan is Joe E. Lewis's old pal, who made a living selling cuff links to Sinatra and other show business people. Some of the cuff links were undoubtedly hot, because Swifty is a character right out of Damon Runyon. Swifty once tried to peddle a pair of cuff links to J. Edgar Hoover in Chasen's Restaurant. Hoover offered him $100 for the set.

"The reward's more than that," said Swifty to the FBI chief.

Nothing was said at the table about the cuff links but the very next day Johnny Grant, an old, old friend of President Nixon, delivered a pair of the presidential cuff links to me.

I still have those, too—a collector's item.

One day I had lunch at the Polo Lounge of the Beverly Hills Hotel with a fetching young actress by the name of Marianne Hill. As is often the case when a young actress lunches with a columnist, she tried to give me news.

"Guess who I had a date with last night?" she said. I couldn't guess. "Henry Kissinger."

I knew she wasn't kidding. This was when the secretary of state, between marriages, was in his Hollywood starlet phase. He was in town because the president was in residence at San Clemente. Remember when that was the Western White House?

So I started asking her questions about Henry as a lover, not a diplomat. Suffice it to say that on a Richter scale of ten, she rated him below five. In fairness to Henry, Marianne said that Secret Service men were always present and didn't lend themselves to romantic dalliance.

"I think," she said, "that if Henry could function alone, he would be all right. But it's very hard to make love when someone is standing around holding a lantern."

I couldn't use those exact words in my column because I do write for family newspapers, but I somehow got the meaning across. By the time the column appeared in print, President Nixon and Henry were back in Washington. I knew Henry was going to hear about the column because three of Henry's other girl friends called me. All of them, as if in chorus, all said the same thing: "Marianne Hill is just a fill-in date. Henry took her to dinner at Chasen's that night, nothing more. He promised me that he wouldn't see her again. I am his one girl out here."

I was impressed by Henry's prowess with the ladies and began to think that Marianne had perhaps downgraded him too much.

His most publicized date out here was Jill St. John, but that was a publicity front. Jill, at the time, was the mistress of someone even more powerful than Henry, and her lover liked the publicity the Kissinger dates gave her. It took the heat off at home with his wife. And, as the lover once assured me, there was no action.

Jill was not one of the three girls who called, by the way. They were all starlets whose names today would mean nothing to the general public. At least one of them told me that she had read the column over the phone to Henry in Washington.

The next night when I came home my wife gave me the astonishing news that the White House had called and would call back. To show you the ego of gossip columnists, I never dreamed it was Kissinger. I immediately assumed it was the president. Before long the phone rang; it was the White House switchboard.

"Just a moment, Mr. Bacon. I'll connect you."

The voice that came on sounded like Conrad Veidt— unmistakably Kissinger.

"Could I talk to you as I talk to the White House press?" he asked. I assured him that he could.

"It's true," he said, "that I took out Marianne Hill, but I won't again. She is the first one who ever talked about me like that. I assure you that that one date will be the only one. As you know, my job requires that I have a certain amount of dignity. The Marianne Hills don't help."

I then pointed out to Henry that he dines with some of our most beautiful actresses in the really chic places to be seen, such as the Bistro. It's bound to get in the columns.

"I like the Bistro and Chasen's," he said, "because I am known there. I don't know where else to go in Beverly Hills. It's not my town," he replied. "I don't object to your writing that I dined with Joanna Barnes at the Bistro, where you saw us the other night. I just object to Marianne Hill getting so explicit. Could I ask you to just write about my dates with Joanna and Jill St. John? It would keep my job dignified. After all, it is very important to our country."

Since he put it on a patriotic basis, I complied.

PART VI

The Biggest
and
the Brightest

Need it be said? Uncle Miltie
and Forrest Tucker belong in
the Valley of the Giants, along
with O.K. Freddy. Other than
that, we have fires, and fewer
and fewer legends.

33

Things People Talk About

WHENEVER I GET OUT OF TOWN, people are always asking me: "When you go to a Hollywood party, what do the stars talk about?"

Well, other than themselves and their latest movie, they gossip a lot, backbite a lot, and invariably, sometime in the evening, the conversation will get around to the size of Forrest Tucker's and Milton Berle's respective cocks. In no place in the world is a large cock held in more reverence than Hollywood. Both men and women will listen in awe when you talk about Tuck and Uncle Miltie. As one who has seen both, I can command center stage at any Hollywood party.

It's a tie between the two—and they both know it.

Everytime they see each other, the greeting goes like this: "East Coast meets West Coast." Milton, a transplanted New Yorker, represents the East Coast champion and Tuck the West.

Tuck, unwittingly, has become one of the great tourist attractions in Southern California—the ding dong Disneyland. This happens via a ritual that Tuck follows almost daily over at Lakeside Golf Club, where he learned to drink with W.C. Fields, John Barrymore, and a few other masters. Tuck primarily goes to the club to play golf, which he does very well every day. He has a few drinks on the course—Lakeside has that bar on the ninth hole—and then comes into the clubhouse and has six or eight more with lunch. After lunch comes a massage in the locker room. He soon falls asleep on the table, which is not hard to do after eighteen holes of golf and eight or ten scotches. The masseur covers his naked midsection with a towel.

And then the parade begins. Members with guests, especially with out-of-town guests, never fail to visit the sleeping Tuck. There's a lifting of the towel, and a lot of oohs and ahs, not to mention looks of envy. Most of these people who take a look at Tuck's big cock are not show business people. They are the doctors, lawyers, insurance men, electronics people, and their relatives and friends from Iowa and Illinois.

I was in the locker room dressing one day when a group of about six people sauntered by the massage table. The member, an airline executive, lifted the towel and commented: "Now you will really have something to tell the folks back home. Fuck the Grand Canyon."

Milton, being more of a showoff than Tucker, and a nondrinker to boot, doesn't have to fall asleep. If you are a friend of a friend, Milton will display it. He's very proud of it, as is Tuck, and rightfully so.

I once was in Milton's dressing room when he was making a movie over at Columbia called *Who's Minding the Mint?* Joey Bishop also was in the movie. One day Joey came to Milton's dressing room and said, "All my life in New York and Philadelphia I have been hearing about your cock. I gotta see it. Show it to me, please, Milton."

Milton, always the gentleman, whipped it out, knocking down two of his brothers in the full sweep. Joey's mouth dropped as he beheld it. Then he walked away, singing, "Why Was I Born?"

Milton and Tucker are both about the size of a small Missouri mule. They really don't look human. I once asked Milton how big his gets when it is hard.

"I don't know," answered Milton, "I always black out."

But big as both these guys are, and there is no real young champion on the horizon, they are still an inch or two short of the all-time champ—O.K. Freddy. Freddy, long gone these shores, measured thirteen inches soft. I once saw Lou Costello put a tape measure to it.

O.K. Freddy was an extra in many movies, nearly every one that Abbott and Costello made. The two comics made sure Freddy got way over scale when he worked on their movies. They wanted visiting privileges for themselves and friends.

"Somehow I never get tired of looking at it," said Lou one day. "It's the Eighth Wonder of the World."

Some famous hostesses—one great Golden Era star in particular—often hired Freddy as a waiter at their parties. His particular job would be to serve something like potato salad or regular salad in a wooden bowl. First the hostess would have a hole cut in the bowl and Freddy's cock inserted in the hole. Then the salad would be poured over Freddy's big thing.

With all the guests tipped off to watch, Freddy would then offer the salad to some unsuspecting, madonnalike star or some pompous, Bel-Air matron. What screams, as she dipped the wooden spoon deep into the salad bowl and came up with Freddy's monstrous cock.

Those were the fun days in Hollywood, before stars started carrying briefcases and taking themselves seriously.

I say there is no real threat to these champions among the younger show business stars, but David Cassidy, the teeny-bopper's idol, is a comer. Several young actresses I know have told me that David is built "long but slender."

And that's a song cue if I ever heard one—"Love is a Long and Slender Thing."

I've got to keep away from Youngman.

34

Champagne Fire

IT WAS JUST ANOTHER DAY on the movie beat. Sophia Loren and I were sipping champagne for breakfast in her suite at the Beverly Hills Hotel. Then her husband came in. Carlo Ponti was all excited: "I have just been talking with Joe Levine, and he said that Bel-Air is on fire. Kim Novak has been called from the set to help save her house."

Here I was, right next to Bel-Air, and I didn't know about the fire. Sophia, Carlo, and I walked out onto the fourth floor patio of the suite. Sure enough, smoke covered the hills.

"It's like when they bombed Naples when I was a child. I have so many friends up there. I hope they save the beautiful homes," Sophia commented.

I called my office on Sophia's phone and told them I was going up to Kim's house first. As I dashed out the door, Sophia said, "Be careful. And that beautiful sports coat, be careful of it."

Going down on the elevator, I must confess I thought about Sophia's last remark. Covering brushfires was routine in a Southern California's reporter's life, but Sophia noticing a new blue cashmere blazer was not.

On the way up to the Bel-Air gate, I came alongside of AP photographer Ellis Bosworth in a compact car. I got into his car because, with all the fire equipment on those narrow Bel-Air roads, we'd have a better chance getting in and out of tight places.

Within minutes, we were in the midst of the fire, past police and fire lines, and heading for Kim's house. Up Stone Canyon, up Tortuoso Way. Kim's house, unless you have been there many times, is impossible to find. As we drove up the road, there was this blonde running. She was wearing a man's shirt, tail out, and black leotards hugging an unmistakable figure. She didn't have to turn around. I knew it was Kim. She got into our car and we drove into her driveway. Her gardener, who had called her from the studio, was manning one hose. On the hilltop above— only 100 yards above Kim's—a magnificent house already was in flames. The smoke was pouring down the mountainside.

I helped Kim up a ladder to her rooftop.

"Jim, take that hose in back of the house and attach it to the faucet here," Kim commanded.

I did, first handling the nozzle end to her. Then I yelled, "I'm turning on the water!" Next thing I knew I was soaked. Kim still had the nozzle pointed my way.

"Sorry," she said.

Bosworth had his camera pointed at Kim.

"Oh, I look a mess! Look at my hair." It was a typical actress's reaction to the situation. But Kim had no time to fix her hair nor to wipe the smudge off her face. It was a Wirephoto that played around the world. The next week *Time* magazine ran the picture and accused a publicity man of staging it. Believe me, it was no stunt.

The house above burned on. Director Dick Quine, Kim's boyfriend, joined the hose line. So did her secretary. Kim, by this time, was soaking wet, her shirt clinging sexily about her. She yelled at her secretary to get her paintings and poems.

"That's all we can hope to save."

Then, suddenly, the winds changed, and the fire coming down the hilltop took off in another direction, away from Kim's house. She came down from the roof. As I looked across hilly Bel-Air, I saw the fire burning furiously in a familiar spot a couple of miles away. We were off to Red Skelton's mansion at 801 Sarbonne Road.

As we drove, I thought of all the times I had spent there, the night after little Richard died of leukemia. I was there that night with Red and Georgia only an hour after he had died. I remembered that we all sat and talked in

Richard's room, how Red had picked up Richard's little suitcase with its underwear and socks neatly packed.

I remember Red's words that night: "He always liked to travel, and he said he always wanted to be ready. I'll never change a thing in this room."

And now here it was, in the midst of the hottest fire in the hills. I knew Red was not at home, that he was in Boston receiving an honorary degree from Emerson College.

A fire truck blocked the road. We got out and walked up the steep hill. Flames were racing up the canyon toward Red's home. Suddenly planes zoomed over the treetops bombing with borate, the white chemical that smothers fires. They were pinpointing the bombs on the flames. When I got bombed, I knew I was too damn close to the flames. That new blue sports coat that Sophia had admired was now borate white.

"Congratulations," a fireman yelled. "You have just joined the borate club."

All around Red's home, houses were burning like matchsticks. All of them were neighbors, or as neighborly as you can get with five-acre hilltop estates. Soon we were in Red's driveway. It was intact, an island in a sea of destruction. At one point, the fire had been stopped just eighteen inches from the garage that adjoined Red's $500,000 showplace, which is probably worth more than $1 million on today's market.

Then I recognized Joe Lombardi, a special-effects man at Red's studio. He said, "We're all experts at fires, setting them, quenching them, controlling them. That's our job. When we heard Red's place was in danger, we borrowed a fire engine from Disney's studio and headed out here." It pays to have friends like that.

The special effects crew had attached their pumper to Red's swimming pool and saved the house. "Doused the house and beat back the flames. It was hot for a while," said Lombardi.

I drove down to the bottom of the hill, where a kindly lady let us use her phone. Amazingly, the whole of Bel-Air was in flames, hundreds of homes going up like tinder. On a fairway of the Bel-Air Country Club, a foursome played golf as if nothing had happened.

As I was using the phone, a man came in and asked the lady, "Will you keep this painting for Zsa Zsa? It's a rented one—and the fire is going to get her place any minute."

We got back into the car and headed up Bellagio Road again, turning off to Bellagio Place. The fire had just hit Zsa Zsa's roof. A lone fireman was powerless to stop it. There is nothing quite like a California brushfire. The fire is so intense that it forms its own cyclones of flames. When one hits a house, it is curtains. Zsa Zsa's house went in twenty minutes. It didn't burn. It exploded.

I thought of all the parties I had been to there, of all the Picassos and Renoirs that weren't rented. It was a sad sight. Zsa Zsa was out of town, but there was little she could have done.

Driving down the block, we saw a home already burned to the ground and—standing in front of it—a sad-faced clown. It was Joe E. Brown.

"The house can be replaced," he said, "but how can you replace a lifetime of mementos? A lifetime of memories?" He fumbled through the ashes with a long-handled shovel. "Sure, I'll miss my home. It was a wonderful place, converted barn—done over in a sort of Mrs. Brown traditional. I think my wife and I will buy a trailer."

The famous wide-mouthed grin broke out with that last remark. Only a clown can smile at a time like that.

"But those mementos. Letters from presidents, vaudeville and circus bills, reviews. I don't care about myself, but my grandchildren would love to have had them. People have written nice things about me. The kids would have been proud of me after I've gone."

He dug into the still-smoking ashes. He picked up a sword. "It belonged to my son Don, who was killed in World War II. It was his dress sword. I'm glad I found that."

There was no more grin. The clown had tears in his eyes. His face looked sad, as only a clown's face can.

It was an unusual fire—no refugees in Red Cross shelters. Most of those burned out checked into the Beverly Hills Hotel. It was probably the wealthiest group of refugees since the Bolsheviks drove the Czar and the Imperial Household out of St. Petersburg. At 6 A.M.—almost a full day after I had left Sophia's suite—I was back in the hotel. The lobby was crowded with some of the most famous names in show business.

Burt Lancaster was there with his ten-year-old daughter. "The kids want me to rebuild it stone by stone. I guess I will," said Burt. The fire had cost Burt $500,000. Fortunately, some $250,000 worth of his best paintings had been loaned to a museum just a week before. They were safe, at least.

Maureen O'Hara's house had been damaged but was still standing. The house next door was a pile of rubble. "It's as if the hand of God were pressed down on my house," said the Irish beauty.

I reached into my pocket and pulled out an envelope on which to jot some notes. On the back I had written down addresses of homes that I had spotted with only mailboxes left standing. The envelope was still sealed, so I opened it. It had just come in the morning's mail. A note inside read:

"Dear Jim: Don [Director Don Weis] and I have so many happy things to celebrate, we would like you to join us for cocktails at our new home, 954 Stone Canyon, Bel-Air, on Sunday, November 19. [signed] Rebecca Welles [the designer]".

I turned over the envelope. There I saw 954 Stone Canyon on the list of burned-out addresses.

No party.

No house.

35

But Will They Do a Movie about Them in 1999?

ONE NIGHT I was in an art gallery talking with Leroy Neiman, the famous artist who is the Toulouse-Lautrec of the sports world. In the group was a pretty singer-actress by the name of Anne Gaybis, twenty-one years old at most. I asked Leroy why he had never painted Jack Dempsey, one of the greatest of the heavyweight champions. Before the artist could answer, Anne said: "Oh, you mean the restaurant owner? I love his cheesecake."

Which means that it is about time to write a chapter about some of the contemporary stars. I have already mentioned McQueen and Eastwood, which leaves Paul Newman, Warren Beatty, and Robert Redford, among the superstars, and Dustin Hoffman, Al Pacino, Jack Nicholson, and Jimmy Caan, among the actor stars.

And who do you have among the women? Barbra Streisand and Cher? That takes care of movies and TV.

I doubt that in 1999 anyone will do a movie about either Dustin Hoffman or Al Pacino, though they be excellent actors both. Redford and Caan maybe. And Newman is a cinch for two-hour special on TV, sponsored by Coors Beer.

Barbra and Cher. Yes.

Currently, the screens are filled with movies on Gable, Flynn, and W.C. Fields, and more are coming on other stars from the Golden Era. Why this cinema cynicism about contemporary stars? It's not that today's crop are not as good actors as the old-timers. They are. And in their private lives they may be just as colorful. But private is the key word. Today's stars are too damn private.

Hoffman, though born in Hollywood, lives in New York. So does Pacino—and Redford, when he is not spending time at his lodge in Utah. Newman lives in Connecticut. Only Caan, Beatty, Nicholson, and the two women live in Hollywood, where they are exposed to the constant publicity that makes legends out of stars.

It's a whole new ball game. When Gable and Flynn made headlines, they were part of a secure working force that got paid every week by studio contract. Pictures were made in Hollywood—not on the streets of New York or Bangkok. Publicity departments told the stars what to do; nowadays it is just the other way around. Dean Martin pays a press agent $20,000 a year and has never once called him. "I've been paying them for twenty years and I don't even know their number," says Dean. He also has three offices and has never been in any of them.

Bette Davis once said that stars lost their color when they started carrying briefcases. "Artists were never meant to be businessmen," says the famed dramatic actress.

I must sidestep for a moment and tell you a Bette Davis story. Right after she divorced Gary Merrill, she told me how, when they lived in Maine, Gary would get drunk at a party and then driving home through the Maine countryside, would open the car door and push Bette out into a snowdrift. At three o'clock in the morning, she would trudge a mile and wake up some farmer so that she could summon a cab to get home. Can you imagine a Maine farmer opening his door at 3 A.M. to find a fuming Bette Davis on his front porch? I wrote the story but in true objective reporting called Gary to ask for balancing comment.

"It's a goddamn lie. I never pushed her into a snowdrift in Maine. Connecticut, yes, maybe a half-dozen times, when she bugged me," said Gary.

See what I mean about the difference in writing about the Golden Era and the contemporary stars? You can't escape the old-timers.

Newman is a natural born hell-raiser, but his wife Joanne Woodward keeps him pretty well under wraps up there in Connecticut. She does allow him to drink a case of beer, minimum, daily. Newman is peculiar. When I see him, which is all over the world, the greeting is always the same: "How about a beer?" He never says ordinary things like hello.

Paul is fifty now, and he's been racing professionally for only the past three years. In 1968 he made a movie about car racing called *Winning*. He did all his own driving in the movie. At the time I asked Paul if he would ever take up racing seriously. "I would if I were twenty years younger." Five years after answering that question, he took it up seriously. You figure that one out.

Back in the days when Paul used to live in Hollywood, he was the only star who drove a Volkswagen Beetle—except it had a Porsche engine in it. I remember riding with him one night up Wilshire Boulevard and pulling alongside some teenagers in a souped-up job. They all recognized Newman and made jeering remarks about his VW. The light changed and Paul zoomed it. You should have seen the look on those kids' faces back there in Paul's dust.

Newman is a superactor as well as being a superstar. But he has yet to win an Oscar. Take the picture *Hud*, for instance. Patricia Neal and Melvyn Douglas both won Oscars in that picture, but can you imagine what that picture would have been without Newman? The same goes for *Cool Hand Luke*, in which George Kennedy won his Oscar. Newman is the modern day Cary Grant. He makes it all look too easy.

The last time I saw Newman was when he and Joanne were honored by a New York film group. He was drinking a Coors. That's because earlier in the day I had located the only case of Coors in New York City and dispatched it out to Newman's home. He came to the retrospective with a dozen cans in his car.

"How about a beer?" he said. Then he added, "I like your style." (Coors is a beer distributed only in eleven western states, if you're wondering about its rarity.)

Redford is another superactor. He and Newman represent the Gables and Ty Powers in our time. I once traveled with Redford the length of Florida in a train while he plugged *The Candidate*. When the train hit Miami after an all-day trip, he took a cab to the airport and headed for Utah. If there is any such thing as a normal actor, then it has to be Redford. He's a devoted family man, and the only time he ever does anything in public is when his wife pushes him into one of her ecology causes.

Their lodge in Utah was built by Bob and an Indian helper. No other star lives in Utah—although it is one of the most beautiful of states. Bob is no Mormon either. He just likes to do his job and then get away from all the fringe irritations of being a movie star. Who can blame him?

Jimmy Caan once was a swinging bachelor in the Errol Flynn tradition, complete with a live-in playmate of the month. Then he surprised everyone—including his brother and close friend—by running off to Las Vegas to marry model Sheila Ryan. At this writing, Jimmy is at least temporarily settled down.

One birthday, his younger brother, who lives with him, brought in a beautiful young chick and put her nude on Jimmy's bed with a candle sticking out of her twat—lit, too. Jimmy blew out the candle and jumped her. "First time I ever fucked a birthday cake," said Jimmy to me the next day.

I first met Jimmy on his first picture, *Eldorado,* starring Duke Wayne and Bob Mitchum.

I happened to be in Tucson touring with Princess Margaret and Lord Snowdon—not as a chum, but as a reporter—and decided to take time out to visit the Howard Hawks set at Old Tucson. The famed director pointed out Caan to me and said: "That kid is going to be a big star someday." I must confess I didn't share Hawks's view at that time, but I should have. Every time at the post, Caan gets bigger and better.

If Jane Fonda were not so immersed in causes, you would have to include her among the new girl superstars. She certainly has the talent, but the last time I called on her she was living in a slum beside the Hollywood freeway. Now what star lives, by choice, in a slum? Her house had little furniture and that looked like early Salvation Army. Most of the furnishings were mattresses on the floor.

"As you see, this place is nothing," she apologized. "All my money goes for the various causes. I'm no do-gooder.

Whatever you call me, don't call me that. I am concerned because I am fighting for my own survival. I am fighting to make America human again."

Jane believes that all her causes are actually—in behalf of the blacks, the Indians, the Chicanos, Women's Lib, and world peace—interrelated. She has no sense of humor about it. At the time, I said I wanted to see the war in Vietnam end—"so we could bring our boys home from Canada." She looked at the door and then me. I can always say that Jane Fonda once asked me out.

That leaves Barbra and Cher.

Barbra got into the Hollywood swing on her first picture. She had an affair with her leading man, Omar Sharif, which is like being listed in the Los Angeles phone book. At the time she was married to Elliott Gould, who took it philosophically.

"Nothing to it," said Elliott. "I was out of town making a movie, and Barbra is cheap. She hates to buy her own meals. Sharif was just somebody to pick up the tab."

Fine. Except that most of the dinners were in Omar's suite in the Beverly Wilshire Hotel. I used to report them regularly, even naming the brand and vintage of the wine, not to mention the main course. Barbra always wondered how I knew those things. Next time when getting room service in a man's room, ask the waiter if he knows Jim Bacon, Barbra. And remember, it never pays for a nice Jewish girl to have an affair with an Arab.

Omar took this all very seriously. Of course, it happened about the same time the Six Days War ended, when an Arab in Hollywood was about as popular as Eddie Fisher at a Planned Parenthood meeting. One night over at the Daisy, Omar confided to several of us that he was seriously thinking of getting circumcized. I told him it would do no good and, at his age, would smart like hell. He never did, as far as I know.

Cher is just mixed-up enough to become a living legend. She's got an undefinable glamour about her. In person, she is not really that great looking, but when those TV cameras hit her, she is gorgeous. That's star quality if ever I saw it.

She and Sonny had a multimillion-dollar-a-year empire

going, but they blew it. For the last year or so of their marriage, it was held together only by William Morris and CBS. Sonny said he never hit her, only shoved her. But then Cher never could take a punch.

I was the first to ever break the story that there were punches thrown in the Sonny and Cher marriage. A friend of mine, a Sonny and Cher nut, had gone to Las Vegas to catch their act twice—once each in separate engagements. He had bribed the maitre d' to give him the best table, tipped the captain, too. Both times, by coincidence, the management announced that Sonny and Cher would not go on. So far my friend had spent about $100 in tips not to see his favorites.

I started checking and found out that the reason for the cancellation in both instances was a Cher shiner. So I printed the story. Against the advice of her press agent, the same one Dillinger hired when he wanted to hide out, Cher called me and while admitting that I had the facts straight, insisted that everything would be patched up.

"I would have gone home to my mother," she told, "but I'm not that crazy about my mother."

Within months, the split was final and Cher went on a sex rampage—first with record tycoon David Geffen and then, in the famous on-again, off-again marriage, with rock singer Gregg Allman. By this time, she may have moved in with her mother. Who knows?

There are two other male stars who are automatically superstars if they would only take time off from their sex lives—Jack Nicholson and Warren Beatty. Both are superb actors and both colorful, especially Beatty.

Warren is a rich man, thanks mostly to *Bonnie and Clyde* and *Shampoo*, from which he has made millions. And what rich man wants to spend all day on a movie set when he could have a woman up in his room?

Warren, for the most part, occupies the penthouse suite at the Beverly Wilshire when he is in town. There's a little old lady, Pasadena type, lives below him. She is always going down to the desk and complaining: "What do they do up there all night?"

It is not generally known, but Warren invented the expression, "What's new, Pussycat?" He once stayed at producer Charlie Feldman's home and was on the phone all the time with some chick, asking, "What's new, Pussy-cat?" It's funny how a little thing like that can mean millions all around. Feldman, of course, made a blockbuster movie out of it. He hired Burt Bacharach and Hal David to write a song of the same title, and Burt got an unknown singer by the name of Tom Jones to make his first hit record by singing it over the titles. All Warren got out of his own expression was laid a few thousand times.

And me? I'm the dumbest of all. I stood with Warren one day in front of the Beverly Wilshire and heard him say the same thing to the pretty secretaries walking by on their lunch hour. One of the prettiest was late for lunch that day.

Warren is amazing. He must take some kind of special vitamins. One night when he was living with Julie Christie, he got out of bed around suppertime and said he was going out for the evening paper. He came back the next morning at 7:30 with the paper, but Julie had moved out. She moved back in the next day.

Nicholson is rated a tiger, too, but he's pretty much a one-girl-at-a-time man. He practices the good neighbor policy with his friend Warren. When Michelle Phillips moved out of Nicholson's house, she moved right in with Beatty.

Michelle is a girl who has always married any man after a certain length of time. So far, neither Nicholson nor Warren has succumbed.

36

How Time Flies

IF YOU SURVIVE LONG ENOUGH as a Hollywood columnist, strange things can happen.

It seems only yesterday when I was talking with Judy Garland in her Holmby Hills living room when Liza Minnelli, maybe ten, got into a hassle with her baby sister, Lorna Luft, who had bitten Liza on the leg. Then before you know it, you are there when Liza the superstar wins an Oscar as best actress for *Cabaret*—and you're working the Jerry Lewis Telethon with Lorna, a talented nightclub performer.

One January Monday in 1953, I was pacing outside a hospital delivery room with Desi Arnaz, Sr. He and I were the only people there. Suddenly we heard Lucille Ball shout happily through her spinal anesthetic: "It's a boy!" And thus was born that day by cesarean section the most famous baby in the world—Desi, Jr. That night every television set in the nation would be tuned to the number one TV show of all time, in which a boy would also be born to Ricky and Lucy Ricardo of the "I Love Lucy" show. The whole thing had been timed perfectly. God knows what would have happened if Lucy had yelled: "It's a girl," instead.

Then, twenty years later, Lucy—still the queen of television—and I are sitting in her dressing room trailer. On the table before us is a newspaper with a front-page story announcing that Liza and Desi, Jr. had broken their torrid engagement. From every side Lucy had been assailed to find out what had happened. Officially, all she could say was that she was surprised. But as the unofficial godfather of Desi, Jr., I could be more blunt: "It's the best thing that could have happened to him. I love Liza, but she wasn't right for Desi."

Lucy gave me a knowing look and said: "From your ears to God's ears."

Her silence was eloquent; my impression was that she agreed. Lucy was very fond of Liza and still is. She never once interfered with her son's tempestuous romance, even though Liza was seven years older than Desi.

"How could I interfere?" asked Lucy. "When men are young, they like older women. When they are old, they like young girls."

A lot of truth rides in that statement.

Lucy and I had been through a lot over the years. I could remember another time not long after Desi was born when his father summoned me urgently to the studio where "I Love Lucy" was filmed.

"Grandpa's fixed it for Lucy," said Desi when I arrived. He showed me a blind item in Walter Winchell's column that said: "TV's top comedienne—a redhead—is a card-carrying member of the Communist party."

This was hardly a blind item. CBS, the sponsor Phillip Morris, and the advertising agency were in panic. Here was a show that had a rating of 80—about the same as the first landing on the moon—and the whole thing was about to go down the drain. Lucy's friends knew she was about as much a communist as John Wayne but Winchell's item was true!

Actually Lucy's involvement with the Communist party was like something out of *You Can't Take It With You*.

Lucy's father died when she was four, and for most of her life she was reared by her grandparents. Grandpa Fred Hunt was an old-time Socialist, always out to revolutionize the world. When Lucy started making it big in Hollywood, she couldn't keep a maid or a housekeeper. Grandpa was always out in the kitchen urging them to strike for more money. He was a born agitator. But Lucy adored him, and anything that Grandpa said was OK by her. So it happened that a Communist once ran for mayor of Los Angeles. Grandpa Hunt took Lucy with him to vote his ticket—and both signed the Communist register to do so.

That was the whole extent of Lucy's involvement with the Communist party. And now Winchell had learned of it, probably from someone connected with the show opposite her on Monday nights. These were the McCarthy days, and it was no laughing matter. Desi asked my advice. I gave him the same advice that I had given Marilyn Monroe a few years earlier when she was faced with the nude calendar crisis—tell the truth, with humor. Everybody loved Lucy too much to take Winchell's dated item seriously.

Certainly, Grandpa's story was a humorous one. Once he got into a fight with the city of Los Angeles because they wouldn't trim the branches on a tree in front of the house. One night Desi was in the house courting Lucy and he heard a thunderous roar of timber. He dashed outside and saw a huge tree smashed down on his new convertible. Standing beside the tree, saw in hand, was Grandpa.

Armed with that and other stories, Desi met the crucial test the next night when "Lucy" was due for filming before a live audience. Only this time the audience was different—the studio was filled with representatives of the media from all over the world.

None of this bothered Lucy very much. She left everything to Desi in those days, and Desi soon had the audience chuckling with stories about Grandpa. Then he ended his speech thusly: "The only thing red about Lucy is her hair—and even that's not real." The chuckles turned to belly-laughs, and Lucy was home free. The panic ended as fast as it began.

The Arnaz kids and Judy's kids aren't the only ones I've seen grow up in this business. Having spent many years drinking with Duke Wayne, occasionally I find myself having a drink with Michael Wayne, the big Duke's producer-son. Like father, like son.

My most unusual session was with the Emmy-winning writer Tracy Keenan Wynn. He has the distinction of being the first *grandson* of an old friend to become a drinking partner. I told Tracy something that his famous grandfather, Ed Wynn, sadly told me before he died.

"There's something wrong about television," said Ed.

"What kind of a medium is it that has Dinah Shore getting laughs and Ed Wynn making people cry?"

It's true.

Ed onstage, in the Ziegfeld Follies, was probably the funniest man who ever performed. No less an authority than Jack Benny told me that.

"No one, not even W.C. Fields, was funnier than Ed," said Jack.

But in his later career on TV, he became one of the medium's finest dramatic actors.

"I have to do it," said Ed. "I have six wives to support. They want tears from Ed Wynn, I'll give them tears—but I'm giving myself tears when I do it. I'm a comic. And it's a saintly gift because we make people forget their miseries."

It was Ed who once explained the difference between a comedian and a comic: "A comedian says funny things. A comic says things funny."

My favorite Ed Wynn story involves his old boss, Flo Ziegfeld.

"One day Flo calls me urgently and I go immediately to his home in Beverly Hills. This is long after the Follies and I know he is broke, so I am not surprised when he tells me he must have $5,000 immediately.

"I was doing well those days as the Texaco Fire Chief on radio, so I came prepared. I had the money on me. I didn't ask him what he wanted it for. I just gave it to him.

"Do you know how he spent the money?"

"He was going back to New York and he needed it to hire a private railroad car. Flo would travel no other way. He had class."

People are always amazed when I talk of Ed Wynn, or Chaplin, or Buster Keaton. It's as if you've mentioned Diamond Jim Brady or Lillian Russell. But nearly thirty years on the Hollywood beat can drum up many interesting memories of stars who are legend now. When I knew them, they were just very vital people.

When I lecture at a university, students invariably ask: Has Hollywood changed for the better or worse in those years?

I always say for the worse.

Look around: There's no Gable today. There's no Bogart. Certainly no Cagney. No Cooper—except possibly for Clint Eastwood.

Today's moviemaking climate is different. In the old days, stars were under contract to a studio. They belonged to a family. They worked hard, but they played harder; hence they were more colorful.

Is Steve McQueen colorful? Is Robert Redford colorful? Probably the most colorful stars today are the British and the Irish—the Oliver Reeds, the Richard Harrises, the Richard Burtons, and the Peter O'Tooles.

Today's American actor lost his color when he started carrying briefcases. Actually, most of them are pretty dull, not on the screen, of course, but to a writer who has to turn out six columns a week. And they are that way to fans, too. Just the other night, Dustin Hoffman was dining with Producer Bob Evans at a Chinese restaurant in Beverly Hills. A young actress, no ordinary fan, came up to greet Evans, whom she knew. Then she spotted Hoffman, one of the most successful actors on the screen today.

"Oh, Mr. Anka," she gushed. "I caught your act up at Caesars Palace."

Can you imagine Clark Gable being mistaken for Paul Anka by someone in the business?

As for me, I find that about 90 percent of my interviews are with young actresses. Now they are colorful.

Now that I think about it, when Gable and Bogart were around, I was still interviewing actresses 90 percent of the time.

So maybe things haven't changed so much.

Index

AVON ◆ THE BEST IN
BESTSELLING ENTERTAINMENT!

☐ **Your Erroneous Zones**
   Dr. Wayne W. Dyer   33373 $2.25
☐ **Flynn** Gregory Mcdonald   34975 $1.95
☐ **Lovefire** Julia Grice   34538 $1.95
☐ **Hollywood Is a Four Letter Town**
   James Bacon   33399 $1.95
☐ **Mystic Rose** Patricia Gallagher   33381 $1.95
☐ **The Search for Joseph Tully**
   William H. Hallahan   33712 $1.95
☐ **Captive Bride** Johanna Lindsey   33720 $1.95
☐ **The Great Santini** Pat Conroy   32680 $1.95
☐ **Starring** James Fritzhand   33118 $1.95
☐ **Legacy** Florence Hurd   33480 $1.95
☐ **Castle Cloud** Elizabeth Norman   31583 $1.95
☐ **Bledding Sorrow** Marilyn Harris   31971 $1.95
☐ **Raising Kids OK**
   Dorothy E. Babcock, R.N., M.S.
   and Terry D. Keepers, PH.D.   31989 $1.95
☐ **Delta Blood** Barbara Ferry Johnson 32664 $1.95
☐ **Wicked Loving Lies** Rosemary Rogers 30221 $1.95
☐ **Moonstruck Madness** Laurie McBain 31385 $1.95
☐ **ALIVE: The Story of the Andes Survivors**
   Piers Paul Read   21535 $1.95
☐ **Sweet Savage Love** Rosemary Rogers 28027 $1.95
☐ **The Flame and the Flower**
   Kathleen E. Woodiwiss   35485 $2.25
☐ **Between Parent and Child**
   Dr. Haim G. Ginott   26385 $1.75
☐ **I'm OK—You're OK**
   Thomas A. Harris, M.D.   28282 $2.25

Available at better bookstores everywhere, or order direct from the publisher.